Down From the Mountain

A novel
by

James MacKrell

 PRESS

DOWN FROM THE MOUNTAIN

Copyright © 2009 by James MacKrell
First Edition: December 2009
10 Digit ISBN: 1-4392-6484-8
13 Digit EAN: 978-1-4392-6484-3
Writer's Guild of America # 1315416

James MacKrell
✉ thebanditproject@gmail.com

For more information, please visit our website at
www.thebanditproject.com

Printed in the United States of America

JMK PRESS

Forward

"Down from the Mountain" is special to me in many ways. First, it is set in the area that my family settled in the late 1800's. Second, Jim writes about agriculture and the struggles producers on the land face every day; the elements, market prices and predators. Third, Jim writes about the special breed of Australian Shepherds, their loyalty, their hearts, love for their work and their owners. Jim has written a superb book about all three. I am so privileged to help. This is a book you won't put down. The Aussies in this story are real, they speak to you. You will cheer for them as you do Javier in his struggles in ranching and taking care of his beloved Aussies and sheep. You will never forget this story. I know I won't.

Judie Manuel, Amistad Australian Shepherds
Winnett, Montana

Acknowledgements

Thank you so much Judy. Without you this book would have never been born. It was through Judie's wide circle of friends that I gleaned the information necessary to make this story come alive. This book is dedicated to two wonderful dogs. **HOF VCH WTCH CH Shope's Goodnight Bandit CDX RTDsc HS HX,** and his son, **Can CH Legends Be Forewarned CD STDc OTDsd.**

These two Australian Shepherds are the living embodiment of everything the fictional Bandit and the other wonderful characters in this story exemplify. Without these two dogs and their loving owners I could never have written this story.

Bandit died while I was assembling this book. I've talked to many, many people who are owned by his offspring and grandchildren and to the person, they all say the same thing, "The Spirit of Bandit is evident in everything the offspring do."

As I write this, Bandit's granddaughter, **Amistad's Falen,** is sleeping at my feet. I have learned so much from her in the short 20 months we have had her in our lives. Falen is the daughter of Warner and Koda, **(C Hangin' 5 Koda of the West),** born on the Manuel's lovely ranch in the heart of Montana. Falen joined this world on New Year's Day, and from that moment on, the lives of the MacKrell family hasn't been the same.

It's the love of Master and Dog and Dog and Master that fuels this story of bravery, loyalty and adventure. Whether on a ranch or a farm, in the spotlight of a dog show, at agility or herding trials, in the obedience ring, or at home protecting and entertaining their families, Aussies are special. If you've never been around one, Bandit will encourage you to learn more about this special American breed of dog.

The people who own Aussies are special too, and without them I could never have told this story. Through Judie's circle of friends I was introduced to **Barbara and Dave Moe**, working sheep ranchers who depend on dogs like Koda to do their day-to-day work.

I can't say enough about the help given by Bandit's human mom, **Anne Shope.** She and Steve live in majestic New Mexico, and being a hall of fame breeder, judge and trial official is the reason that we all enjoy Bandit's offspring. Anne was particularly inspiring when, as she read the fictional accounts of Javier's Bandit, she cried tears of joy and sorrow, since the passing of the great Bandit was so near. The storybook Bandit took on a special place in Steve's and Anne's hearts.

Shelly Hollen, Karen Keller, and my dear friend **Karen Fremuth** all encouraged, edited and provided invaluable information. I have to add as well **Dr. Dan Kainer, DVM,** who handled all of my questions with patience and charm. My friend and fellow herding dog fan, **Lucian Williams** read every word of this story and encouraged me each step of the way. And thanks also to my dear cousin, **Sue Smith**, who with her beautiful and smart Dobermans rooted for Bandit as the story unwound.

But as you will learn, Bandit is one half of this story. Bandit would never have survived that first Montana winter without his adopted mother, the beautiful Gray Wolf, Sheena. I used as a model for Sheena a living wolf named **Mystery** who lives out her life in the comfort and security of **Jean LeFevre's St. Francis Sanctuary in Montgomery, TX**. Mystery was mistreated and near death when a Texas Game Warden found her and transported her to St. Francis. Under the great care and good heart of Mrs. LeFevre wolves like Mystery will live out their lives in peace and contentment. They will never be sold, moved or hurt for the rest of their lives. In the book when you see a picture of Sheena, think of Mystery and her friends at St. Francis.

Lastly, without the aid, editing, spelling, general good cheer, love and respect of my family I could have never finished this two years of work. My wife of 51 years, Cathy, and my beloved daughters, Catie and Lisa, who were as involved in this project as me, are the reasons I was able to complete Bandit's story. For countless nights, days, weekends and late hours they all strived to make this a reality.

Again, another important thank-you to our editor **Dane Wilkins** who lent his professional talent and brains to the editorial effort; He is a pro in everything he does.

And to my friend and fellow writer, **Bud Connell,** who never let me forget that I had to "just sit down and write," I say thanks.

Also to **Lin Bolen Wendkos**, former VP of Programming for NBC, who saw promise in me years ago and has remained my muse, supporter and friend through the years.

Lastly, to my little **Rowdy,** our black tri Aussie with the big eyes, while not big in stature is enormous in heart. Without his constant companionship, I would have never learned the gift of canine affection.

Here's to the dogs, be they big, short, loud or tall. May they live in love and companionship, having their lives fulfilled by loving and appreciative masters.

One last thought. Throughout this book there is an obvious connection between the animals and the *Spirit of the Day and Night.* I believe that to be true. I believe that all of God's creatures are responsive to his will, guidance and love. It is in this belief that I present to you, Bandit's story: **Down from the Mountain.**

Book One
Let the Dance Begin

Chapter 1
"Up unto the hills..."

A horsefly's bite sent a quiver from the gelding's tail up through his entire body. Javier re-sat the saddle, placed two worn hands on the horn, and let a breath ease out into the crisp morning air.

He clucked to the horse he called Bayo, and with a shake of the reins moved out toward the pasture. The mountain breeze ruffled his worn blue shirt. He massaged the ache in his right leg with a scarred hand. At his age, hurt was just something you lived with.

"We'll let these ewes eat their fill, then let'em nap a bit." Javier rubbed Bayo's mane as he continued to explain to the horse what his plans for the day were. Alone with the flock Bayo was the best thing Javier had to talk to. He continued, "Late in the afternoon after they've grazed some more, we'll move'em and us home for the night."

He ducked a low-hanging fir branch and noticed how fast the grass was turning brown. It wouldn't be too many more weeks before they would have to move the sheep into winter quarters.

He squinted as he surveyed the vista ahead. How he loved Montana, with its mountains, its valleys, its forests and streams. If he could paint his conception of heaven, it would look like Montana.

"I'm glad Mr. Jim left you for me, old hoss," he said as he rubbed the bowed neck of the animal. "You and me, we been trottin' along for a good long time." He smiled, gently urging the horse forward.

The memories of his arrival in Montana remained as vivid as the morning in front of him.

Javier Coronado, a Basque herdsman, had moved to Montana with his friend and employer, Jim Townsend. As they had stepped off the train in Big Timber three decades ago, both men were overcome with the beauty of the Big Sky country. All of their hopes were pinned on the sheep in the cattle cars they were bringing to their new ranch, just outside Big Timber, Montana.

"A lot more open than back in California," Jim said with a laugh as he gazed at the surrounding mountains and their snow-white peaks.

"Mr. Jim, we're gonna have a lot of room for our sheep here."

"It's going to be just you and me, old boy. We've got a lot of work cut out for us."

"Don't forget the dogs, Mr. Jim. We've got our dogs and they are the best helpers."

A brisk wind snapped Javier out of his reverie. He noticed ominous thunderheads building up over the western mountains. The air smelled of moisture, but he believed there were a couple more days of grazing before he wintered the sheep.

* * *

Jenny carefully watched Javier and the band of ewes moving up the path toward the pastures. Her body sagged with the feeling of uselessness. Why was she locked up like a wayward pup? She longed to be about her business. A sudden throb shot through her midsection. The effort of expectant motherhood tired her. She stood up and moved into the sunlight again, circling in an ancient canine ritual. When she was satisfied with her resting

James MacKrell

place, she plopped back down and breathed a heavy sigh. Resigned to her solitude, the sheepdog turned her head away from the spectacle on the hillside. As the morning sun climbed, its warmth made her drowsy. Perhaps she might sleep until all had safely arrived home again. An unborn puppy twitched, and an involuntary reflex shifted her sluggish body into a more contented position.

On this Indian summer day in the foothills of the Absaroka Mountain Range, the band of sheep flowed like sea foam in rising water up the rocky passage toward the grazing pastures high in the foothills. Australian Shepherd dogs, looking from the distance like multi-colored balls bounced around the edges, urging the moving mass up and up. The familiar routine made Jenny tremble with anticipation. Oh, how she wished to be there.

"They'll probably need me," Jenny uttered to no one in particular.

* * *

Small clouds of moisture escaped with each snort as the bay Morgan horse slowly picked his way up the rocky path he had been climbing for the past thirty years.

"Bayo, you and me are getting a little long in the tooth for all this work," Javier said with a smile as he wiped his handkerchief across his chestnut brow. He tugged at the rope attached to the pack mule, Sarah. "Yep, too soon we get old." Taking a deep breath he continued, "With lambs to be born next spring and Jenny with her puppies, I guess we have to keep trudging along." He complacently chuckled.

The land was his, owned lock, stock, and barrel, since Jim Townsend, childless, had bequeathed some 3,000 acres to his faithful friend and employee.

Javier's favorite stock dog, Jenny, was an Australian Shepherd directly from the intensive breeding program started back in California by Jim Townsend's father and grandfather. In fact, her bloodline could be traced back to a dog called Perro, that Javier's grandfather brought with him from Australia.

Jenny was a shepherd, a working stock dog now bred to the number one stock dog champion in the whole northwest. Being pregnant was new to her, working sheep wasn't.

Just before she let the afternoon's warmth overcome her with sleep, she glanced again up the trail to where her littermate, Blu, and the other Aussies were going about their work with precision. She let her black head fall to her paws and soon was dreaming of better days. Jenny didn't know that soon black clouds would be hanging over her head, delivering life changes to her, those she loved, and those she would come to love.

James MacKrell

Chapter 2
"The price of motherhood..."

Sleeplessness hounded Jenny most of the night. The chill fall temperatures caused her to curl into a tight fur ball, which was difficult due to the enormity of her belly. Before dawn her exhaustion overtook her and let the mist of sleep lull her tired bones. Her restless legs pantomimed running. Every apparition caused her sleeping eyelids to twitch. As deep slumber approached, a bright light forced her awake. Golden beams causing long, cool shadows from the foliage signaled the beginning of another day. Vivid yellow leaves on the aspen and cottonwood danced in the sunlight to the accompaniment of wind.

The dog shook herself to cast off all the night's aches and pains; she stretched as far as her lying body would let her. The weight of motherhood reminded her of her delicate condition as she struggled to get her paws beneath her. "Oh, my," she grumbled as she stood erect, looking through the chain-link fence. "Here I am stuck in this kennel again."

A picture of ewes grazing skipped across her mind. Her absence from the flock only made her predicament worse. Oh, how she loved tending the sheep, listening for the herder's commands, all the while keeping her keen eyes riveted on the grazing stock. Each movement of his hands sent her to correct some errant ewes, or perhaps a ram that had exerted his independence and strayed from the group. She let her brown eyes play over the partially green hills. Caring for those wooly sheep was her way to show Javier how much she respected him and wanted to attend to his every request. Sometimes her tenacity and drive to work sheep overrode her need to please Javier, but those times when she had selective hearing were rare. Blowing her flews as she sighed, she remembered fondly how Javier always said he loved a working dog that could think on its own. Jenny could certainly work and not be totally dependent upon Javier for her every move when working sheep or cattle. Jenny was an Aussie whose toil was Javier's bread and butter.

Her head snapped around at the loud clang of the kennel door. Lonnie, the freckle-faced neighbor boy who came over to help Javier feed the animals, opened the door, stumbled a bit, but still balanced the kibble that rattled in a shallow tin pan. The black dog settled back in the hay on the floor and pretended to give little reaction. She gave a disinterested sniff in the direction of her feeding dish. Quick eyes darting between the hillside and the pan of waiting food gave no hint of her misery.

"I don't think my belly will hold a crumb with all these puppies jammed up inside," she grumbled, the Aussie's white lip curling in a half-smile knowing she could utter whatever she pleased. "Dog speak is beyond human comprehension," she barked.

Javier stepped gingerly out on the coarse wooden porch and stood for a moment leaning on a rail. The wind rattled the windows of the rustic wood cabin he had called home for the past thirty years.

A cup of hot coffee created wisps of steam in the frigid air. The tang of his aftershave wafted across the restless morning breeze. Jenny's black nose stabbed the air, trying to find the source of the familiar scent. A loud yawn, suggesting he hadn't slept well either, broke the morning silence. Two startled crows squawked and leapt from the branches of a gnarled old evergreen near the house. A worn brown hand rubbed his forehead with a ragged red and white bandana. The handkerchief was as much a part of Javier as the faded Montana State baseball cap constantly perched on his balding head.

After a deep swallow of coffee, he ambled down the porch steps and wandered out into the yard. Missy, the old spotted momma cat dashed for imagined safety as his heavy boots left proof of his passage in the frosted grass. The last smoke trails from the house's rock chimney ascended the clear blue sky like prayers reaching to heaven. Night temperatures had left a glaze of white on the porch and roof that would soon burn off with the rising sun.

Javier's weathered face broke into a crooked smile at the sight of a red squirrel doing a circus trick, hanging off the edge of the roof trying to pillage the bird feeder.

"You little thief! I hope one of those big Magpies pecks your criminal head off."

Secretly he loved the old squirrel, even though the rodent always found a way to steal some of the birds' food.

"What a wonderful morning," he sighed. Old Emma meandered out the cabin door and found herself a sunny spot on the porch. She snuffled a contented sound, agreeing with her master. Javier glanced back at the elderly Aussie.

"You're right old girl. It's good to still be alive."

Emma glanced in his direction and then firmly plopped her head down on the porch to resume the task of getting as much sleep as she could.

A glimpse of the sheep pens reminded the herder of the old days when Emma and Mr. Jim ran things at the ranch. Now that she was approaching the age of fourteen, she moved a lot slower. "You old pooch, now you're just in charge of sleeping."

Emma grunted. She would always grunt.

Emma raised her head and stared at Jenny in the kennels.

"I know how you must feel, young momma," she said, "but when you've brought the pitter patter of feet, wet noses, and wiggling butts into the world, working dogs that carry on our great lineage and help Javier, the miracle of motherhood will erase the misery of carrying that extra weight around. Some of Javier's working dogs are getting old, and he needs new blood coming up. He's depending on you. Plus, Javier is getting an itch to trial competitive again. Maybe his competition partner will be one of your pups," Emma said thoughtfully.

If dogs could grin, Emma would be showing all teeth. A fly lit on her nose and she let out a breath through her nostrils, not caring whether or not the fly stayed or went.

If the Townsend Sheep Company had a matron, it would be Emma. In her merle coat of many colors she reigned over the entire ranch. No one crossed Emma; no one dared to disagree with her at all. Even the chickens, who didn't mind anyone, paid close attention to the wishes of Miss Emma, as they called her. Chickens were all well aware of Miss Emma's one blue eye and couldn't tell when it was watching them, so they stayed on guard all the time when Miss Emma was in sight.

She enjoyed trips to the pasture, where she liked to stretch her legs and take potty breaks. She formerly chased rabbits at breakneck speed. She would also take cheap shots at Javier's small band of milk cows, for whom she had little respect. Those trips were less frequent now. Not long ago, the cows were quick to move out of her way for fear she would give them one of her famous surprise nips on the back heel. Just for fun, she'd grab a nose and make them change direction because she knew she could, and

James MacKrell

they would if she demanded it. The dairy cows probably knew she was old now, so she was a bit more respectful and gave them more leeway when her old bones allowed her to meander into the pasture. She didn't want to learn they weren't as dumb as she first figured, so she tended to her business without interfering in theirs. Oh, how she did love it, when Javier used to let her take the cattle from one pasture to the next or help him gather calves at branding time, assisting him in loading a stubborn group of calves into trailers. Now, she had to be satisfied with watching the other dogs do these tasks. Javier kept dairy cows mostly for milk; his main income was the sheep. His Aussies, however, true to their stock dog heritage, would be capable of working both.

* * *

Jenny lifted her black, copper, and white trimmed head, and with a probing nose searched for Javier. She saw him coming and flipped away as if not to notice. Her feelings were hurt by his apparent rejection; she felt that today would be no exception.

"If he doesn't care for me anymore, I will just ignore him."

Her big heart couldn't let that happen. She was totally devoted to the Master and could not help herself, no matter how hard she tried, but obey his every beck and call. That was the law. That was the bargain between Aussie and herder.

"Hey, old gal, how's my number one helper this morning?"

Jenny couldn't believe her ears. It was the boss, in her kennel, stooping to stroke her. She heard him before she saw him. Although he knew it was for her own good, he hated to pen her up, so he'd make sure to stop and stroke her each morning when filling her water pail and food dish. He made sure Lonnie would do the same on mornings he attended to the feeding chores. This morning she heard his feet coming down the steps from the house and his spurs jangle on his boots when he crossed the yard.

A thrill ran through her body, causing warmth to flood her being. She looked into the face she adored. Her eyes beamed. She wasn't forgotten. She was still loved. Australian Shepherds are known for singling out a human and attaching themselves at the hip, never wavering in their devotion to that one person. They're always worried they aren't loving a person sufficiently. Javier's Aussies' needn't worry; he loved them without reservation. These dogs were his family, his ranch hands, his buddies.

The woolen shirt he had chosen this morning started to feel a little too warm. Temperatures were predicted today to climb to the mid sixties. After all the years in Montana, Javier knew the weather could swing in either direction as fast as a mountain bird could swoop on an insect.

"If it stays this warm tomorrow, my Jenny Dog, I will let you take a walk with us up the lower mountain. You probably need a little exercise and I'm worried about leaving you in your condition. This way I'll be sure you're okay." He ruffled her collar with a familiar stroke. "Plus we'll take it easy, and I've missed having you with me."

Jenny was the top herding dog on the place. She had earned it, and with her new puppies he was hoping that one of them would grow into her stature. Secretly he prayed one of the puppies would be so great and so grand he would become the number one stock dog champion in all Montana, surpassing his sire, Warner. Javier competed in stock dog trials when his time allowed, which for the

James MacKrell

past couple of years had been minimal. He had a hankering to try his hand at it again. It was a great hobby that kept his handling skills sharp. Plus it was fun and winning was in his blood and always on his mind. He liked proving his dogs both on the ranch and in competition.

Jenny's hind leg reached forward to scratch her left ear, not so much because it itched but more to prove she was awake and this promise of escape was real. Two magpies lit on the kennel floor, trying to pick the last couple of kibbles left in the pan from this morning's feeding. She didn't care.

She had something to live for; puppies or not, she would be about her master's business tomorrow.

The morning couldn't come fast enough for Jenny. Javier would take her with him tomorrow, she was assured. For the first time in weeks a belly full of puppies didn't bother her.

A cold wind swept around the barn into Javier's face as he returned to the house. The chill stopped him short. He glanced at the dark clouds building up behind the mountain chain to the west. While the Indian summer winds trickled across the foothills, dipping toward the lake and rising again to slip down the hills toward the cabin, the sight of dark clouds bellowing in the west was something to heed. He made a mental note to check the weather forecast again.

James MacKrell

Chapter 3
"An invitation to the dance..."

Javier, still mad at the TV, stomped into the frosty yard. Last night he had fiddled with the old set, hit it, punched it and cursed it, but to no avail. No TV, no way. Weather is the only thing he ever watched and when he missed Tom Spillman's forecast he felt lost. Two things a rancher has to worry about: weather in all its forms, and the markets and their fluctuations, but when your livelihood depends on Mother Nature and the whims of speculators, those are life-changing worries. He had climbed up on the slick roof to adjust the satellite dish because he couldn't bear not hearing the forecast. Even with all his prying and pushing, he still had no picture, no sound, and as he exclaimed to poor old Emma, who didn't really care, "no nothing!"

On the roof he had an unobstructed view of the snow-covered mountains to the far west. The snowcaps glistened as the evening sun slipped below the Absaroka-Beartooth Mountains. The view was particularly dramatic due to the ominous clouds that formed a backdrop that splayed the setting sun's rays into a palette of crimsons, brilliant yellows, and oranges.

"Weather," Javier mumbled. "It's a hard thing to figure out sometimes." His booted foot gave way on the slick, wet shingles. Steadying himself with his hand, he nearly grabbed the satellite dish out of its mooring.

He plopped down on the roof, getting the seat of his pants wet. He could feel the cold in the wind. Mad at the TV, he climbed down, stomped into the house, threw his

Down from the Mountain

gloves on the floor, and went to bed in a fury. Emma sauntered over and picked up the gloves and returned them to his chair. "There," she thought, "Now I can get some sleep. Forget all this pounding on the ceiling." Emma ruffled up the rug at the foot of the bed and circled until it felt just right. Then she plopped down with a grunt.

When morning dawned Javier was still peeved at the TV contraption. With the billowing clouds still on his mind, he looked up to survey the twisted satellite dish. He paused and looked at the mountains again, this morning glistening with the sunrise. A frown crept onto his sun-browned face. He glanced at Jenny's kennel where the Aussie was already standing by the gate, wiggling her entire back end. A huge smile chased the frown from his face. He had forgotten. Today was Jenny's day.

Waiting at the gate for her Master, Jenny was ready to go. She had eaten light last night and hardly touched her kibble this morning.

Out of the corner of her eye she saw the blue merle matron with her copper leggings and snow-white face. Emma had a worried look and Jenny knew that was the precursor to a lecture. The Matron had a way of slipping up to the kennel fence without directly looking at the dog inside. She stretched herself out, took a minute to roll in the dirt, righted herself, and gave a little bark to get attention. She didn't have to do all that; Jenny was glued to her every move.

Jenny stared at the elder Emma, anticipating the upcoming sermon. Emma always had a sermon, not a word of advice or praise but a full-fledged oration of fire and brimstone. There wasn't a dog among the shepherds who hadn't at one time or another had their ears rung out for some minor infraction. Even the two Great Pyrenees,

James MacKrell

afraid of no one, man nor beast, stepped gingerly when Emma was near the flock.

Jenny, sure that even Javier didn't argue with Emma, canted her eyes toward the ground and steadied herself for the sermon.

"How do you feel, darling?" Emma queried.

Jenny's head jerked up with shock; the only thing that could have startled Jenny more would have been a bucket of cold water in her face. She shook her head from side to side to make sure she heard correctly. Sure enough, Emma stood there with a pleasant smile on her face, waiting for a reply.

"I, uh, I'm uh, ah, pretty well, thank you for asking." She thought a moment and added, "If it wasn't for these confounded puppies tumbling around in my belly."

Emma smiled, shifted her position and resettled in about the same spot she had been in.

She continued, "Jenny girl, you have a great and wonderful responsibility bestowed on you."

Jenny's ears perked.

"Bringing life into the world is the greatest gift the Spirit of the Day and Night bestows on his creatures. It is a holy task. A task in which the Creator allows his created to join him in the dance of life."

Emma sat up. Her blue eye glowed with an inner light, her other eye, the amber one, radiated with understanding.

When pure wisdom is spoken, the listener needs no verification; when truth is presented, no substantiation. All Jenny could think about was the "unborn luggage" flailing around in her tummy, but the message of what Emma had said reverberated in her brain like a gong. The dance of life; the more she thought about it the more confused she became. "I, uh, uh," goodness knows she didn't want

Emma to think she didn't comprehend what she was talking about. "Uh, I totally agree, Miss Emma." And with full attention focused on the old Aussie, she continued, "and I look forward to doing that dance when it comes along."

"Oh, it will come, little girl, it will come. If you listen carefully you might hear the music beginning." Emma stretched her back, gave a good scratch to her midsection, and without another word turned and sauntered back toward the cabin.

Jenny would have been pondering Emma's words all day if Javier hadn't strolled up to the kennel door with his shepherd's crook in his hand. Jenny jumped to all fours. No puppies bothered her this time.

"Come on, old gal, let's take these ewes to get something to eat."

Coronado believed Jenny was at least a week away from her due date, so he felt this trip to the pasture would be all right.

"I want you to take it easy, no working the sheep at this time. The other dogs can do that. You just tag along and take it easy. It's a short trip and I'll keep my eye on you in case you get tired. You can ride in my arms if you do. Bayo won't mind. He and I have carried many a sheep back to camp or back to the ranch when they are hurt. We can do the same for you. I have to graze these sheep and I feel more comfortable having you with me where I can keep a sharp eye on you."

The shepherd dog went immediately to heel at Javier's left awaiting his next cue. She stayed so close to her Master her wavy coat brushed against his pant leg.

A shower of yellow leaves riding on a cold brisk wind blew across the dirt road, raising a little cloud of dust as it passed. The sky above was a clear cerulean blue. From the valley where the cabin sat, the foothills climbed like stairs ascending to a throne. The rocky road was littered with dried autumn leaves, their many colors resembling a royal carpet laid before herders. Jenny glanced to her right toward the sheep pens. Black and spotted gray faces stood at attention like a legion of soldiers ready for the day's march.

Bayo neighed his readiness for the task ahead. His saddlebags were jammed full with food, and there was a piel de cabra full of water and an extra ten gallon hat for Javier slung over the saddle horn. The big gelding pawed the ground impatiently.

Jenny flicked her eyes to the gnarled fir tree by the cabin porch. Where were the crows? She listened for their constant cawing about one thing or another, but all was quiet. In fact very few of the mountain birds of any kind could be seen. Javier's squirrel didn't even show himself. Most of the leaves from the cottonwoods had settled on the ground. The white bark of the aspen stood silently on guard, giving a glimpse of what was to come.

Blu's watchful eyes never left the sheep still in the pen. The guard dogs mingled with the flock. The Great Pyrenees, Mike and Gabe, were named after Javier's two favorite angels to whom he constantly prayed for protection. Both dogs had lived with the sheep since they were ten months old. They smelled like the sheep, and with their great shaggy gray-white coats, they looked like the sheep. Many coyotes or wolves made fatal mistakes when they assumed that these placid giants were an easy mark.

Javier treasured Jenny's independent mind and endless energy. When the other dogs napped while the herd was grazing, Jenny would be running around harassing butterflies if nothing else was around. Coronado loved to call her too rowdy. He was sure it aggravated her, but he felt she could take the teasing.

As his foot slipped into the stirrup, he grabbed the saddle horn and swung himself up on Bayo. The Morgan bent a little to the weight of the man, took in a deep breath to make the cinch strap a little more comfortable, and finally let out a noisy snort signaling a readiness to begin the day's work.

Jenny moved to her accustomed place on the horse's left. Javier signaled Lonnie to open the sheep gate and headed his horse and troop up and onto the pathway.

It was like every morning. The band of Suffolk sheep nimbly picked their way in pursuit of the shepherd, bobbing their heads at the grass along the way.

Jenny's head was up and alert. Her amber eyes sparkled. She was working in her mind but was ever so mindful not to actually work, lest she be rowdy. Nothing pleased her more than pleasing Javier.

James MacKrell

Chapter 4
"A change in the weather..."

The morning had been just like Javier and Jenny liked best, a little breezy but cheery and pleasant.

But by afternoon the wind picked up with a vengeance. The air cooled rapidly, a precursor to a sudden storm typical of Montana in late November. As the temperature continued to drop, the first snowflake hit Jenny squarely on her nose. Cold and wet, the crystal was completely unexpected. She tucked her head down into her ruff, trying to keep the building wind from drying her eyes out; she didn't see the concern etched on Javier's face. Despite his size, Bayo skidded sideways at the force of the gust, nearly unseating Javier with the sudden lurch. Blu began to circle the flock as if alerted by some secret message from the gods. Two flakes, followed by three others, and then it were as if someone swept back a curtain; the snow began to pour down on the sheep and shepherds. In a matter of minutes the sky had darkened, first a slate gray, then speckled with black and swirling bubbles of clouds.

No more rays of the sun's face penetrated the soupy mass of turbulence. The snow kept spinning in a dangerous dance of mayhem, and the winds picked up, whipping and howling through the trees and down the gullies.

Jenny watched Blu and the other Aussies trying to bunch the sheep. Javier rode from one side of the pasture to another, all the time urging the dogs on. The Pyrenees boldly pointed their faces into the wind at the pasture's edge to discourage any prowlers from taking advantage of the panic that could sweep the entire flock. Javier's voice remained calm, though heavy concern started to show in his eyes. A tremble ran through Jenny's body. Some force she didn't understand kept screaming in her mind, "You must protect the puppies at all costs." These new reactions countered all of her desires to dash forth and help gain control of the flock, to do Javier's bidding no matter what. All the complaining and fretting over her discomfort and general malaise disappeared. Every fiber of her being sensed the danger. The snow quickly nearing blizzard conditions caused Jenny to blink and squint so she could no longer make out the forms of Javier or the sheep she knew should be right in front. The driving snow picked up in strength and made it more difficult for her to make her way.

A miserable hour had passed and the depths of windswept snowdrifts piling up all around her slowed her progress as much as the howling wind. The weight of her stomach was like an anchor being dragged on the tide. She was falling farther behind Javier's scramble to get the sheep to safety. She could hear the urging barks of the Aussies. She could hear her brother, Blu. His voice seemed more and more distant. She just couldn't keep up.

Her coat was heavy and wet with sticky snow as she plodded on through the deep drifts toward the bleating of the band of confused and frightened sheep.

A stiff and sudden gale of snow-laden wind slammed across the mountainside, causing her to stumble back into a deep drift. Struggling to get up, an inner engine working overtime propelled her forward. No matter how tough the going, Jenny was going to be a survivor.

His blue eyes flashing with a spark hinting at the fire in his gut, Blu's bark had a sound of urgency to it. Through the snow he plunged.

James MacKrell

He circled the strays, calmly urging them on while not adding to the flock's uneasiness. His head spun in the direction of any sheep headed astray.

Mike and Gabe were just ahead, staring blindly into the whiteout, probing the air for any danger from wolves, wildcats, or coyotes that would use the disarray to single out a lost or elderly ewe for slaughter. Attentive to his task, Blu also took on the responsibility of making sure the other herding dogs performed well so they could get down the mountain and pen the band of ewes before any were lost to the storm.

Something caused Blu to stop dead in his tracks. Jenny's littermate felt a wrench deep in his heart.

It was a pang of anxiety, as if something was missing, and he was too busy to search for it. Grief gripped his insides, yet to his alert mind everything had to keep working to enable Javier to get the sheep down without losing any of the precious flock. The herdsman worked his ranch on such a small margin that disaster at this time could financially wipe him out. Javier would again, late in life, be compelled to attend someone else's sheep, make money for someone else, no longer be his own boss. After being with Javier all these years, since Blu and Jenny were puppies, Blu had learned from Miss Emma how much this ranch and its livestock meant to the old Basque.

Emma told Blu she remembered the tears dripping from Javier's cheeks as he read the will of his dear friend and boss, Jim Townsend. I bequeath this Townsend Ranch and all its holdings to my trusted friend, Javier Frances Coronado. Emma said she sidled up next to Javier, rubbing fondly against his leg. She could sense the joy bubbling up through his soul.

This story Blu never forgot. It gave purpose to his shepherding and his love for the flock.

Blu and Jenny were parts of Javier's heart, and neither would ever let him down.

The gust of wind rounded the fir cliff like a wall of water pouring down a tunnel. Blu, blown off his feet, scrambled to right himself. His questioning mind spoke in a still voice. Blu, where is your sister, Jenny? "Where is Jenny?" he barked.

His searching eyes scanned the snowscape for a glimpse of her tri-color body plodding along behind, but safe. He didn't see her; he couldn't smell her familiar scent. Should he backtrack to find her, help her?

At that moment a ewe, with panic painted across her black face bolted for the trees, camouflaged in a sea of white. Blu's attentive eyes caught her movement, and an instinctive impulse jolted him into action to head off the panicked sheep. In a flash his concern for Jenny was shoved aside by his need to corral this escapee. Instincts embedded in his DNA forced him to save the wooly charges regardless of the danger to himself.

"Bayo, easy now, my big boy, steady," Javier said as he gently rubbed the neck of his horse.

If ever Bayo needed reassurance, it was now. His black mane coated with ice made tinkling sounds as the bay bobbed his head, trying to focus his eyes. Each time he snorted, a gust of steam rose from his nose. The worn saddle slipped as Bayo's coat became wetter and slicker and the cinch strap loosened. Javier nearly lost his balance as he stood in the stirrups, scanning the surrounding area. The wind and snow worked hard to freeze his eyelashes, making his eyes sting, causing tears to slip down the herdsman's cheeks. He tried to brush the salty drippings away and clutched the scarf around his neck, pulling it over his nose so he could breathe easier. The cutting wind pierced the core of his body. One gloved hand held the reins as the other reached to pull his collar tighter against his neck.

"Easy, Blu, get around." His voice was calm yet very loud and assertive. Although the dogs were also trained to respond to whistle commands as whistles carry farther, Javier didn't plan on needing his whistle this trip so he left it at home. Now he wished he had it. Hysteria was trying to grip him, but he shook it off as he tended to his flock and his dogs. He knew he must keep his wits about him.

What little of the sky Javier could see in the west remained black as pitch. Under his breath Javier cursed the broken TV again. He had missed Tom Spillman's broadcast of the weather, something he never did. Nearly all of the ranchers and farmers relied on Spillman's weather report since their lives, and livelihoods, depended on it. Ranching is difficult in the best conditions. Those dedicated people who sustain a living out of soil and livestock depend on luck and knowledge to protect themselves from the forces of nature that can wipe them out in a moment's notice. For Javier this was one of those times.

If he didn't get the sheep down to the pen and soon, he risked losing a major part of the flock.

Each sheep represented money, and money was hard to come by.

He cupped his hand to his mouth and shouted Brady, come by! He urged the red Aussie, who had come close enough to hear him in the storm, to head in a clockwise direction around the sheep. He could sense them drifting off as the path down the mountain started to narrow.

Blu pushed from the rear of the band, closing the gap between the sheep and the herder's horse.

"Get out!" He directed this command to Mate, an older dog with great experience under pressure. Mate reacted automatically and eased off the group of sheep he drove toward the herdsman.

Bayo's front hoof grazed a rock hidden beneath the snow; his right shoulder buckled a bit, causing Javier to lurch forward. His hat fell and was snatched up by the whipping wind. The sombrero was quickly buried in a drift. Javier's eyes never left the sheep and the dogs. He prayed that together they could get the sheep down the lower mountain and penned.

Mike, the big male Pyrenees, started a ruckus at the edge of the woods. A wolf was stalking slowly toward a group of sheep bunched against a pile of fallen trees.

The wolf bared his fangs and dropped his head in a menacing manner, preparing to attack. In response two hundred pounds of white fury lunged at the would-be attacker. Mike sank his teeth deep into the wolf's neck. Before Gabe could join in the defense, the gray wolf shook free of the great white dog's grip, turned tail, and disappeared back into the forest. Mike, barking loudly, took a few threatening bounds after the wolf, watched the beast dissolve into the cover, then turned back to the flock and to his quiet, gentle self.

All the Aussies took note. They knew they had nothing to fear while the guard dogs patrolled.

It became harder to walk. The snow piled into deepening drifts and the darkness seemed to crash in all around them. Javier's eyes squinted, blinded by the snow and cold, in search of all his sheep.

"Hunt 'em up." he said to Blu and Brady. As both dogs headed out running hard to round up any strays, Javier's face froze in panic. "Where is Jenny, Bayo?" He strained to look for the black dog.

"Jenny! Jenny!" He shouted hoarsely against the wind. "Jenny, come! Jenny, come!" He whistled through his teeth, hoping the sharp sound would cut through the howling storm. Javier ducked his head as heavy coughing wracked his body. His mind was focused on Jenny, and his heart was beating fast with fear and dread. He was choking with grief, not just from the storm. Blu's head popped up. He could hear the Master's voice. All of a sudden a chill, having nothing to do with the weather, cascaded like ice water through Blu's body at the thought… "Where is Jenny?' "Our Jenny is lost!"

James MacKrell

Chapter 5
"Utterly alone…"

Jenny pawed the air trying her best to get a foothold on something solid to break her fall. The ground seemed to have disappeared beneath her. Just seconds ago as she crept her way forward, more by hearing than anything else, she stepped onto what she thought to be a part of the path covered with deep snow. Jenny's misstep onto the perceived path put her instead smack on top of a drift, which collapsed immediately with her weight.

Her side slammed into a protruding rock, bouncing her to the right as she plummeted downward, still paddling her frost- covered legs in wild, desperate movements, reaching for anything firm. The dense snowfall obscured her vision. She couldn't tell up from down. Her black body ricocheted off the gully wall, causing her to tumble head over heels nearly twenty feet to the bottom.

Jenny slammed against the frigid ground which knocked the air from her lungs. She lay gasping, unable to move. Cold, bloodied, and semi-conscious, she managed to raise her head enough to glance around, but nothing looked familiar. She had a huge gash just above the copper colorings over her eyes. Her thoughts were a jumble. She whimpered as she stared upward into the white veil. A cloud of confusion enveloped her mind as sound mingled with strange flashes of light produced ghostly apparitions before her eyes. The wind's howl down the fissure drowned out her pitiful cries for help. She wanted the roar of the storm to stop. She tried vainly to cover her ears with her mangled, dirty paws.

"What about your puppies?" a small voice deep within her seemed to say in what sounded like Emma's voice.

The throbbing in her side stopped. One eye was bruised and nearly closed. The salty blood in the corners of her mouth didn't alarm her as much as the question about her puppies.

She tried to leap to her feet, but nothing worked. Her copper and white legs that moments ago had been fanning the air, now wouldn't move. For the first time in her life she wondered if she would die. Jenny had seen other things die. An animal would lay there, its body cold to the touch so no matter how much she might poke or paw the form, nothing moved. The eyes had no light, no sparkle. They looked back at her with a vacant stare. Jenny would sniff around the animal's nose but no warm breath could be detected. Soon someone or something came and took the corpse away. Gone! Where she didn't know, why she didn't know, just gone. Now for the first time she faced the fact, that she, just like all the animals preceding her, might be gone as well, *"but to where?"*

A tiny movement deep in her painful belly grabbed her attention. She couldn't move, but something moved inside her. Not the jumping and cavorting of the unborn puppies that had, pestered her for weeks at home. No, this faint twitch, and then another, signaled a flicker of life, an answer to her prayer. Despite the winter detritus and a wet mangled coat, sudden warmth started in the depths of her belly and spread throughout her freezing body. Life, not death, oozed, filling all the holes in Jenny's being. The question, what about the puppies became a song, a song of survival, a song of life. Jenny began the dance. Her thoughts were choreographed in step to her memories.

James MacKrell

She tried to curl her head back down to lick her bruised under-belly. "Emma must have known." With that thought a small light sparked in her eyes.

Jenny now was determined to join the dance, as Emma had called it, to immerse herself in the song of life.

* * *

All the sheep were penned and mounds of hay were shoveled out so that food would keep their metabolism working, providing warmth. The edges of Javier's eyes stung with ice that formed on his lashes. No matter how he bundled up, he wasn't warm. He worked at break-neck speed; the exhausted sheep dogs never wavered in their work. The Great Pyrenees' shaggy coats were covered in ice. Their feet left bloody footprints in the snow. Ice burrs formed between their toes, making every step painful. Every second counted. Everyone, man and animal alike, knew disaster was only moments away. Blu, Mate and Brady could smell the fear in the ewes. The dogs governed their movements to avoid a panic in the flock. Javier's voice was steady and calm, yet his heart beat to a different rhythm.

"Blu, where is our Jenny?" His voice cracked with emotion. Blu didn't seem to be paying attention; his intensity was on the sheep, yet a stabbing shot ran through his heart as he thought of the plight of his sister lost on the mountain. "Oh, Jenny." he whined. "Oh, my little Jenny." Two black-faced ewes bolted toward the partially opened gate and Blu, barking with intensity, dashed to herd them back.

The mane of the gelding was frozen solid like a stiff brush. The heat from the horse's body provided some warmth for the old Basque. Bayo knew as soon as the sheep were safely bedded down from the storm he would be carrying the Master back into the teeth of the storm to look for the Jenny dog. It was the least the great Morgan could do.

From the forest with trees bending nearly to the ground with ice, other eyes were watching the performance. Hidden eyes looked hungry, as they peered from the darkness, seeking the errant ewe that could become food to warm a wolf pack. The scent of the predators rode the ice crystals in the air and both of the giant guard dogs rushed the fence, furiously barking and snarling to ward off any attacks.

This night all of Javier's band of sheep would be safe, against both the cold and the threat of being eaten. The spent dogs would curl up in their kennel barrels, warm from the outside and comfortable in their assurance of a job well done -all but Blu. He would spend the night awake, worrying about his littermate, hoping for her well-being and safe return.

He caught sight of Javier and Bayo as they rode back into the snowstorm. Javier's voice was becoming weaker as he plaintively called his lost dog's name.

Jenny knew that if she didn't find cover she would surely die. Her wounds were freezing over with the ice and snow that was accumulating in the bottom of the gully. The blood on her face turned into a crimson icicle. She licked her paws, trying to keep them warm, hoping to massage them into working. Jenny's heart was racing with a fear she had never known before.

With trembling paws she stretched out her body to try to get a grip in the freezing slush on the rocky wall. Each nail of her paws extended like a cat's in an effort to pull herself up the side of the gully. If she stayed in the bottom she would soon be covered in snow. Her sense of

James MacKrell

survival warned her to reach for higher ground. Oh, how she hurt. The muscles in her tired legs bunched under the strain. Each step left a blood mark that would have been easy for a predator to follow. Her life hung tenuously to a cord of willpower that seemed to be fraying.

Jenny looked up but saw nothing but the coverlet of white that roofed the gorge. She shook out her coat in an attempt to cast off the snow and wet, hoping to keep her body heat in. Everything around her looked fuzzy and out of sorts.

"If only I could get out of here," she whimpered searching the sides of the ditch. "If only Javier could find me."

As the question crossed her mind she already knew the answer.

"Javier won't find me," she thought. "I am the only one that can save me and my puppies."

For an instant her clawing stopped. She settled and let the importance of the thought sink in. Jenny wasn't used to thinking of herself as independent of anyone's help. The realization of her helplessness dawned on her, causing her eyes to dim. Her kind always had humans to care for them. Someone brought her food, fixed the kennels, provided shelter from the cold. Somebody petted and loved her, and comforted her when she was sick or injured. Someone had always been there. Not now. Solitude covered her like the falling snow.

* * *

Ronnie cursed as he slammed the window closed for the forth time, his hands knocking over an empty whiskey bottle. The bottle bounced against the stone holding the door shut and burst into a hundred pieces skittering across the dirty floor. The heavy winds outside pushed at the windows of the cabin already weakened by age and neglect. Spencer's house, if it could be called a house, was really no more than a dilapidated lean-to hidden from the main road down a dead-end dirt lane. The gate had a hand-painted sign that read, "Spencer's Kennels, Home of America's Best Protection Dogs." This evening the sign lay beside the highway, covered in snow, blown down by the strong winds.

Ronnie Spencer was in no mood to put up with the window not working. He was cold, hung over and in a foul mood. This sudden storm had caught him by surprise. He had to rush to cover the kennels with an old tarp and stuff hay in the stakeout barrels in an effort to keep the dogs from freezing. Whether driven by the cold or just the madness of being constantly kenneled, the dogs barked incessantly to Spencer's extreme annoyance. Chilled to the bone he rushed in, shedding dirty wet snow off his stamping feet and off his jacket, to build a fire to keep as much of the shack warm as possible. Through the cracks in the warped sideboards the cold air streamed at will.

"Shut your mouths, you mangy curs! You're good for nothing, anyway. All you bastards do is eat and bark."

The barking continued; in fact, it got louder. Out in the makeshift kennels one female wasn't barking. She stood against the wind and cold just like her kind had for thousands of years. Her gray coat ruffled against the weather, her silver-tipped ears erect and listening. Her undercoat provided the warmth needed to brave the elements. Yellow eyes stared at the cabin where the screaming was coming from. If only she could get at him. She would make sure he would scream at them no more. He would no longer beat them or abuse them or hold them prisoner ever again. Hers was a deep hatred for the Man.

James MacKrell

The only sound she made was a deep, guttural growl, the growl of a wolf.

James MacKrell

Chapter 6
"A life without love…"

Charles "Hoss" Wilson was a bully, a mean and deceitful person since his childhood. He had hung kittens by the tail over clotheslines. Set fire to cats just to see them run. His experience with dogs was limited to a little Rat Terrier owned by an aunt. While visiting in Gary, Indiana, his mother sent him into the backyard to play so she and her sister could gossip about their husbands. A pitiful yelp stopped them in mid-sentence, and they rushed to the back porch just in time to save the small dog from being hung. Meanness followed Charlie "Hoss" Wilson like stink on a skunk.

Distrusted in his neighborhood and hated at work for his lying and his unruly temper, Charlie thought owning a wolf-dog would command the respect he had longed for all his life. Charlie stared at his computer screen with a grin. He smashed out his cigarette and said to himself, "Things are going to be a lot different around these parts." He was looking at a website with an advertisement that read, Guard your property and family. Own a piece of the wild. Guaranteed wolf-dog hybrids. Charlie beamed and made a hasty phone call to set up a meeting. "After all," he muttered to himself, "it will take a full-bodied guy to tame a wolf." All the way out to the kennels, Hoss flexed and released his forearms by squeezing the steering wheel. He wanted to pump up his muscles to impress the kennel's owner.

"Good Morning," the trainer greeted him. "Hope you didn't have no trouble gettin' here?"

"Naw, it was a piece of cake. I got me one of those GPS handhelds and poof, just like magic, I was at your place."

Wilson's eyes were wide with amazement as he entered the yard of Protection Kennels, just fifty miles due west of downtown Chicago. From around the back of the yellow frame house a dog stuck out his head, and quick as Charlie might blink his eyes the massive animal begin charging full steam at the two men. Instantly, a cold sweat popped out on Wilson's forehead, his heart began racing. He edged a little closer to the man who had identified himself as simply "Sarge." The camo-clad owner of the kennels barked a curt command, "At rest, Trooper." The huge black and tan animal skidded to a stop not three yards from Charlie Wilson. Wilson let out a deep sigh, and a weak smile broke out across his rotund face.

"There is a good example of the ability of my wolf hybrids to listen and obey commands in an instant." He sauntered over to the sitting dog and gave him a tertiary pat. The dog never took his eyes off Charlie. One thing Sarge left out was the fact that Trooper was a full-blooded German Shepherd, professionally trained by a Schutzhund handler. Sarge had purchased the attack dog when the former owner passed away and the estate put the dog and other animals up for sale. Trooper was a whole different story from the wolf-dogs Sarge had advertised for sale. While dogs like Trooper had been bred for generations to be companions and workmates for men, wolves had survived for thousands of years by following their own inner light and putting their survival above any other need. All dogs carry wolf genes, yet temperament and domesticity varies greatly between species. Those who have captive wolves or so-called domesticated wolves also prove this almost daily by the failure of these experiments.

James MacKrell

Sarge, trading in on his combat appearance, preyed on unsuspecting potential owners who envisioned the pride of taming one of nature's predators. Such was the unsuspecting Charlie, who arrived with hope that the acquisition of a wolf-dog might finally make him the man he dreamed of being. He wanted to be a man people would look up to and admire. Mostly he dreamed they would secretly fear him.

On the way back to Chicago, the sleeping 8-week-old cub, nestling next to his leg in the cab of the pickup truck, looked docile enough. Charlie couldn't wait until his Sheena, he named her after his favorite comic book heroine, grew into a full-grown wolf. As the miles clicked by he smiled at the anticipated reaction of his next-door neighbor, who for the most part ignored the fat, little man.

"I'll show him," grumbled Charlie, nearly drooling as he spoke. The vision of his neighbor being afraid of Charlie and Sheena danced in his mind.

A year passed, and Charlie proved as inept at training Sheena as he did everything else in his life. He read that dominance was the trick, and to Charlie dominance meant a cowering pup. He would tie the young Sheena to a post in the yard and yell 'Sit!' at the top of his voice, and then beat her down with a cane shaft when she didn't obey. After the beatings and the chains didn't work with Sheena, Charlie started fearing for his life. At nearly a year old she weighed just under eighty pounds and seemed much more menacing. One day the lock on her collar broke and she charged him baring her fangs and growling in a deep, deadly voice.

"You damn bitch! You get away from me. Get away!" He swung the stick in his hand at her and moved faster than he ever had before, grabbing the kennel door and slamming it shut in Sheena's face. From that day forward he never again went into her cage.

Charlie resolved to rid himself of the "Silver Fury." He saw his opportunity when he came across an ad on the Internet: "Wanted-wolf-dog hybrids. May be full grown or puppies. Top dollar paid." Contact Ron Spencer, P.O. Box 1256 Big Timber, Montana." The ad went on to give a phone number manned 24/7 by a recorded answering machine.

Wilson hired some professional handlers to medicate the wolf-dog and help him get her into a crate for shipping. As they loaded the dog into the back of a pickup truck, Charlie looked up to see his neighbors all standing around in their yards laughing and pointing. He never felt more humiliated in his life.

Chapter 7
"She moves to the mountain…"

Ronnie Spencer purchased Sheena and brought her to his so-called kennels deep in the mountain valleys of south central Montana. Her indoctrination into the cruelty of Man continued. Sheena learned to mistrust humans. Distrust lead to fear and fear to aggression. At almost one hundred pounds Sheena would be a formidable foe for man or beast. She was tall with a heavy cover of grizzled fur. Her nearly white face gave the wolf-dog a look of mystery. Sheena's father, a native-born North Country Timber Wolf, had been trapped by poachers and sold to the Protection Kennels in Chicago to be used at stud. He was never tamed. However, due to the medication the kennel owner kept mixing with his food, he remained tranquil enough to be used in breeding. The giant wolf was intoxicatingly handsome and regal. So beautiful, the kennel owner, the man called Sarge, used an enticing professional photo of him in his advertising as a lure. Evidence of this beauty and presence was readily witnessed in Sheena.

Now at Ronnie Spencer's place, Sheena gazed into the next run, thinking the ten-year-old male there was the most beautiful wolf she'd ever seen. With his luxurious grizzled-gray coat, wise and battle-worn face, and utter self-confidence, he was the essence of the alpha male in a wolf pack.

Behind his piercing yellow eyes beat the heart of a strong hunter and defender of his territory. The other wolves knew the imposing male as Scar. A bullet's path across his strong face left a gaping wound from the corner of his mouth to the back of his ear.

Another rifle's bullet crippled him and brought him under submission. Neither did he indicate that he was in pain nor did he ever show the man any fear. Deep in his proud and free heart he longed to die. To live as a captive was more than he could stand. His wild spirit was dying.

Sheena had spent most of her boring days staring in silence at Scar. He returned her worshipful gaze with loving eyes, totally enamored with her strength and beauty. In the wild they would have mated for life. Here, cooped up and prohibited from being together, their love had to be day-to-day.

Ronnie used the wolf to breed Sheena in an effort to encourage his interest in the other bitches that were in heat as well. Scar eagerly mated with Sheena but refused to mate with the bitches. The bitches harbored a human smell that was as stinging to Scar's nostrils as acid. He hated the humans, and he venomously loathed captivity. The only thing left of his life in the wild was the wolf-hybrid in the pen beside him. It was in her that Scar found the only solace in this human prison. Only Sheena aroused him. Spencer had no background whatsoever in the husbandry of animals, and he assumed that a male wolf would act like a male human when around available females. What he failed to learn is that the female still must arouse the male; without arousal there can be no breeding. Spencer had the idea that he could excite the big wolf with Sheena and quickly substitute the others before he could impregnate the she-wolf. When Scar mounted Sheena, Spencer thought he could poke him with an electric prod attached to a long stick to interrupt the act. Scar accepted the pain and disobeyed the man's command. The wolf and Sheena were tied up in mating and nothing was going to separate them.

James MacKrell

In a melee Sheena was consummated and the other females were not.

Sheena's aggression scared Spencer. He knew she would be hard to handle, but he had no idea the beautiful wolf-dog would turn lethal. "When that bitch has puppies and they are anything like that devil wolf she's bred to, them little bastards would probably come out ready to eat a full-grown man."

His saner side knew the extremely belligerent hybrids were harder to place since no one could control them.

* * *

"Mostly I just shoot 'em." The tobacco-juiced grin caused Spencer to take a swipe at his mouth. At the thought of how much fun it was to turn the evil little bastards loose and "just shoot the hell out of 'em," he started to laugh and some of the tobacco phlegm slipped down his gullet, causing him to choke.

Sheena grew to hate the man more every day. As the cubs in her stomach grew her sense of protection deepened. She paced the double-wired cage constantly, only stopping to eat when she became nearly exhausted. She spent a fitful night. Due to the coldness of the steel barrel propped against the back part of the enclosure, her bones ached incessantly. Sheena got no pats, no warm words, no love of any kind. Ronnie wasn't the type of man who understood affection. He showed no kindness to man or beast.

With each passing day, as she watched every move of Ronnie Spencer, her hatred grew. Even on the coldest of nights she lay curled in her barrel thinking of ways to get to the man, plotting his destruction, planning her escape.

One night Sheena was awakened by a dream, a disturbing series of thoughts filled with dread. She stirred in her kennel and listened as low moans came from the adjacent kennel. Even with the freezing cold of the air, the big male was lying on his side stretched out on the ground, near the wire fence separating the two runs.

He strained to lift his gray head, and with his dying breaths the great hunter spoke in short gasps to Sheena. She got as close to the fence as she could. Her ears tuned to the slightest utterance.

"Dearest Sheena, take pride in your kind." The old wolf groaned as the pain in his heart grew sharper. As each second ticked by it became more difficult for him to speak. He tried to raise his head but the effort overcame him and his head plopped back down on the freezing ground. Sheena whimpered and crawled on her belly to try to get as close to him as possible. She needed to fill her snout with the odor of his maleness, smell the life still in his body.

He hacked dry coughs as he spoke. "You have been chosen my beloved; carry my cubs well, for someday they will make all of our ancestors proud." With that he breathed a long sigh, his eyelids open as his mighty yellow eyes went dull with the exhale of his last breath.

A stabbing pain shot through Sheena. Struggling to get to her feet she raised her pale face to the blackness above and from the depths of her soul pierced the night with the wolf howl for the dying.

* * *

Four weeks after the big blizzard hit, Sheena had her puppies. Three little boys and two girls, all born strong and healthy, nursed the necessary mother's milk to give them

James MacKrell

the antibodies and sustenance they needed to start their first day in the world.

Sheena beamed with pride. She even said to the night air, "This little one looks just like his sire. I hope he will grow up big and strong."

Her mother's tongue massaged the cubs, making sure each pup's internal organs worked and they were able to pass the waste from their bodies. Sheena loved being a mother. The song of motherhood danced in her brain as she swore allegiance to these newborn babies and vowed to give them the protection they would have received in the wild from their father. The dance of life was very strong in the mother wolf-dog; her caring eyes gleamed as she looked over each and every one.

The morning burst upon the world bright and frosty. The sun shining through the wire of the run created a dappled effect on the ground. Sheena roused from a deep sleep and probed the hay in the barrel to count each pup with her nose just to make sure they were all there. She never tired of counting, licking and nuzzling her babies. For the first time in her captive life she felt she had a purpose.

The sting startled her. Sheena's hip began to throb and little by little she could feel a burning sensation spread from her hip over the lower part of her body. Cold fear gripped her as she realized she could not move her legs. She could not even feel them! Her mind was spinning. She wasn't thinking clearly, nothing made any sense. The warm, numb feeling kept creeping up into her midsection. Rolling around she fought and fought to keep her eyes open, but the harder she struggled the more everything became fuzzy.

He shoved the remaining tranquilizer darts into his front pocket and lowered the blowgun. "There, that will

hold that bitch until I get them devil-babies out of there."
Ronnie Spencer loved to hear himself talk. He figured as
long as he talked to himself he would be assured of an
intelligent listener. When he was sure Sheena was
unconscious, he quietly climbed into her cage and picked
up all five puppies. He tossed them into a barrel full of
water and held them down, ensuring the end of each and
every one. It didn't take them long to die. The cubs
weren't big enough to give him the pleasure of seeing them
run for their lives.

It was late afternoon and the shadows became
longer and longer as the anesthesia started to wear off.
Groggy, Sheena raised her head and sniffed the air for the
familiar scent of the cubs. All she could smell was the
putrid odor of Ronnie Spencer.

She staggered to her feet, a glaze of panic in her
eyes as she panted loudly, searching in vain for her brood.
The lingering scent of drugs and the overpowering reek of
tobacco assaulted her nostrils and left her nauseated.

The water bucket was pushed aside, the bedding
pulled from the kennel barrel. She scratched and dug the
earth around the edges of the cage trying to find any hint of
her babies. A violent surge gripped her insides. She
vomited out pure bile. Sheena's mighty head swung from
side to side, sucking at the air, trying to get a taste of the
scent of the missing puppies. The more she gulped the
smell of tobacco, the more she hated that human.

All night she stayed awake plotting her chance to
attack Spencer.

She groaned like she was sick, hoping he would
come in the cage to see if she was hurt. If she could only
get to him, he would pay for all his cruelty. Her spirit told
her that someday he would. She wanted that day to be
now.

James MacKrell

Sheena paced her cage trying to find a corner or position near her crate to shield her from the stabbing wind and cold. It had been two days since Spencer killed her pups. Every hour her anger grew. She snarled and snapped at anything and everything that approached her cage. This night the cold only added to her discomfort and made her more determined than ever to escape.

Chapter 8
"Dash to freedom..."

The steep hill next to Ronnie Spencer's place rose from the valley floor behind the kennels straight up nearly 300 feet. Tall fir and spruce trees that formed a wall up the hillside stood vigil against the night. The wind-whipped power lines jerked and strained at the tenuous connection to the decrepit shack, causing the lights inside to flicker. Puffs of smoke bolted their way skyward from the chimney. The scene from the hilltop looked desolate, but to Sheena it was the sight of a horror she had just fled.

Three weeks earlier, the heavy winds from the devastating snowstorm clipped a huge limb from an aging tree directly over Sheena's run. As the tenacious winter winds blew, the large branch finally broke loose and crashed down, hitting the weakest parts of the makeshift compound, ripping the rusted chain links like torn canvas. Sheena pushed and jumped at the cleavage in the fence until it was wide enough to afford her a chance at liberty. With a silent leap she cleared the tumbled wire and dashed up and onto the hill. In seconds her gray form blended with the rocky hillside and the sparse patches of snow and disappeared into the storm that freed her.

Finally unchained of her prison, Sheena made her way deep into the blackness of the forest. The huge, swaying spruce and fir trees held back the strongest force of the wind, as she wolf-trotted away from Spencer's place. Her ears primed for any sounds of danger, she kept a steady pace down an old deer trail that wound through a thick stretch of woodland. Sheena didn't know where to go. She only knew her path took her further away from the nightmares of Spencer's hellhole.

Some way down the trail the woods opened up to a large, grassy copse.

A small hillock rose on the other side and before it lay the random, scattered remains of trees and debris deposited there by years of wind and rain.

Exhausted by the unaccustomed exertion, Sheena sought out a niche in the rotting pile of timber in which to escape the damp and biting cold. Her nose checked each piece of wood and crevice for the scent of other animals. Satisfied she was the only occupant, she twirled around, scraping at the leaves and debris strewn beneath her tired feet until a pattern was worn that served as her bed. Her exhausted legs curled under her body as she laid her beaten head on the pile of leaves. She wasn't warm, but she also wasn't freezing cold. This night offered something she had never experienced; tonight she would sleep in freedom.

* * *

In another part of the mountains, Jenny fought for her life.

After scrambling a third of the way up the arroyo's windward side, Jenny's aching paws reached a cavern's edge. All of her muscles strained nearly to the breaking point as she pulled herself up and climbed into the dark hole. The cave offered shelter from the icy wind. She leaned against the rocky wall and relaxed. The violent shivers wracking her body began to subside.

Outside the snowstorm railed on, but the closeness in the natural den gave her comfort and succor.

Jenny massaged her aching muscles, pausing to lick the most grievous wounds. Warmth returned to her limbs

James MacKrell

and they became a little more manageable. Her constant licking around her belly also caused the unborn to respond with a twitch. Not as much movement as back in the security of Javier's kennel, but enough to tell of an inner life.

Suddenly she breathed a familiar scent. "Could it be?" she thought. A faint but familiar scent wisped by her nose and jolted her to attention. It smelled like Javier. *"Had he come back to find her?"* Driven by hope she scooted inch by inch farther back into the crevice. The blackness made it difficult to see any form, but it sure had Javier's odor.

One paw pushed deeper into the darkness as far as possible without having to move her entire body. The left paw touched something soft and woolen. With her claws she stretched to pull the object closer to her. Crusted with dirt but dry, the material definitely seemed to be something she had encountered before. As the soft object loosened from its mooring in the side of the cavern, the scent of Javier grew stronger. The woolen mass proved much larger than Jenny first surmised. As both paws clawed the cloth closer to her the smell became more identifiable. The fabric appeared to be a mackinaw with red and black checks that Jenny had a vague memory of seeing on Javier.

"How did it get here?" she wondered. Jenny curled it around her so the bouquet of her master would fill her head. Exhaustion from fighting the wall and the storm gave way to sleep. A deep slumber filled her head with dreams of hope, hope that sometime soon her beloved master would find her and rescue her from all the peril she was suffering.

So ended the first day lost, her dreams being her only solace.

Jenny, in response to the tremors in her belly, shifted position and buried her head into the sleeve of Javier's lost coat.

* * *

The first contraction jolted Jenny out of sleep. The squeezing in her stomach grew in rhythms and soon engulfed her body in waves of pain. Her mouth dried. The pupils of her eyes dilated with each undulation of her stomach cavity. Unnaturally cold, she fidgeted, as the area about her birth canal grew warm with an oozing of body fluids. The Dance had begun.

In a dirty rock-littered cave, miles away from the security of Javier's ranch, Jenny gave birth to her puppies. One at a time the babies escaped her body. Her natural instinct told her to lick and massage the little ones until each took breaths on their own. The harder she worked on the first puppy the more she understood it was in vain. Her heart was breaking; the first three puppies entered the world lifeless. All of the urging to protect her puppies now seemed fruitless. *"What have I done?"* Her eyes glazed over with guilt, her breath came in short pants. *"I didn't save my babies! They are dead."*

Three lifeless forms lay as cold as the night air. Jenny fretted. She had failed. The life that grew in her was gone. Then another contraction gripped her body. *"Oh, no,"* escaped her tired lips. The pain increased and another puppy slipped into the world, only this time, the little bundle wiggled and let out tiny yelps. It was alive, and that life awakened Jenny's will to live.

She licked and massaged all over the pup. The puppy yelped more, her little sides writhing with each breath. She nuzzled her mother's warmth. A pink nose

James MacKrell

burrowed into the middle of Jenny's stomach; soon her mother's milk flowed into the little Aussie. The pride in Jenny's eyes beamed enough to almost light the darkened cavern. As the baby nursed, Jenny continued to lick and caress its little form. Her baby girl was alive.

Another sharp contraction drew Jenny's attention from the red colored pup. Again her womb gave forth life. This time a black puppy with a startling white blaze down his chest emerged yelping. He too, just like his sister before him, wriggled and gulped the air, seizing as much life as he could. The black bundle of fur scooched into the furry belly of his mom and drank deeply of the milk of life.

James MacKrell

Chapter 9
"The glimmer of life…"

Stones strewn around the tiny cavern's floor caused no discomfort for Jenny this night. She was too full of pride and love for the two mewling puppies snuggling deep into her midsection, each seeking the source of their mother's milk.

Exhausted, her maternal instincts guided her through sleep, guarding the litter's safety. Fat and full, each little Aussie found the pillow of flesh and fur on Jenny's stomach. Each burrowed in. The diminutive black male and red female settled and spent the night in security and calm without a thought of the danger just outside the opening of their cave.

* * *

All day Emma searched the ranch grounds for any hint of Jenny. Determined to find her, the old dog probed every nook and cranny around the house, the barn and any outbuildings where Jenny might have been trapped.

By the time she dragged herself inside the cabin and flopped at Javier's feet, fatigue permeated every muscle in her body. Javier sat in the overstuffed chair holding his head in his hands. Tight worry marks etched his face as the herdsman gave in to the ache of his heart. He had nothing to be ashamed of but felt remorse; his tears were forms of prayer for his missing dog.

Emma rose in response to Javier's tender strokes across her graying head. Sorrow and worry weighed down both man and dog and would stay with them through another sleepless night. The old Basque fought the panic to get up and return to the mountainside again to search for Jenny.

In the days following the storm, Coronado busied himself getting the mandatory work done at the ranch so he could traverse as timely as possible back through the deep snow drifts looking for tracks or signs of his lost Aussie. He figured he'd be able to safely leave tomorrow.

At first light, Bayo struggled with the snow-covered and craterous hillsides as Javier rummaged around piles of fallen timber and deep brush, probing any area that might have ensnared his dog.

"Jenny? Jenny?" He called down canyons and ravines into which she might have fallen. His voice, weakened by grief, echoed with no response. Blu's keen sense of smell queried each shift of wind for any scent of his lost sister. Once again the trio of horse, dog and man returned home without finding as much as a trace of Jenny.

* * *

The crisp morning broke with clear blue skies and a temperature of 15 degrees. The herdsman limped a bit due to the sleeplessness caused by tossing and turning all night. Javier rounded the corner by the house to the garage for his pickup truck.

Blu ran at his heels, eager to go with him and anxious for the ride. Gloved hands turned the key in the truck causing the quiet V-8 to purr into action. Warm air poured from the vents as Coronado pulled out of the driveway onto the road leading to the main highway. From his usual seat up front, Blu eyed the passing countryside in case, somehow, Jenny might be seen. Signs, written in

James MacKrell

black marker, described the lost dog and the location where she was last seen. The word "REWARD" was bold and placed at the top. The posters lay on the front seat between him and Blu, and he had nails and other materials needed to post the flyers.

"I hope I didn't miss anything on these signs." He couldn't stop glancing between the leaflets and the road. An antacid fished from his pocket provided relief for his nervous stomach. Javier began fiddling with the radio, turning it on and off, and clicking his fingers on the dash to help ease the tension in his body. On the other hand, Blu's steely eyes never left the road, searching from side to side. A quick blur of black and white dashing alongside the road caught his eye. He strained against the side glass, tense and ready for the rescue, but decided the streak was only a stray cat probably chasing some doomed chipmunk. Javier's eyes never left the road in front of him. Driving by remote control, he continued to grip the steering wheel, working the muscles in his hands absently. Blu glanced over at him and whined. He shared the Master's distress. His head drooped, waiting for the accustomed reassuring pat, but that warm touch never came. Javier was too heartsick, too sidetracked.

* * *

One squiggle too close to the mouth of the cave caused Jenny to grab the pup by the nape of his neck and yank him back to the safety and warmth of the old jacket. The woolen cloth served as both bed and whelping blanket and became the only world the red puppy and her black-as-night brother knew. The snow outside started to diminish; it had snowed continuously for the past week. Outside the temperature stayed consistently below freezing, but finally started warming up due to the sunshine playing peek-a-boo through the menacing, boiling gray clouds. Jenny's pups resembled guinea pigs more than dogs as they scooted around the floor of the grotto, feeling their way because of their sightless eyes. Mostly, they searched for their mother and something to eat. The next several days proved routine for the little family. Jenny subsisted on what she could find near the opening of the cave. Her system needed food to produce enough milk for the pups. Food was scarce, but she managed to find just enough small animals to keep her going. The puppies grew each day, and Jenny loved them more and more.

* * *

A push on the driver's side swung the dark green door open. "Blu, stay!" The command bolted the Aussie to the seat, content to obey and watch all the action in Big Timber, Montana, from the cab of the truck, as Javier swung down, his arms loaded with posters. Located just off Boulder Road, west of McLeod, the Townsend Ranch backed up to the foothills of the Absaroka Mountains. The wilderness area that forms the Absaroka-Beartooth Mountain Range is possibly the most beautiful raw land anywhere. Wild and untamed, the wilderness was a daunting place to travel any time of the year. In the winter it was almost impossible. The canyons were short and deep with rocks protruding like monoliths from the soil to great heights. The higher the elevation, the more sparse the vegetation, but down in the foothills where Javier grazed his flock the grass was tender and full of flavor. Even as late as his last trip, it was worth the trouble for the sheep to graze. The heights of the mountains made it a virtual wall to the southwest. Sudden storms like the one that caught

James MacKrell

the flock were unpredictable, quick and furious. They were more deadly because of the deep canyons and the lack of workable trails. The area was mostly deserted during the extreme winter months. Javier's only hope was that one of his fellow ranchers or a hunter could have come across Jenny and was holding her for safety. He spread the flyers from Livingston to McLeod, with his last stop in Big Timber.

The green pickup wedged its way in between several other trucks parked at an angle in front of the Crystal Café, a favorite of the locals. Javier was certain he would find several of his friends in town for supplies or feed or just looking for an excuse to run into neighbors.

He stomped the snow off his boots before entering. The welcome bell hanging over the front door jangled as he entered and he slipped off his hat.

"Coronado! How goes it?" said a rancher in greeting. Most of the people in the café were familiar to Javier and after greeting sever of them he slipped into a booth with Charles Goodson, a neighbor on the next ranch over from the Townsend spread.

"Coronado, you look terrible! You look like you haven't slept in weeks!"

"I nearly haven't. We didn't have much of a Thanksgiving." He blew on his coffee for a moment and stared into the blackness of the cup.

"Charlie, I've lost my Jenny dog in that storm we had. I took her up with me to the lower pastures, and we got caught in that damn blizzard. By the time I got the sheep down, I couldn't find her anywhere." His thoughts made him relive the ordeal. A catch in his voice gave away the sadness in his heart.

Charlie Goodson didn't say a word. He stirred the cream in his coffee, making little swirls of milky clouds.

These men who make their living from the bounty of the earth don't need a lot of words to express their feelings. Each man and woman knows the importance of the sheep dogs, their worth and the bond between the ranchers, and the animals working with them.

Javier pushed several of his flyers across the table. "Charlie, could you help me by putting these flyers around?"

Javier could rest assured that Charlie would not let one flyer go un-posted. With half a cup of tepid coffee left in his mug, Javier shook hands with his friend, said goodbye to several others and headed back to continue his search for Jenny. Blu was sitting behind the steering wheel, resisting the urge to blow the horn to hurry Javier up, something Blu did when he thought Javier had been gone too long.

They rode on in silence, stopping every now and then to post a flyer in hopes that someone might just get a glimpse of her or be able to offer some information that would bring her home.

James MacKrell

Chapter 10
"Their lives depend on me..."

Jenny's every thought concerned the puppies and their dependence on her. She scavenged for what little food was available in an effort to keep herself nourished. Melting snow quenched her thirst. The puppies grew. The little black one, a burrower, easily got lost in the sleeve of the mackinaw serving as their bed. His sister's bright red color, white face and copper markings stood out even in darkness.

Javier's lingering scent left among the threads on the old coat filled Jenny with longing. The sheep dog yearned to go home. Three weeks had passed since the puppies' birth. How much she wanted to show off her babies, but she realized the icy conditions barred her from leaving the cave except for fleeting absences to rummage for food.

The entrance to the refuge stood about five feet above the floor of the ravine. The Aussie managed to make the climb up and down but realized it would be impossible for her to move both puppies without endangering their lives. As the days wore on, the initial storm and passing snow showers subsided, but the hillside remained frozen. The elements made travel nearly impossible. Jenny grew thin and drawn as the demands of feeding the pups drew on her strength and stamina. She rested as much as possible knowing all the energy she saved would be better put to use producing the milk needed for the puppies' survival. Once she thought she heard her name being called. Straining to hear the distant voice, her body tensed with anticipation.

She cocked her head toward the opening of the fissure straining to hear, but as quickly as the sound came, it faded. Her brown eyes dulled with depression from malnourishment, worry and fatigue.

"My babies are so alive, so wonderful." The joy seemed to change in mid-thought to worry.

"How am I going to keep them alive with these horrid conditions?"

Her heart skipped a beat, either from exhaustion or fear. The things she had worried about seemed so trivial now. How selfish she felt. If only her time at home had been different. At home! Her head lay quietly between her front paws, the babies pulling on her tummy. She had to live; her dance of life had to continue. As she pushed her muzzle further into the warmth and scent of the old coat, she heaved a sigh full of dread.

"If anything or anyone can help me, please hurry. Spirit of the Day and Night, You, who give all things life, protect my babies and me. We don't know what to do, and we don't know if we will live or die! Oh Spirit, please help us to live."

A cloud of sleep eased over Jenny's mind. Tonight, in this forgotten hole in the ground, Javier's prized dog lay with her puppies in deep slumber. While she slept, a warming wind whisked down the ravine and found its way into the cavern that had become Jenny's home.

* * *

The same day, Sheena ruffled her fur in an effort to warm her freezing body. The joys of escape from Spencer were short-lived. Lonely, afraid and totally confused, she wondered what to do.

James MacKrell

"How will I live? What will I eat? Where will this freedom lead me?" The jumbled pile of thoughts ricocheted through her sleepless brain. Sheena had never experienced the bile of fear. It seemed to her so distinctive from the hatefulness that had grown in her spirit for so many months.

A sharp cracking sound exploded near the pile of wood. Sheena bolted awake. The tips of her ears tingled with strain trying to heed each noise. Her yellow eyes pierced the maze of dead limbs searching for a hint of movement that might give away the source of the noise. A dark figure loomed from the tree line. It had a strange scent to Sheena; the odor caused the sensitive cells in her nose to burn. Clearly the monster was the largest thing the wolf-dog had ever seen.

Watchfully she followed as the black mass ambled over the piles of wood, snapping fallen limbs like twigs. Every nerve in her body sounded the alarm to the danger.

The animal lumbered leisurely toward Sheena's makeshift haven. The creature's face appeared much longer than wide. Great tuffs of hair sprung from the area around the ears, which were twitching to and fro. Slowly, snatching at pieces of dead grass exposed through the snow and tree bark from the fallen limbs, the creature strolled closer to Sheena's hideout. The wolf-dog intently eyed the beast trying to discover if it presented any danger. She slunk lower in the branches but kept her head where she could monitor the odd looking mammal's movements. The moose wasn't in a hurry, browsing the forest edge for anything edible, stopping from time to time to test the air for anything out of place.

Another crackling of broken wood at the forest's edge drew the wolf-dog's attention. Behind the enormous creature, two smaller and lighter skinned animals followed a short distance behind the cow. A low growl started rumbling from Sheena's throat to sound a warning, but it was stifled for fear she would divulge her hiding place. She had strange feelings about these beings, but fear didn't seem one of them. Smaller than its sibling, the calf in the rear had a tougher time stepping over some downed tree trunks. Sheena noticed it moved more slowly than the first calf, and with a slight limping gate. The baby moose's right hind leg bent at an unusual angle, inhibiting her ability to keep up.

Surface winds blew across the piles of deadwood stirring up frozen fall leaves. A dusting of snow slapped her in the face, stinging her eyes and causing her to flinch. In that split second several timber wolves exploded from the cover of darkness, two charging the mother and first calf, three others surrounding the cripple. The wolves attacked swiftly with a well-rehearsed, precision battle plan. The cow ran hysterically for about ten yards and in her confusion inadvertently allowed herself to be trapped in by a steep embankment. With a bellow of anger, she whirled to face the slaughterers head on. The other calf tried to make herself invisible using the mother's body as protection. The elder moose's eyes burned with a red glow as hate poured from her soul. Her babies were in danger. With her head lowered, the moose charged the attacking horde. She landed a blow to the head of the closest wolf, gashing the side of its face with her sharp hooves. She reared and slammed down on the gray mass again and again, causing the predator to crumble under the mighty blows into a mound of bloody fur. She whipped her head around as the second wolf grabbed a chunk of her backside.

As she battled the snapping wolves, thrashing about with both front legs, using her hoofs like scythes, she beat back the attack. The gray hulks of terror whirled and, as quickly as a thought, retreated to the refuge of the forest. Her sides heaving, the moose staggered over to the corpse of her crippled baby. Her heart was broken. The calf was ripped asunder and its lifeless body's cavity was split open in the assault. The moose's head nuzzled her dead calf with her velvet nose. Heavy in heart, she slowly and deliberately turned her back and walked away.

Sheena hadn't moved during the entire attack. Her long gray snout, pointed toward the violence, inhaled great gulps of air. The air smelled of blood, and death, and the smells all seemed familiar. Her bowels grumbled from hunger and the spectacle she witnessed stunned her, yet the smell of red meat awoke in her a deep hunger. The primeval part of her brain grew excited by the kill. She recognized the fight for what it was: the battle of the fittest for the food to sustain life. Sheena's nature boiled up from the depths of her soul. Like the millions before her, she was and would continue to be a wolf. And starving wolves are killers.

Chapter 11
"Where the winds blow…"

"The Chinook conditions could be with us all week and the temperatures should jump by at least 40 degrees."

Javier raised the volume on the TV; the information was vital in the aftermath of the storms.

A too-easy smile broke across Tom Spillman's tanned face, due to the makeup he piled on before each broadcast. His hand poked out of his baby blue coat sleeve, pointing to the numbers on the screen backing up his predictions and working the clicker to change screens. The TV picture flickered as Spillman continued.

"Ah, the warming winds, and don't we deserve a break from all the heavy weather that gripped this southwestern part of Montana for the past few weeks. It's like an early Christmas present, isn't it?

He gave the viewers a reassuring grin and turned back to the weather map filled with numbers pointing out the lows and highs of the past weeks.

Javier sighed and hit the power button on the remote, stared at the blank screen, yawned and picked up his copy of Louis L'Amore's Collected Short Stories of the Frontier from the table over-stuffed with books and newspapers. He shuffled off toward the bedroom with Emma in tow. Coronado read himself to sleep most nights with Emma curled up by the side of his bed, wheezing in her sleep. He never tired of L'Amore's word pictures of the Old West. Any story set in his beloved Montana he liked to read over and over again. This night his reading would be sporadic; he just couldn't concentrate on anything but his fears about Jenny.

He fluffed his pillows and slipped the blanket covers back, turned, making sure the windows were tightly shut against the night's cold, slipped into his worn flannel pajamas and started to climb into bed. A thought stopped him as he sat on the bedside.

With the Chinooks coming full steam tomorrow, all that snow and ice that made searching for Jenny so difficult should melt away pretty quickly.

Javier remembered Chinooks of the past and one wind in particular. It swept out of the southwest over the 10,000 foot elevations of the mountains and poured down the leeward side with dry currents of air warming the region in such a way the snow almost disappeared as if by magic. One such wind in recent memory caused a temperature fluctuation of nearly eighty degrees. It's no wonder locals described the Chinooks as the Native Americans had: "Snow Eaters."

* * *

After the wolf pack ate their fill of the slain moose calf and slunk back to the shelter of the forest, Sheena moved in on the remains of the carcass and managed to scavenge enough to satisfy her nagging hunger.

Her muzzle bloodied, she cast a glance around her before turning away from the scene, the gleam in her yellow eyes revealing a knowledge embedded deep in her wolf heart.

The ecstasy of the hunt, the excitement of the kill and the pleasure of raw meat were ancient delights lying dormant in her DNA.

James MacKrell

With every step she bounced with excitement. The coppery tang in her mouth and the salty lick on her lips invigorated her every move. Her snout sniffed the air for signs of anything living. Her gray head swung back toward the carcass of the calf. The wolf pack would probably come back, and instinct told her to put as many miles between her and the pack's kill as possible. Her paws beat the ground with a steady rhythm. The wind was picking up speed as the gust of warm air cascaded down the slopes of the mountains. Sheena's paws splashed through puddles of melting snow. As she rounded the corner of a wall of spruce, she made her first kill. It was easy, an older rabbit with no defense against the raging attack of the wolf-dog. She wasn't particularly hungry: it was her thirst for blood that needed to be sated. Sheena knew nothing of a wolf pack's behavior, nothing of the ways of the wild. Her anger had built up for so long that the ability to let it explode seemed vindicated in her troubled mind.

* * *

Peering out the opening of the small cave, the Aussie searched the blue sky for any sign of movement or any sounds of humans. Never did she lose her conviction that Javier would save her, well sometimes she fretted, but fretting was just Jenny's way.

In the past four weeks the puppies grew, doubling in size from their birth. On rubbery legs they explored the cramped cave area. Strong enough to survive on their own for small periods of time, they snuggled in the mackinaw, soaking in the smell of the man. For dogs and wolves alike, being born in the North Country, their bodies were given extra padding and coat to assist keeping them warm against the piercing elements. As the spirit of winter's cold first raises its frosty head, the animal produces a thick cottony undercoat of insulation. Even an extra growth of hair on their paws saves them from the painful cuts from frozen ground and ice.

This wasn't Jenny's first Montana winter. Her downy undercoat offered extra protection for her babies as well.

This morning the babies lay fast asleep wrapped in Javier's woolen jacket. Jenny jumped from the opening to the bottom of the arroyo, splashing in the melt-off running at the base of the crevice. Over the gully, the strong Chinook winds blew, eating away at the snow and raising the temperature into the high fifties. Jenny ventured a little farther down the break, taking in deep breaths of the warm air. One paw grasped a fallen tree in the ravine, her nails dug into the surface of the thawing bark. The other paw pulled her weakened body up so that step by step she could climb up the wooden incline to peer over the gully's edge to survey the land on either side.

During the freeze she couldn't have reached this height, since the tree trunk wore a mantle of ice and her paws wouldn't be able to sustain a grip. Gully walls protected her from the gale, like currents of the Chinook winds. The tremendously warm and dry air served another purpose as well; sounds aided by the constant wind carried for miles. At first she thought she imagined it, her ears remaining erect, listening intently for any vibration of sound. Other animals started their cacophony, drowning out the slight sound Jenny perceived to be someone calling her name.

"Oh please, again! Call me again, I know it's you. I thought I heard Blu's bark, but now all your sounds are gone." Two rabbits peered down from the edge of the crevice; they looked into Jenny's face and wheeled,

James MacKrell

hopping madly away from being someone's dinner. Just before Jenny could back down the incline, a hawk swooped with the speed of a fighter jet, beaming in on a field mouse that had only wanted to be warm for a change.

* * *

The sleeve of the abandoned jacket covered the little black boy completely. His little sister with her Joseph coat of many colors squirmed up blindly, seeking her mother's warm side. Tiny cries whimpering into the soundlessness of the cave weren't answered.

"Where is our mom?" she squealed as her tiny red nose scratched against the woolen material filled with the scent of their little family. The black beauty was flopped on his belly, turning his white chest up to the air, completely covered in the sleeve of the black and red cloth. Climbing back into the makeshift den, Jenny crawled over to her too-active puppies, counting noses. The red baby was on top of the coat, squirming with her head bouncing up and down. She could smell the little black one but had to shuffle through the folds of woolen cloth before she retrieved him.

The next morning the golden slanted sunlight came streaming through the windows. Emma pulled the covers from Javier's bed in an effort to wake him. Javier's body felt warm, which wasn't the usual greeting for a person in the beginnings of winter in Montana.

With his eyes barely open, he wanted to spend just a couple more minutes in half-sleep. Emma kept working the blankets until they slipped from the bed to the floor. The covers piled on Emma's head, burying her in a mound of quilts and blankets still warm from sleeping.

"He's got to get up. He's got to go and search for Jenny. The weather is warm, the snow is melting.
"I just know he can find her."

Chapter 12
"The search for that which is lost..."

Even the trees seemed to be smiling over the weather change. Wiping the sleep from his tired eyes, Javier stumbled down the stairs and headed toward the barn to fetch Bayo. Emma ran ahead, knowing she was too old to accompany Javier, Bayo and Blu on this rescue mission, but wanting to add her two cents before they left.

"Blu will help. Blu is young and strong."

Emma's front leg buckled as her old knee caught, causing her to nearly stumble. She soldiered on.

"Well, I can pretend can't I?" she said to herself, admonishing her own desire to be in the middle of everything important.

Several chickens decided they would get into the hunt as well, joining Emma and Javier on their brisk walk past the outbuildings to the stable. The drip, drip of melting snow made little splash marks in the ground. The Chinooks continued to blow, the resulting warmth melting the snow even more quickly.

Hoisting the saddle up on the horse's back, the herdsman said, 'This is a good day, ole friends. With the snow clearing so quickly we will surely find signs of our Jenny, and we can get her home." Cinching the strap, he grabbed the reins in his left hand and swung up on the gelding's back. He was full of hope. This misery had to come to an end one way or another.

He just couldn't lose his adored Jenny. He had to find her. Bayo neighed his complete and utter agreement.

On this morning, hope was the watchword for all on the Townsend Ranch.

* * *

In the foothills, her paws soaked with melting snow, Sheena the wolf-dog trotted along the edge of the woods, keeping in the shadows to hide her presence. The wet that had clung to her coat for days had completely dried as the warm winds blew. With the rising temperature, the forest seemed to take on a new energy. All of Sheena's life had been spent in a cage. She could only look out at the world passing her by. Now she was a part of that elusive world. Unsure what her new world demanded of her, she rested in the knowledge that she had seen wolves in action and felt pack life was where she fit in.

She skidded to a stop and her head and body slunk down low. Something thrashing in the brush ahead riveted her curiosity. Her shy wolf nature prompted her to seek concealment lest she be discovered, and instant quiet engulfed her body.

"Is this another of the long-faced creatures?"

Sheena's steely concentration never wavered.

"If this is one of those creatures, will the wolf pack come back and attack again? Will they let me join them? Can I be a part of their family?"

With the exception of the short time spent with the sire of her brood, Sheena never felt attached to anyone, or anything. In her experience as a puppy with Hoss Wilson, she had no memory of a soft touch or a kind word. An abusive life reaps terrible rewards.

Her yellow eyes honed in on the mammoth creature rolling its way from the dense brush into the middle of the trail. The coffee-colored body suddenly stood erect,

James MacKrell

waving paws the size of buckets and nosing the air, throwing its massive head vigorously to the left and right. This wasn't anything Sheena had ever seen before. No long-legged, sunken-faced cow; this was a presence that exuded danger in every direction. The closer it got to where Sheena hid, the larger it appeared. She backed up on her haunches and hunkered down to make herself as undetectable as possible.

"If only the wolves would come back, they could drive this monster away."

Sheena's faith in the effectiveness of the pack was slightly overblown. The ferociousness of a pack of wolves wouldn't affect in the least the seven-foot tall grizzly bear with three-inch claws blocking her path. No training, no lessons, no words of warning were needed for the wolf-dog to cower in the presence of the North Wood's great predator.

Her tail plastered between her legs and her ears laid back in a very submissive way, Sheena was afraid for her life. *"This thing, this giant could kill me just as the wolves killed that calf."*

The lonely wolf-dog immediately learned the major lesson of the wild. If you can kill, you can also be killed.

Her bushy tail still firmly tucked between her legs, she slunk away hoping not to arouse any more attention from the giant bear.

In another part of the mountain, Jenny rose to full height, turned around and settled back down as close to the puppies as possible. To the tiny Aussies, everything, even in such close quarters, was new and exciting. Each day brought new adventure, new discoveries and a new strength in their little bodies as they wormed their way around the cave like little guinea pigs. With the sudden warmth, they played even rougher. The red and gold little girl would crawl on the back of her black brother, with all four paws. Teeth flashed and tiny mews filled the stillness. Jenny fidgeted over a dilemma growing each minute with the melting of the snow.

"Now is the time to escape this cavern, but how?" She squeezed her eyes together to concentrate all her senses to find a solution to this life-and-death question.

"How on earth can I carry these two puppies to safety?"

Jenny was calculating whether to carry one to the top of the gorge, leave that puppy and return for the other one, or try to manage both at once.

Her thoughts vacillating between her longing to return home and the wellbeing of her offspring caused her eyes to dull over with worry.

Something in her spoke: *"The warm weather won't always last. It could turn cold again in a moment."* Urgency gripped her along with a fear of losing her little family. Fretting, Jenny would have paced the space, but the cave was too confining. She longed to be free of this prison and her worries over the weather, her pups and how to find her next meal. She just wanted to go home.

* * *

No thought of going home ever entered the wolf-dog's mind. She had no conception of home, only places of misery and abuse. Since escaping Ronnie Spencer's hellhole she breathed deeper, the air tasted sweeter and her heart beat much more in rhythm. She ventured out into the opening between the deep forest and the stark mountains for the first time. It felt good to her; bouncing like a puppy she chased butterflies and harassed chipmunks and field

James MacKrell

mice. Her only uncomfortable feeling was the mother's milk left in her too-full teats.

An errant ground squirrel scurried from under Sheena's nose, hurrying back to the safety of its burrow. She followed the gray animal's antics without giving chase. She wasn't hungry, and the brush that was peeking through the now- crusted snow scraped across her stomach, irritating her low hanging teats. Just as the squirrel plummeted down the opening to his underground home, movement down the hillside grabbed her attention. It looked at first like moving dots slip-sliding up the trail toward Sheena's Valhalla.

"Could this be danger?" A warning device clicked on in her brain. After her encounters with the wolf pack, the moose and the bear, she was becoming used to the strangeness of her new world. As still as granite, Sheena's eyes locked on the procession moving up the trail, watching the parade from so far away. The figures appeared as tiny as the ground squirrel fleeing to avoid being the wolf's dinner.

As she watched the mysterious parade move closer and closer, though, she had no idea of the important part they would play in her fitful life.

James MacKrell

Chapter 13
"Keeping the faith…"

Earlier that morning, before embarking on the rescue search, Javier dressed, filled his mug with extremely stout coffee, and sat for a minute at his kitchen table. Not hungry, he nibbled at a stale biscuit and once again read the story of the Good Shepherd.

His fingers played across the lines "He forsook the ninety and nine in search of that which was lost."

"Emma, we must find Jenny!" Javier leaned over and stroked her head. She looked back up at him with the same determination she saw in his eyes.

Javier played the morning's thoughts and prayers over and over in his mind as the trio ascended the trail toward the high pastures. The wind continued but had lowered its velocity. Blu's face darted from side to side with an eagerness compelling the herdsman to hurry.

"Bayo, this might be our last trip up the hills before this hot wind ends and we are again in the middle of ice and snow."
The Morgan bounced his head up and down, not constrained by the loosely held reins.

Up ahead on the trail Javier saw the footprints of the animals that ventured forth into the open air, taking advantage of the dry spell.

Melting snow caused the ground to be a bit muddy but passable. The surrounds weren't any wetter than the cheeks of the herdsman as he plowed upward for what might be a fruitless trip.

"I have to try this one more time." He pulled up the collar on his corduroy jacket against the fresh cold mingling with the warmth of the fading Chinooks.

Blu raced farther out, testing the air for any familiar scent. The gelding's back seemed to sag like the shoulders on Javier and even Blu, each willing to try but so afraid of failure.

The trail took a circuitous swing up the high side of the grasslands and turned back toward the foothills on the left. The deep forest bordered the half-mile width of the pasture, with the mighty Montana Mountains rising like barren monoliths out of the jade timbers protecting the hillsides. In the open air, wind currents played peek-a-boo around the outcropping of rock and slithered deep down the crevices that split the floor of the valley. Bayo's hoof prints had dug into soil so often the bay horse almost followed his own trail.

As they approached the area where Javier and Blu lost sight of Jenny during the blizzard, Blu became more agitated. Running ahead he frantically barked in as loud a voice as he could muster.

"Jenny! Jenny! It's me, your brother, Blu." He raced round in ever-widening circles and continued his frantic barking; *"Javier and me, we are looking so hard for you, my sister, answer me! Call back to me. Let me hear your voice."*

As this drama played out, little did Javier, Blu and Bayo know, they had an audience of one.

"What is this strange being?" Sheena rolled the question over and over in her mind, again trying to figure out if she had ever seen an animal with four legs and a man growing out the middle.

"One thing is for sure, I am not getting any closer...."

James MacKrell

Slinking her way around the timbers, she remained hidden. Little of the morning light touched her silvery body.

The dark shadows provided the perfect cover for the wolf-dog since the man and horse stayed in bright sunlight. Even the strange dog with a spotted coat of blue and white appeared not to be hunting so much as to be looking for something specific.

Sheena stalked Javier, Blu and Bayo, keeping her distance. The threesome turned away from the side of the forest where she hid and crossed the open grassland back toward the left.

Oh, how she wanted to get closer to them, to see what they were doing, and to find out if they offered any danger to her. The trio became very agitated. Loud shouts filled the quiet. The blue dog dashed across the ground and then disappeared before Sheena's startled eyes. She inched further into the grass to get a better view. Careful to stay downwind from them to avoid being detected, she assumed nearly a crawl position, furtively moving closer for a better vantage point.

In her eyes the strangest thing happened. With all of the shouting and barking, the strange being separated as the man-looking creature became distinct from the four-legged being and walked around on two legs of his own. Sheena was bewildered.

* * *

"What is all the noise, babies?" said Jenny, in the middle of a nap lifted her head, cocking her ears to figure out if that was barking she was hearing or just another illusion of hope.

"I believe it's Blu." She spoke softly to the puppies, trying to give them a sense of security she only dreamed of for herself. There it was again. This time the barking was closer and accompanied by what appeared to be the voice of Javier.

Her body trembled, so great was the thrill. Maybe she and her puppies would be rescued and returned to the safety of her home. Almost laughing Jenny barked, *"Here I am, here I am. You are near, I can feel it. Here we are, I can feel it. Please hurry, we are waiting."*

Jenny thought about jumping down from the cave and racing to the sound of Blu's barks. But didn't. She was tied to the puppies. Their safety had to come first. She licked each one. The red tri pup scooted close to the edge, while the little black male didn't want to be disturbed and retreated to the darkness of the sleeve of the coat his mother said smelled like the Master's.

James MacKrell

Chapter 14
"He will know his own…"

The herdsman was having difficulty catching his breath. He watched Blu dart down the steep ravine barking at the top of his lungs. Dropping the reins on Bayo's bridle to the ground, Javier ran as hard and fast as possible to the side of the arroyo that had virtually swallowed Blu. He had to stop again for a minute, with his hands on his knees because his sides hurt from the exertion, plus the joy pumping through his body with every beat of his heart. He knew the Australian Shepherd Blu; he was an honest dog who was hard to fool. If Blu sensed he had found something, believe it, he had.

Blu scrambled over the fallen trees in the bottom of the crevice, slipping a couple of times on un-melted ice. All the while 'Aussie chirping,' his barks echoed down the crevice. Blinking back tears, the herdsman watched as the sheep dog bounced from side to side, over and around fallen debris, desperate to reach his goal. Climbing down after the dog, the old Basque had to use both hands to keep from falling, grabbing first one limb and then the edge of a rock sticking out the side of the gully wall. An errant step on a wet rock caused him to fall, banging his knee and tearing his pants. No pain would deter his search. Jenny had to be here, she had to be alive.

* * *

"What shall I do? If I leave the puppies they could get hurt, yet if I don't answer Blu we might be left in this forgotten hole."

Jenny decided to bark as loudly as her voice would let her. She wanted to direct Blu to her hiding place and he would bring the Master. So she cried, *"Dear Blu, I am over here, just a little bit farther. Please, just come down the gully a little bit more. You will find me, I am sure."*

Blu, excited by the sound of Jenny's voice, remained motionless to better hear his sister's pleas for help. His blue eyes darted up and down the rocky walls, then, there, just ahead, he spied an opening in the wall and from it he believed came the voice of Jenny. He sprang forward, not worrying about hitting the side of the walls or being jabbed by the loose branches that stuck out like sabers. With his steely eyes he focused only on the opening. When he reached it, he stood on his hind legs with the top of his head just above the entrance.

At first, Jenny wondered if it was just an illusion. She scooted close to the opening of their cave home without losing touch with the little girl puppy who seemed permanently embedded in Jenny's side. The black puppy was snoring peacefully, wrapped in Javier's long lost jacket, and seemed to care less about all the commotion going on with his mother.

Then, the eureka moment! Jenny saw the face of Blu peering in the cave as he stood on the tiptoes of his hind legs. Never had a face looked so good.

"Oh my goodness… Oh my…" Her heart was so full, full of joy, full of excitement, and full of thankfulness. She could only say in whimpers of pleasure, *"Oh Blu, oh Blu, oh Blu."*

Catching up with Blu, Javier peered into his beloved Jenny's face and let the emotion of several weeks

James MacKrell

explode in sobs of gratitude. Prayers of thanksgiving poured from his lips, in Spanish and English all mixed together. His brown hand, bloodied by the scratches from the underbrush lining the ravine, felt the warmth of Jenny beneath the gentle caresses of love.

"Jenny, my Jenny! Oh, how I have missed you, my girl. It's so wonderful to see you again!"

Blu never moved, his tongue lolling out of his mouth, tired and dry from all his barking.

Their faces, steadfast in devotion, locked in on their Jenny at the end of the hunt for that which was lost.

When the face of her beloved master entered her sight, she could only shiver and tremble. Blu barked and Javier called her name. Never had two sounds thrilled her more. A voice deep within her consciousness whispered, *"Our dance continues, sing the music of the dance."*

* * *

Javier's big arms reached for Jenny, and in doing so touched the fuzziness of the puppy by her mother's side. His joy doubled.

"Blu, Jenny has a puppy!" He stroked the puppy's back. For the first time the baby Aussie experienced human touch. Javier gently reached in as far as his arms would allow, the opening large enough for a dog, but not wide or tall enough for a man. He gathered the puppy in his hands. Lifting the baby from the cave and backing out, he carried the tiny puppy back to the top of the ravine to stow her safely in Bayo's oversized saddlebags. He came prepared: if Jenny had been hurt or even worse, he brought blankets to carry her home. Javier gently wrapped the puppy in a woolen blanket and safely laid her in the giant bag that hung on the left side of the horse. Little did he know there might be more than one passenger. Blu stood vigilantly by the cave opening, guarding the spot for fear if he left they wouldn't find Jenny again. His eyes never strayed from Jenny's face.

Javier slid partially down the embankment in his hurry to return to get his dog. All the way up carrying the puppy and back down to get Jenny, he mumbled under his breath, "Thank you, God, thank you, God."

He reached in to pull the Aussie mom out. Jenny struggled against his efforts. She cried and squirmed. All that seemed to Javier as fighting against being pulled from the hole.

Jenny feared Javier might miss the little black puppy wrapped and hidden in the old coat.

She struggled, trying to make him understand. *"There is another puppy, Master, don't forget the little boy."*

Javier looked down to make sure he had a firm footing. There, near his foothold he saw the remains of the three stillborn puppies.

"Blu, the other puppies must have died." He looked back up at Jenny, trying to imagine the distress and pain she must have felt in losing such precious parts of herself. With another glance down to make sure he wasn't disturbing their tiny remains, he pulled harder to free Jenny.

"My girl, it's going to be alright. I will get you home and fed and covered in a warm blanket for you and your baby. We'll be fine. We'll be just fine."

Blu became agitated and barked incessantly at Javier trying to warn him about Jenny's fear. Jenny kept up her desperate cries, now joined by Blu. *"Don't forget my baby boy! He's just back there under your old coat. Let's get him and carry him to safety, and then come back and*

James MacKrell

get me. Please! Please!" It wasn't that Javier ignored the pleading of his dogs, it was like Emma had stated earlier, humans just didn't understand dog talk. Javier gently carried Jenny up the incline and climbed aboard the gelding. The ride back down the mountain was uneventful. Jenny rode snugly across the saddle horn held by the loving hands of Javier. The puppy snuggled warm as toast in the oversized saddlebag bouncing along to the gait of the Morgan. A frigid current of air moving down from the north seemed to chase away what remaining warmth there was from the Chinooks. Jenny was exhausted, long tired and skinny from her ordeal; she didn't have the strength to struggle anymore against the wishes of Javier. With the red tri pup wrapped around her midsection blithely nursing, the fight to save the other puppy seemed lost. Exhaustion replaced fright, and weariness replaced anxiety.

Javier rode down the mountain with Blu merrily bouncing alongside, the herdsman singing an old Spanish victory song. He would be able to sleep tonight, and he laughed to himself, So would that rascal, Emma. She wasn't going to keep him up another night.

* * *

From the time the horseman and the dog first appeared at the bottom of the hill, until they rode back down the mountainside, Sheena's eyes followed their every move. She never showed herself or made a sound. Stealthily, she followed the unfolding drama from a safe distance. When the man and the dog disappeared down the arroyo, she moved a little higher on the hillside so she could see every movement and action of the duo. It was confusing to her. They didn't appear to be after food, yet they pulled another dog from the side of the gully and what appeared to be a cub, and toted them up and rode off with them both.

"Does the man intend to eat them later?" She plopped down to ease the pain in her stomach from the abundant mother's milk she was carrying around. She didn't know that soon the milk would start drying up and she would return to normal. All she knew right now was that it hurt.

Satisfied that the human and dog were long gone, Sheena rose to her full height and slowly, paw after paw, eased toward the side of the ravine. She moved quietly so as not to arouse anything that might have been left behind. As she reached the cusp of the side from behind some bushes along the rim, she peered down into the crevice. There, just at the bend in the channel, she noticed the side of the wall bearing scrape marks and all around the base just below a large opening in the wall of the cut about four to five feet up and about three feet across. Inside the hole was dark. Because of the overhang little sunlight got in.

She slipped over the edge. With the ease of a slithering snake she wormed her way down the steep side toward the bottom. Man scent was everywhere, and so was the strong smell of dog. All those years and months at Ronnie Spenser's taught her well the odor of dog and the stench of humans. Silently she crept, paw tracking paw, leaving no sign of her presence.

As she reached the floor near the small stream that flowed with water from the melting snow, she sniffed the objects large and small around where the drama had taken place. The slightest ripple in the wind current caused her silver and white head to pop up, testing the air for danger.

"I smell something, something different and strange."

Without making a sound she eased up on her hind legs and stared into the void at the mouth of the opening. It had the smell of life. Something was alive in there. She knew it. With an acrobatic leap she scaled the wall and landed her front paws inside the mouth of the fissure. Her back legs digging into the wall and her front paws locked in the cave's opening, she scrambled up and into the cavern. All was black. Her yellow eyes adjusted to the dark and she made out a pile of cloth or some substance located farther back in the hole. From the middle of the bundle of cloth she first heard a tiny whimper. She remained motionless, seeking the sound with all of her might. Sheena was now prone on her stomach with her front paws stretched out toward the unknown material and her back legs protruding out of the opening. Crawling inch by inch she reached out and pulled at the abandoned jacket. When she pulled on the cloth the whimpering grew louder. As the cloth easily moved toward her, it unwrapped a bundle of black fur, yelping as loud as it could and screaming for its mother. Sheena's head shot up. This was a familiar sound, not the same as the only night she spent with her own, but very, very similar. The black puppy squirmed his way toward the wolf-dog and without the slightest hesitation began filling his belly with the milk of Sheena. At first she was surprised, then a bit frightened, but as soon as the milk in her teat started flowing she relaxed. She closed her eyes and wrapped her knees around the wiggling black package of life. The baby Aussie drank deeply, and then, as puppies are wont to do, belched, rolled over on his side, and burrowed his face into Sheena's stomach ready for another nap. Sheena was bewildered but also extremely pleased. It wasn't her puppy, but it needed her oh so desperately. For the first time since she escaped Spencer's horror, she wasn't alone.

Book Two
A Song of Survival

Chapter 15
"Out into the light..."

Since Sheena had entered the gully cave, she studied the red and black jacket shoved in the back corner of the hole. The odor of puppy and dog wafted from the material, but another distinct scent permeated the cloth. It smelled of human, but different from what she remembered human stench to be. This had a fragrance, crisp and clean, almost pleasant to her nose. One front paw pulled the fabric toward where she laid with the puppy and bunched it up like a pillow.

More comfortable, she was able to turn so she could survey the little life suckling on her teats.

"He is dark. He resembles no wolf or dog I've ever seen. He doesn't even have a tail!"

She licked his tiny body, cleaning him from head to toe. His blackness intrigued her; the copper touches above his eyes made the fur around his face appear like a mask. Under his jaw, a white splash extended down between his legs. His paws had just a touch of copper coloring to set off the white markings on his feet like snowshoes.

"I should give him a name. Each living thing needs a name, something to be called by."

Sheena loved her name, even if the name came from the mouth of the despicable mound of flesh, Charlie Wilson. She knew nothing about the comic book character she was named for. To her, the name, *Sheena*, flowed, hinting of grace and poise. The pup ended his morning meal and quick as a flash headed for his hidey-hole in the abandoned jacket.

"He's as speedy as a thief in the night," she mused. *"And since I've stolen him away, I shall call him my little Bandit."*

A soft sigh slipped from her lips. *"Bandit, my little Bandit, what a wonderful name."*

He stopped in mid sleeve. *"Bandit. That amazing dog is calling me Bandit. What does Bandit mean?"*

The wool was reassuring to the puppy because it reminded him of his mother. He missed Jenny but rationalized. *"She must have sent this great dog to feed me and protect me until she returns."* With a full belly and a secure mind, the black puppy burrowed into the black and red woolen coat and soon fell fast asleep.

* * *

The morning sunlight barely reached inside the rocky enclosure. Sheena, lulled by the darkness of the cave, slept much later than normal. When she awoke she felt little Bandit gulping up his morning breakfast. Sheena's stomach growled from emptiness but she waited to feed herself until the puppy ate his fill and drifted again into sound sleep. Bandit climbed into his mackinaw sleeping bag and began dozing loudly in a matter of minutes.

"He seems bigger than yesterday. Do cubs grow that fast?"

Sadness engulfed her memory like floodwaters. She knew she had no experience with growing puppies. She never got a chance to be with her own cubs past the first day. Now she had little Bandit, and she wanted to pay special attention to everything he did.

She moved quietly out of the opening so as not to wake him and jumped down, on padded paws so as not to

James MacKrell

frighten any nearby prey. Quickly, she made her kill and gulped down the meat. Satisfied, she rushed back to the opening in the gully wall to check on Bandit.

The small creek bed at the bottom of the arroyo had filled with water from the runoff of melting snow. Now that the winds were turning cold again she knew she would have to quench her thirst on whatever snow fell. As Bandit grew she brought fresh meat back to the cave for him to learn to eat solid food. Day by day the routine became more familiar, and daily the bond between them strengthened. Bandit grew too, until the small cave seemed almost too little to house a full-grown wolf-dog and a developing Aussie. Days turned into weeks and weeks into months. The winter faded into spring and the glorious Montana grasslands and forest sprang to new life.

Bandit grew and prospered under Sheena's nurturing eye, but at no time did the thoughts about his mother stray from his mind. *"Someday I will see her again. I will tell her how much I missed her and how glad I am to be back with her where I belong. Someday, I am sure."*

The morning dawned exceptionally bright. The dark days of the past months were now blended into April skies. Cold temperatures remained, but the sun facing west warmed the Montana mountains with life-giving rays. Sheena's face turned up to the sky, testing the air. She crouched in the opening of the makeshift den, her silver back scrapping against the roof of the grotto. In back of her, up on his paws to make himself appear taller, Bandit stood ready to face the world, as long as Sheena led the way. With a graceful leap Sheena sprang from the hole and landed across the water lightly and in complete balance. Bandit's turn next, he looked straight into Sheena's eyes, to gain encouragement, and determined not to be afraid,

Down from the Mountain

launched himself into the air. Sheena turned her head so she wouldn't see Bandit crash in the cold water. She only saw half of him hit the water. With a face dripping wet, and a muddy bottom, he straightened up and gave her his best grin and said, *"Ok, it's not perfect but I jumped, didn't I?"*

She pointed her nose upward and led her pack of two to the world beyond the ravine.

Just below the opening of the abandoned cave Bandit crossed over a small pile of bones left behind. As a paw accidentally stepped down on one of the tiny skeletons, a shiver ran through his black body. The feeling lasted only a moment but in his mind it rang of another time and place. Sheena turned back, caught his eye, and resumed her climb over the broken branches and fallen trees that had washed down from the topside. Pausing for a moment, Bandit was startled when a giant frog catapulted his body from just from between Bandit's feet. He bounced back on his hind legs, but not in time to keep the splashing water from striking his face.

The wet staggered him and the look of the offending frog surprised him even more. Sheena kept heading out and upward, determined to leave everything in the gully behind. A world Bandit had never experienced awaited them both. For Bandit it represented growing up; for Sheena, a life of freedom and a chance to live without being alone.

James MacKrell

Chapter 16
"Life at the top..."

Out from the gully, Bandit saw the splendor of the Absaroka-Beartooth wilderness for the first time. How clear the streams were, how giant the evergreens that poked their emerald heads to the sky. Beyond the forest stood the granite faces of some of the most beautiful snow-capped mountains in the lower forty- eight states, some of the peaks reaching 12,000 feet into the heavens.

Brown-and-white chipmunks and starchy-tailed gray ground squirrels dithered between the rocks in the foothills, looking for the sweet water from the flowing stream. He had fewer memories of his sister each passing day, yet the sense of his Mother remained rooted in his consciousness; but that is how sons are about mothers. As his white paws touched the level ground on the right side of the fissure for the first time, his brown eyes feasted on a thrilling sight. The land seemed alive, the grasses grew green and tall, and the butterflies zipped around as if chasing the bees flitting from flower to flower. Wildflowers in full bloom, the lupine, the fairy slippers, the shooting stars, lent an artist's palate to the rising meadows. A gentle wind caused the taller grasses to sway like dancers and the trees, rocked by the higher and stronger winds, swayed to the beat of an unseen drummer.

Five-month-old Bandit operated pretty much on his own, steady and graceful except when his giant paws tripped him up. Extremely interested in the disappearance of a squirrel that had moments before been right in front of the Aussie's nose, he turned for a second to make sure

Sheena was still there, and when he looked back all he saw was an empty hole. A sharp retort split the air, dissecting Bandit's nature studies. It sounded like a piece of dead wood breaking underfoot. The sound sizzled in the cool air.

"We must hurry and get out of the open; we need find refuge my little one." Sheena nudged the baby's butt and turned to trot off toward the nearest stand of trees. Bandit followed in line, playing a child's game of trying to step only in Sheena's footprints. Off to the left of the ravine, up on the hillside, humans were making sport of shooting rabbits, little rabbits experiencing life for the first time just like Bandit. Sheena led the pup quickly across the grasslands, careful to stay in the deepened grass to hide the pair from the hunters' rifle sights.

Bandit and the responsibility for his upbringing taught much to Sheena. The wolf-dog's hatred was quenched by the tiny dog's presence. Bandit was innocent and innocence has a soothing effect on a hateful heart.

Bandit and Sheena fled across the meadow of one of the most magnificent wilderness areas in the United States. Much of Montana's wild lands are just that, a look back at a time when most of the world was unspoiled. Wildflowers covering the landscape shot up to the sun reaching for life-giving warmth and nutrients. The dense forest looked to be covered with an emerald canopy that few human eyes witness. Bandit moved just in front of Sheena and the two canines fled to the safety of those deep woods. Soon they disappeared from view of the humans who were still firing guns up on the hill.

Having been born and spending the first five months of his life in a cave, Bandit wasn't bothered by the dimness of the forest a bit. . His black coat blended in with the shadows cast by the colossal trees. The

James MacKrell

underbrush thinned due to the lack of both sunlight and nutrients and presented a bed of needles, soft to the pads of their paws. Lingering snow patches stood in contrast to the budding grass in the meadow. Life in the gully hole had another distinct advantage for little Bandit; his eyes adjusted to darkness quickly. Sheena's yellow eyes also gave her excellent night vision.

Neither Bandit nor Sheena was aware of the roving eyes scrutinizing them from the time they emerged from the arroyo, across the grassland, until they set their paws into the woods. The rise and fall of the land gives many opportunities for watchers to remain hidden while observing others. This morning, unbeknownst to little Bandit, both Sheena and he were being sized up as a potential meal. Not only because of the watcher's hunger, but because Sheena and the pup had wandered into a territory already claimed. A mountain lioness ruled the area as her own, and she enforced her control by claw and fang. She moved behind the wolf and cub like oil oozing down cracks.

A five-month-old puppy's concentration is about that of a gnat's. Bandit mustered up all his strength and focused intently for a second or two, but then a chipmunk would zip by and he would be off into another world. Under current circumstances Sheena needed him to focus only on her. She had an instinctive sense of danger and suddenly her hackles began to rise. She scoped out the surrounding area for an escape route. She didn't have to glimpse the cougar behind them to know their lives hung in the balance. More importantly, she knew Bandit was extremely vulnerable, so she shoved the little Aussie under a fallen tree, pushing him back into a tiny space and hiding him with the mass of her body. Then she saw it, or rightly she heard it, and what she saw and heard proved every bit as horrifying as she had imagined. The light brown head of the big cat poked through the bushes first with its mouth open in a petrifying snarl, the hissing sound piercing the stillness of the forest. Almost a human-like scream boiled up in the throat of the huge predator. The lioness lowered her head and settled on her haunches, ready to pounce on Sheena. The angry, determined glare in the wolf-dog's eyes gave the big cat pause. Facing the attacker head on, with her tail covering Bandit, Sheena took a defensive position. The cougar didn't need any further reminder her foe had the lethal force to fight to the death. From deep in Sheena's soul, a blood-curdling deep growl announced her readiness. Her lips curled and her fangs dripped with saliva. Her yellow eyes glowed red with the inner fire blazing in her belly.

An ear-splitting sound rebounded in the timber as the cougar hissed again. An equally threatening roar answered the snarl from the silver beast. Sheena feinted toward the cougar. He drew back in response to the wolf-dog's quickness. The cat turned sideways, its long tail switching back and forth. When it moved a little to the right, Sheena turned in that direction, but she didn't move to strike. She intended to keep little Bandit covered, knowing that if she followed the cat's lead and uncovered Bandit, the big cat's focus would divert to the pup and before Sheena could recoup, Bandit would be lost in the teeth of the attacker. In an instant, the puma changed direction again, looking for a vulnerable spot for the kill.

Bandit held his head low and closed his eyes. He didn't know what was going to happen, but he knew it might be bad. How bad, he didn't know, but his trembling little black body shuddered and his breath came in short, dry pants. He scooted back as far as possible into the

James MacKrell

safety of the tree trunk, but tried with all of his might to keep touching the body of Sheena for reassurance.

The wolf-dog had shown a ferocious nature before, but the threat on her life and the natural drive to protect her cub drove her to near insane proportions. Normally if confronted with a marauding cat, a wolf flees instead of standing and fighting. One of the basic laws of the wild is that avoidance is always the best option. But if cornered or defending young, wolves became killing machines. Sheena made up her mind that Bandit's life was more important than hers, and she would fight to the death to protect the cub she'd been given.

The puma didn't advance and the wolf-dog stood her ground, a perfect standoff. All snarling and hissing, the growling and vocal challenges grew in volume.

In the area around the fight nothing moved.

When the life-and-death struggle began, birds hastily flew away and small animals hid. Some, like little Bandit, holed up in safe places, figuratively covering their eyes and ears so as not to be part of this dance of death.

As the cougar risked moving in closer, Sheena backed deeper into the fallen tree, making sure the big cat couldn't attack from the rear.

Suddenly a sound like a shot, or a loud explosion, interrupted the skirmishing pair. The wolf-dog and the cougar ceased their vocal battle as ears on both animals flicked to attention, twitching to locate the source of the noise. Whatever this racket, it seemed more threatening to the combatants than the struggle they were pursuing.

In the lull of the fight, human voices yelling and screaming over the mechanical roar of engines burst on the scene. A well-traveled trail used in the spring and summer wound its way through the wooded area and passed only about 20 feet from the battle site. Sheena's white face lifted, trying to get a better look while keeping her attention on the killer cat. The cougar's ears pinned in a more defensive maneuver as she searched for the easiest escape route. A loud retort from the exhaust of the all terrain vehicle set the cat back on her haunches. Sheena backed even closer to the tree trunk. Knowing the frightening sounds seemed to come from in back of her, she felt trapped. A wolf's nature is to jump and run, but she had to stay to protect her baby. Little Bandit wiggled into the fur of Sheena's backside; if he could have, he would have climbed inside her.

Another shriek from the humans sounded to the cougar like a war cry and in an instance the puma fled. Sheena followed the cat's movement and slunk down to avoid being seen. Her body settled and her breathing slowed. Her silver coat melded into the gray of the dead tree as she pressed against Bandit, trying to keep him as quiet as possible.

As quickly as the ATVs came, they left. The machines' noise abated as the speed of the pair of snowmobiles with their frolicking riders sped down the trail. As the forest quieted, Sheena ventured forth, in tiny slow steps, to be able to scrutinize the surrounding area and test for the smell of danger. Bandit didn't move. His little black body was curled into a tight ball, and he wasn't going to move until Sheena told him it was all clear. Sheena had a wolf's patience and wasn't anxious to venture out to where she could encounter the cougar again. The forest became quieter. Little by little the songbirds returned and leaves rustled as ground squirrels and chipmunks hustled by.

An hour passed and Sheena felt the danger had subsided with nothing more to fear from immediate attacks. Her white face turned back to Bandit and she licked him all

James MacKrell

over in a comforting way. He whined with pleasure, relieved of the fear that had consumed him minutes before. His breaths became deeper and more sustained. Sheena stood and moved out into the clearing that had been the deadly battleground. Bandit stood as well, rising to his full height and trying to show confidence as he strolled after Sheena. That's what he tried to do, but his little legs were still a bit wobbly. The future great warrior tumbled right over on his face. Sheena pretended not to laugh, but her lips that had been snarled in a mask of death now turned up into a slight grin.

She turned and the twosome set out for further adventures. Tonight she would find a safe, clean den, and they would sleep their exhaustion away.

James MacKrell

Chapter 17
"Life has to go on..."

Jenny lay on the porch, listless as her red-tri puppy played over, around, and on top of her. The late April sun climbed overhead and the black Aussie dozed, her body half in and half out of the sunshine.

Javier crossed the yard, pulling his work gloves off to get a drink of cold water from a pitcher on the porch rail. Blu cavorted at his heels as though in a dance of thanksgiving for the warm weather. Across the yard the aspen and cottonwood stands were budding, ready to fulfill a promise to provide breathtaking color to the hillsides.

Emma raised her head to check out the Master strolling toward the house, glanced at Jenny, and rolled closer to the wall, avoiding the prying paws of the five-month-old mound of red, white, and copper fur. When Javier first brought the puppy and Jenny home, he bathed the baby and held her, wrapped in a warm fuzzy towel. She looked to him like the spitting image of one of the most famous dogs of the Townsend Ranch back in California, a nationally known stock dog champion called Falen. Since finding the puppy and her mother, Javier doted on the little girl, remembering the strong line of Australian Shepherds in her background. She mirrored the great Warner, her sire, the number-one stock dog champion in the entire northwest. Javier remembered Jim Townsend telling him that the name <u>Falen</u> meant "granddaughter of the king" and royal was the way he felt about her. Five months old and already a princess in the Basque herdsman's heart, she cavorted and chirped, calling to everyone and everything in sight, announcing her presence and declaring her rule. Blu tried to avoid her and keep a distance from her needle-sharp teeth. Falen chewed, bit, and mouthed anything she could get her snout around. Jenny wasn't in any mood to play. She loved little Falen but depression gripped her, knowing as each day passed the chances of her boy baby being alive were more and more remote. Now several months after her rescue, Jenny's heart had given up and she grieved, believing he had died.

Blu bounded up on the deck, skirting Falen's mouth by inches, and licked the ear of his sister with love and kindness. Javier crossed the porch, grabbed the doorknob, and stepped over Jenny while balancing the glass of water and the almost empty pitcher. With his hands full, he let the screen door slam shut behind him. Emma raised her head, grumbled about the noise, and lay back down. Javier was waiting for the foreman of the shearing company he had contracted to harvest the wool, so he put on a pot of coffee. As he reached for the percolator his hands showed the scars of sheerings long past. The old herdsman was skilled in the art, even having taken a complete course at Montana State University. Still no one man could handle all the sheep. Since the hired workers could strip a sheep in about three minutes, Javier long ago decided to provide the coffee and food and let these youngsters do their work.

Framed by the rising hillsides, the green forest, and all the budding trees dotting the yard, the Townsend ranch house resembled an advertisement in one of the magazines about ranch living in Montana.

Young Lonnie fed the Aussies this morning, while Javier attached the milking machines to the cows. He gave Bayo an ample supply of fresh oats and tended to the needs of the ewes and lambs. All had wintered well, and only a few lambs were counted lost to local predators. Since the infusion of new wolf packs from Yellowstone, ranchers found more and more depredation. The carnivores found lambs and calves an easy target, in contrast to the wild elk and moose higher up in the mountains. Javier depended on his guard dogs to keep the marauders at bay. The Aussies also contributed by causing a ruckus when they spotted a lone wolf. Single wolves usually fled from any confrontation with dogs, but from time to time an unseasoned dog would attempt to follow the retreating wolf back into the forest and run flush into an ambush of the wolf pack. When a pack charges together, there is very little that can withstand their ability to kill.

Javier survived the heavy snowstorms and the extremely cold weather of the past winter, and now that spring was upon them he viewed it as a continuation of the cycles of life; a life he loved because he did the work he knew best.

He took a deep breath, inhaling the pure air of the Montana hillsides.

* * *

Her eyes squeezed shut and her white face turned into the sun. Sheena lay in foot-high grass and soaked up the mountain air in all its freshness. Bandit was enthralled by a speck, high in the sky, circling around and around. He watched as the hawk made bigger and bigger circles. In fact, his gaze was so intense his little black head started circling in the same pattern the hawk flew. He made himself dizzy, and if it weren't for a ground squirrel springing right in front of him, he would have hypnotized himself. He was so startled he just about fell over. As he tumbled in the grass a meadow bird sprung into flight.

"What is this strange creature walking in the air?"

He tried at first to sniff it but the bird flushed and landed about ten yards away. He bounded to where it landed and decided he would taste whatever it was. *"Yeah, that's the way to find out."*

He snapped as fast as his little jaws could but only got a mouthful of air. No bird, no way. It seemed to have disappeared.

Just to his left the grass parted and began to sway on its own. He stood to get a better view and sniffed the air. The grass stopped moving. Bandit crept a little closer and the grass parted again as if by its own power. Bandit's brown eyes fixated on this strange movement. He watched as the split in the grass moved in a zigzagged fashion and seemed to head for a trunk that had long ago lost its tree. Bandit learned from Sheena not to get too ambitious about new things, so as he had seen the wolf-dog do many times, he inched closer and closer on stealthy paws. Then, he froze in his tracks. A spitting hiss came from the grass and he soon saw what caused the movement. A Rocky Mountain Rattler coiled and faced the dog. Full of deadly venom, the cornered reptile raised its lethal head, about to strike. The snake's rattlers sounded the alarm. Bandit peered into the beady eyes of the assailant, almost frozen by what he saw. Stock still and enraptured by the spectacle, he never saw the silver mass swoop down on him and grab him by the neck. Sheena whisked the puppy out of the snake's reach, her heart pounding as she carried him in the opposite direction. She dropped Bandit down and growled a deep reproach, *"Never, never do that again. That is a snake and he will kill you. When you see them or smell their foul odor, leave the area. Do you hear me? Never…"*

Bandit felt she went on and on. He got it the first time and hated it when she lectured him over and over again. He may hate it, Sheena thought, but part of living wild is to know all the dangers lurking around each corner and every part of this land. Bandit soaked it all in, but he hated when she fussed at him. He was beginning not to like this old forest anyway.

Sheena watched as Bandit returned to puppy play. She noted he acted differently than the cubs she'd seen before. Bandit was confident, assertive, and in Sheena's eyes, a little bit foolhardy. He exhibited none of the shyness typical of her kind.

* * *

Up the far side of a nearby steep hillside, covered with trees and still wearing a blanket of snow, a wolf pack moved in unison, weaving through the trees. The alpha male always led with his alpha mate close behind. Other male wolves didn't challenge his right to lead. A wolf called Shifty bore the scars from an encounter with Stone. Stone, about five years old, had ruled the pack since he deposed the old male. They fought to a bitter finale and Stone chased the former leader off into isolation. The hardest thing for a timber wolf is to be forced to live alone.

Several months later, Stone and the Absoraka pack came across the carcass of the once mighty leader. Stone stood near the old wolf's head and for several moments just stared at the remains. The rest of the pack fidgeted, peeking to see Stone's reaction. They nipped at each other during a restive dance, leaving about a 20-foot perimeter between them, the new alpha, and the corpse of the old.

Stone turned his grizzled muzzle away from the smell of death, raised his head, and howled a lament to the old warrior. He then walked away, his head drooping and his tongue lolling out of the side of his mouth. The rest of the North Country wolves avoided his eyes and would avert their heads if he looked their way. Death has a sobering effect on all creatures.

* * *

This was an important money-making time of the year for the ranchers of Montana. Lambs were being collected and the ranchers packed the sheep's wool that made Montana's clothing industry famous. Young hay sprouted, promising a full harvest.

At the stockyards at Three Forks, Javier piled out of the green pickup with Jenny close at his heels. Blu stayed in the back in his crate like he'd been trained. He only got out when invited. A quick whistle and Blu's body sailed over the top of the truck bed and, without missing a step, fell in with Jenny and Javier. Strangers to the sheep and cattle industry are always amazed by the ability to control such dogs with the tiniest of whistles. Each sounded the same to human ears, but spoke volumes to working stock dogs.

"Good morning, Mr. Coronado." "With a tip of a worn wide brim hat, Otis Millman greeted his fellow rancher and neighbor.   "Lonnie tells me your dog is home and you got a new puppy." Otis's bottom lip quivered at the coming joke.

"Man, that's something. Lose a dog and get two in return," Otis laughed easily. His six foot-three-inch, two-hundred-fifty-pound frame bounced in time with his chuckles; Millman always enjoyed his own jokes the most.

"Otis, just take a look at my girl. She's fat again and just as feisty as ever."

Jenny turned her head away from the two men, hoping they didn't recognize a dog's blushes. Blu eyed another Aussie in the back of Doc Williams' SUV. The

108   James MacKrell

Aussie named Ruthie had her nose elevated and her eyes canted back to catch every move the Blu dog made.

"If only, if only," she thought. She lived for the day that her owner would ask Javier to allow breeding between the two.

Doc Williams came out of the hardware store and put his hands up to his forehead to shield the bright sunlight.

"Morning, men, how goes it?" Doc was a consulting veterinarian for the Montana State University agriculture program. He supervised sheep and cattle breeding programs and worked closely with the Montana State University sheep project.

"That Jenny girl looks pretty good for a dog you threw away." Otis laughed even harder at Doc's humor.

Javier blushed and found no words for retort. Otis nearly split his pants laughing. "He's got you good there, Javier," Otis gently slapped Javier on the arm. "I never knew you to throw anything away, especially one of the best stock dogs in this area!"

"Listen, I am not going to stand for all this…" His voice trailed away into a big grin.

Blu never stopped gazing at Ruthie. Jenny seemed preoccupied wondering what trouble little Falen might be getting into at home. She had left her alone. Then it dawned on the mother dog, Falen had enough relatives to more than meet her needs. Just give her something or someone to chew on, and Falen was ecstatic.

As both Jenny and Blu got within reach of the three ranchers, absently their hands reached down with reassuring pats. Sometimes action of the farmers' hands on their dogs is so automatic, they don't even realize they're doing it. But in this country where partnerships are so

important, the bond between ranchers and stock dogs is
enduring.

Chapter 18
"No room for newcomers..."

Living alone with her cub in the forest, Sheena became extremely stealthy. She blended in the background and stayed so still her breathing could barely be heard. Bandit learned as well, that quiet equals safety and quiet lets you see a lot of things that normally go unnoticed in the wilderness.

A major wildlife highway dissected the range of mountains, an old deer trail probably older than many of the residents in the region. Strong winds high in the tops of the giant spruce and fir created a constant rush. The whistling amongst the branches masked many sounds on the ground. Sheena took advantage of any camouflage available, both visible and audible. Alone, with a growing pup to care for, she faced the scores of predators who roamed day and night. Living in the wild the search for a source of food is constant and you must always defend it.

The wind blew across the path right into the face of Sheena and Bandit, blowing away their scent. Both hunkered down behind a scrub of bushes and rocks, allowing them a clear view of activity that passed. The soft padding of large paws sounded a steady four-beat rhythm as Stone and his pack in single file trotted through the broken sunlight of the morning. Bandit's nose bore the scars of disobeying Sheena when told to be silent. He didn't need any more lessons on standing still.

"My goodness, he is magnificent."

Sheena sighed under her breath for fear the gray wolf would hear. She couldn't tell if she said it aloud or only thought it, but she knew it was the truth.

Not since Scar had she seen a wolf so powerful and striking to look upon. Sheena's heart seemed to burst through her ribs. She imagined it must have been the way Scar carried himself when he roamed free.

Close behind came the alpha bitch. Her name was Beauty and all who saw her agreed.

She pranced on paws so light she looked as if she were walking on air, but her demeanor was proud and steely. Second in importance, she followed Stone only a few feet away. The rest of the pack marched along, never venturing ahead of the alphas.

Stone stood nearly three feet tall at his withers, and weighed about 150 pounds. His jaws were twelve times more powerful than a pit bull's. His front paws, larger than those in the rear, reached out as he carried himself in perfect poise and balance. His countenance bore the look of kings. At this time of day the sun caused his fur to glisten like highly polished silver.

Sheena watched, jealous of the alpha bitch. Beauty had nothing that Sheena didn't have, except a mate. Without a noticeable move, the wolf-dog gently stroked Bandit's back with her nose. She hoped he too would to take in all the pageantry of this parade. In her dreams Bandit grew into a mighty leader. She often forgot her Bandit wasn't a wolf; he belonged to a species so far removed from Canis Lupus only the most prehistoric of genes survived in his body. Bandit was a dog, a servant and partner of mankind, a canine that existed in total harmony with humans for tens of thousands of years. Bandit's kind loved everything Sheena hated.

James MacKrell

The Gray pageant moved on down the trail at a steady pace. Stone's pack covered over 25 miles a day and tonight, far down the trail, they would hunt and sleep confident of their safety because of the mighty wolf's leadership.

Sheena, however, needed to find a new den. Only then, while the little guy slept, she would have the time to hunt food for them both. In the morning they would feast on her kill. Bandit knew that Sheena brought food but he didn't give much thought to who had died, so that he might live.

* * *

Back in the comfort of the ranch, Falen never met a food bowl she didn't like, and the crunchy kibble presented to her three times a day melted in her mouth like manna from heaven. She disliked the raw meat they were forced to eat in the wild. The strong coppery flavor with the odor of spoiled meat caused her to gag. But these brown little rocks of goodness smelled wonderful to the growing puppy. Since she ate on the porch old Emma would stick her nose into the dish, shove her little face aside, and snatch up the remaining morsels. It drove Falen crazy. It didn't take the little Aussie long to figure out if she devoured each bite in a hurry, not leaving any Emma would have to eat out of her own bowl. Emma had been eating dry food for years and she loved it until she got a mouthful of puppy chow. The Grand Dam thought the baby food tasted like butter rolling off a sweet cake.

Falen stopped in mid-bite, noticing the old squirrel reclining near the bird feeder. In a flash Falen's head popped up with a mouthful of kibble still between her teeth, and she charged out, not to do any harm but to find someone to play with. Food occupied her young mind right ahead of play, and this morning the squirrel didn't want to be bothered. Up the crooked evergreen he scampered, leaving the raiding of the bird feeder to another time. Falen was left reaching as far up the porch post as possible, standing on her hind feet's tiptoes. In a split second Falen spied a magpie landing on the lawn.

Desperate to make friends Falen bounded off the deck, turned end over end then righted herself, still looking for the strangely marked bird. From the top of the gnarled old tree, the multi-colored bird squawked at the puppy. Tempted to swoop down and give her assailant a good peck on the head, she continued her shrieking at the pile of fur still landlocked. Before the bird could make up its birdbrain, Falen's attention scampered off to other adventures. All of the running around caused her to want to visit the kibble bowl again, but she knew old Emma had already eaten it.

* * *

Just as Lonnie shut the door on the feed bin, Javier's truck pulled into the gate of the ranch property. Blu had fallen asleep in the crate in the back of the truck, probably dreaming of Ruthie, and Jenny, in her accustomed place in the front seat riding shotgun, didn't comprehend what all the discussion had been by Javier, Otis, and Doc. It seemed to trouble her Master a great deal. Worry lines around his eyes appeared deeper and more pronounced. He mumbled to himself as his hands gripped the steering wheel like squeezing lemons. Jenny's body, already tense from trying to keep her balance, pushed even closer to Javier's side. Driving faster than usual, the herdsman anxious to get

James MacKrell

home stared straight ahead. He played the words of his friends over and over in his mind.

The truck whipped around in the driveway and before the engine barely shut down, the driver's door swung open. Javier jumped down like a rodeo rider exiting a two thousand pound bucking bull. Jenny followed, as did Blu, up the stairs and through the front door without acknowledging any of the animals stretched out on the deck.

Javier tossed his Montana State baseball cap at the hat rack and stomped into the kitchen to brew some coffee. Grumbling to himself, he poured the water, put in several spoons of strong grounds, and flipped the switch on the automatic percolator. Then, almost like a collapse, he fell into his front room's over-stuffed recliner. Jenny eased up to her Master and gently laid her head near his hand. With the softest of eyes, she looked up into Javier's face, trying her best to figure out what bothered him so much. She couldn't think of what she or the other dogs did that would have riled him so. Thinking back to the conversation with the three ranchers, all of their words became more heated after a story Doc had related. Jenny wasn't good at remembering anything except dog things, but she was sure the conversation had something to do with the sour mood that clouded the herdsman like a fog.

Javier reached for the phone, but thought better and sank back down into the rocker. Before he could relax, the timer on the coffee pot did its incessant beeping so he pushed out of the chair, crossed into the kitchen, and poured a mug of coffee. Just then Blu started barking furiously and Emma joined in. Jenny ran to the front door yapping the same message she heard from Blu and Emma, *"Stay away, you've been warned! Stay away from our home."*

Javier started for the front door and saw a sheriff deputy's car pulling up in front, honking to announce his presence. The lawman exited the patrol car and waved a greeting, slipping off his hat to show this was a friendly mission.

"Mr. Coronado, Doc and Otis told me about your conversation in town and I thought I might just ride out and fill you in on all the details."

Javier took the deputy's outstretched hand, said many thanks, and invited him for fresh coffee.

"I will tell you, Tom, this could be a hell of a mess before it's over," Javier said as he turned to lead the way back to the house. "We got enough to worry about trying to wring out a living off this land without outside troubles and outside problem-makers." Tom nodded his head in agreement. Both men entered the house and all of the Aussies returned to their duties of lying around.

Chapter 19
"The threat from within..."

Most folks knew Javier lived a solitary life. He didn't mind, but to some, the loneliness would drive them mad. Javier had plenty of friends, but not enough time to visit. He laughed; they didn't know how much companionship an Australian Shepherd can give, especially to a person so used to being alone. His Aussies tended to listen to his stories without interrupting, along with a Morgan horse he used as a sounding board for his troubles, and a band of sheep who never complained about his old Spanish folk songs. The sheep didn't understand Spanish anyway.

What was shared with him in Big Timber brought to the front a problem no one had ever faced before. The threat from a person within their midst that could destroy the peace and their livelihoods rippled through the ranch community like shock waves. The community was the ecosystem these Montanans fought diligently to protect. The law and order of the land was paramount. Ranching was tough enough, having to battle the wind, rain, and other elements, without having to face an intruder who could unbalance the system they all depended on.

Blu and Jenny and the other stock dogs would give their lives to protect their home and livestock. Ranchers would give their lives as well. That is why the subject of illegally breeding wolf-dogs appeared so serious and why Deputy Tommy Hampton took the time to come all the way out to discuss the situation with Javier. Hampton believed this might blow up and wanted to head it off if he and the

Sheriff's Department possibly could. Otis and Doc worried that Javier, living alone, might be a target of the renegade's anger.

To hide some of his concern, Hampton glanced down at the uniform hat clutched in his hands and started the conversation easy. "Javier, seems like the lambing is going along fine, he sipped the strong coffee Javier had brewed. "And there's a lot of naked sheep in them pens."

Jenny crawled up into Javier's chair, as much an integral part of the conversation as either the deputy or Javier. Emma couldn't be bothered and Blu and his niece, Falen, weren't through inspecting each and every nut and bolt on the patrol car.

"So far, so good. I haven't lost many newborns and we've been pretty busy with all our other chores." Javier raised the mug to his lips, took a long swallow, exhaled, blew on the hot coffee again, and looked up at the deputy with a big smile.

Tom had been around herdsmen most of his life and the lawman knew talk needed to be sparse and full of important holes. You don't rush a man to speak when he's spent almost a half a century whistling at dogs and singing to sheep.

Tom played with the band of his trooper hat, drank some coffee, and squirmed in the chair. The old Basque's face continued to smile yet his eyes were dark and apprehensive.

"We've got a potentially explosive problem here. One the Sheriff's department doesn't want to erupt into violence."

Javier nodded his head, and stared at the deputy. "Doc first found out about this guy called Spencer at a meeting at the University. Spencer's place, I believe he rents the spread, backs up to federal land, and a lot of the

118   James MacKrell

ranchers in his area have been losing livestock to what they thought were wolves or big cats."

At the mention of wolves Jenny raised her head, suddenly much more interested in what the men were talking about. She poured herself off Javier's lap and sat erect near the foot of the chair.

Tom crossed and uncrossed his legs, put the mug of coffee on the table, and went on. "What the ranchers found had none of the markings of a pack kill. These seem to be loners who will strike in broad daylight. Tom Rafferty even told Doc that two of his Border Collies had been killed with their throats ripped open." Emma rose and moved just next to the deputy's chair.

"This all sounds like a State problem, Tom. Why's the sheriff getting mixed up in this?"

"I wish we didn't have to worry about this, and if only it was the livestock killed, or if only it were them wolves, then the game wardens could handle it."

He sat back and looked off in the distance for a while, not knowing how to say what had to come next.

"Oh Lord Almighty, I do wish that was the case, but as I told Otis and Doc this afternoon, the Anderson kid was shot at near the so-called Spencer kennel. The kid wasn't doing nothin'. He was just riding on an old mountain trail on the hill behind Spencer's ratty old place, and two shots zinged by his head. One bullet clipped the top of his hat."

Tom broke into a half-smile grateful for a chance to break the tension. "The kid practically crapped his pants, to hear his daddy tell it." When Javier didn't laugh the deputy plastered his lawman's serious face back on. "I mean that crazy bastard could've killed that kid."

Javier nodded, stroked Jenny's head, and stared down at the floor.

"What I mean to say is this; if the drunken SOB starts shooting at people, we are going to have a world of trouble. We can't arrest him for something we only think he's done. We're gonna to have to catch him in the act. I'll tell you this, I'm glad I'm not one of the State officers who is going to have to drive in there and interview him."

Tom drank some more coffee, and left the air silent between the two men, apparently hoping Javier would join in. He didn't.

Tom cleared his throat and went on. "We know Spencer has been in town yelling up some of the ranker watering holes. In fact he nearly got into a fight with Sarge over at that motorcycle hangout, claimed he was cheated out of his change and wanted to take on all the others in the whole bar."

At this Javier's eyes smiled. "If I know those truckers and cowboys who drink there, you would have carried Spencer out in a box like so much manure."

Tom smiled and fidgeted with his pant leg, glad Javier had finally joined the conversation.

"All I know is this crazy guy thinks he's some kind of bad soldier, wearing fatigues and a Vietnam crush hat. The drunker he gets the braver he becomes. I'm just afraid he'll decide to take it out on some of our ranchers, lashing out against everyone in the county he thinks has done him wrong."

Javier understood the implied message. Javier being all alone would make a good target for Ronnie Spencer's pent up anger at all the ranchers whose lands surrounded where he raised all those wolf-dogs.

They discussed the fact that more than likely Spencer's hybrids were tormenting the sheep and cattle on the reservation. They were becoming bolder and bolder the hungrier they got. Everyone believed as drunk as Spencer seemed to stay, his dogs could run off at will. He would probably never miss them, the ones he didn't use for target practice.

* * *

Later that night as Javier turned in, one of Spencer's hybrids bedded down in the dugout far up in the mountains she and Bandit called home.

Chapter 20
"No place to go, without a family…"

Bandit rolled in the snow for a while, jumping up to pounce on an imaginary foe. His growls had become deeper and his legs grew like new trees. Sheena loved to sit and watch him. She still didn't allow him to go with her on hunting trips. She didn't know why, but she had a deep desire to keep him from watching the killings. She brought back the meat and Bandit tore into it as if he hadn't eaten in days.

The couple's routine remained consistent. Their den was deep enough for both to sleep and eat without bumping into each other all the time. It also offered cover from the elements and any enemies roaming in the vicinity. They were snug and warm during the last night's deluge, the April temperature bottoming out at about 25 degrees causing them no discomfort. The morning brought slate gray skies but warmer conditions. Patches of snow remained where the melting rays of the sun could not reach, creating a quilted pattern across the forest floor.

The memory of Stone and his wolf pack played in Sheena's mind. The night before she had even dreamed she was the alpha female, his mate, his support in fights and on hunts. She awoke to a warm backside curled against her and for a moment she thought of Stone but realized it was Bandit, snoring away the morning. She had laid the results of last night's hunt far enough inside the den opening so that other animals couldn't steal it. As soon as Bandit's eyes opened his mouth did as well. He was a growing boy, strong and tall, and he pleased Sheena in many ways. The only thing that puzzled the wolf-dog was why he didn't have a tail.

* * *

Jenny followed Javier everywhere, into the kitchen, as he picked up the dishes from last night, even when he went to the bathroom, where she waited outside the door. She sensed tension. Awakening several times during the night, she would open one eye when he got up to get a glass of water or go to the bathroom. When he went into the living room to sit in his overstuffed chair and stare out the window into the darkness, she inched her way from the bedroom to his side. Resting her head on her paws, she lay as close to his leg as she could get.

The moonlight cast a searchlight's glow over the front yard. The cold in Big Sky country made the stars seem almost reachable. The brightness of the night sky played games with Javier's imagination. Shadows took form and then danced away. Dark apparitions seemed to emerge out of the nothingness. They only added to his growing anxiety.

"What to do?" he mused. He bent over and rested his elbows on his legs, placing his hands near his temples and massaging them as you would worry beads. Jenny moved, bumping against his leg, and tried to re-settle herself without bothering her Master.

His eyes dropped to the Aussie he loved so much and had grieved over during her absence.

"My sweet girl," he warmly said, dropping one hand from his head to stroke the dog's back. Emma came strolling in to join them with little Falen close behind. All around his leather easy chair the dogs perched, like ladies in waiting circling the throne of the king.

James MacKrell

A deep ache started to rumble in his heart. He tried to speak to the Aussies, but the sight of little Falen made tears well up in his eyes.

Javier worked. That is how he had spent his life. Death held no mystery for him; he never worried about his own mortality. At the funeral of his beloved Rosario, Javier placed her wedding ring on a gold link chain, which he wore night and day. At times he could feel her presence reaching out from the ring into his soul so he never felt alone. With the loss of Clara Townsend followed by that of the ranch owner and his dearest friend, Jim, Javier depended on Rosario's ring for strength.

Alone now, the ranch became his love and companion. The lives of the Australian Shepherds he and Jim carefully bred and raised were his focus in life. He placed the dogs' needs over his own. Javier, truly an unselfish man, trusted God and never forgot to be ever-thankful for his bounty.

On this night, one of the first times in a long time, he thought of himself. What would happen to all of his possessions if someone, something, took him away?

Jenny seemed to read his mind. She had the experience of loneliness and despair. She lived through dark nights of terror. Jenny wanted with all her big heart to speak to Javier in a human way so she could express how much she recognized his fears.

Javier read the Aussie in ways she could not fathom. Looking down into her up-turned eyes, Javier whispered, "Thank you, my girl, thank you for your love." His work-worn fingers played through the silky black hair on her nape.

What the deputy told Javier didn't frighten him as much as it made him aware of his vulnerability living alone. Sure, he had the dogs to warn and protect him, but not against the malevolence of a person out of control and bent on doing harm.

Many a day Javier had finished his daily chores before the sun finished its race across the sky and dipped behind the mountains. With spring bursting forth, each day only signaled more work and less time to stop and smell the bounty of spring flowers. Now this trouble with the unruly outsider gave a new set of worries for the families living along the valleys and rivers of south central Montana.

The sudden sound of activity some distance beyond the fence broke the sleepy silence. Jenny leaped to her feet and forced her nose hard against the window, peering into the darkness for any signs of movement. Alert barks filled the area as Blu, Brady and Mate all sensed the threat of intruders. Gabe and Mike's giant white masses milled among the flock in the pens, searching for any danger to their charges.

With her feet firmly planted on the window sill, Jenny growled through the glass, *"Blu, search every corner. Do you need me? Shall I come out to help you look?"*

Blu's ears flicked, listening to Jenny as he strained against the chain link of the kennel. The warning had been sounded, *"This is our territory and you had better be warned that to approach it could be your last mistake."*

The commotion sounded real enough to propel Javier into his jacket, armed with a powerful portable searchlight, and out into the yard to investigate. Opening the kennel gates, he didn't shush the dogs. A command to be quiet might tell them they were doing something wrong. They weren't, they were alerting the ranch of perceived danger, and to a rancher living alone any warning is a good warning.

Gabe made it to the western-most portion of the fence and seemed transfixed by something just on the edge of the woods, perched on a cliff overlooking the pens.

Jenny stood by Javier's side, as did Blu, Mate, and Brady. Little Falen stayed on the porch within easy reach of the door left ajar. A tiny growl boiled up from her heart, a way of telling Mom and her uncles that she was with them, but would stay near the house just in case she wasn't needed. Emma was restless and continued her survey of the inside of the house.

Blu rushed ahead of Javier to the outside edge of the fence, staring up into the darkness.

"Gabe, what do you see? Am I looking in the right place?"

"Look a bit higher up on the edge of the cliff. I noticed movement just seconds *ago, but now it seems to have vanished."* The Great Pyrenees put his paws on the metal rungs of the fence to get a better view.

"Don't go up there, Blu!" Gabe never wavered in his attention to the rim of the cliff. *"It might be a trick to make us run into the pack!"*

Mate and Brady, who were on the opposite sides of the sheep, raced to the backside, warning off the attackers.

Jenny and Javier got to the section of the fence where Blu and Gabe stood. With a pat of assurance to Blu and a 'good boy' to Gabe, Javier trained his light beam up the side of the hill and stopped on the rim. He didn't know what to expect but he knew his dogs, and this threat wasn't a false alarm..

Jenny stood in front of Javier. Her paws were firmly planted and her haunches a little lower than her withers. She was poised for action; ready to defend those things she cared for with her life. Brady rounded the pen and came up on the left side. Gabe's massive head reared and a menacing growl filled the still air. Javier trained the searchlight to the top of the hill and slowly played the beam back and forth, letting the white circle creep down toward the rim of the outcropping.

"There, did you see that?" Jenny softly whined. The other Aussies' eyes were following the field of light. All of the dogs were as still as steel statues, each carefully studying the widening disk of brightness as it swept back and forth. Then Javier saw them. They appeared as red dots against the black background. While Javier kept them in the frame of the searchlight's beam, two other red dots shone just to the edge of the white island in the darkness.

As the full force of brilliance surrounded the cliff line Javier saw the red dots were the reflective pupils of a gray wolf-like creature. He flashed the beam back at the other two who had now moved ever closer to the edge of the rocks. There, standing side-by-side, two more beasts looked down on Javier. He thought the intruders resembled dogs more than wolves. The first had the white face and mask of a Malamute; Javier noticed the curled tail over the gray body. Yet as big as Malamutes get, this animal seemed small for its breed. It lowered its head, ready to lunge. The ears on the companion were erect and twitching, listening for any movement, a signal to attack. Each of the animals stared down on Javier and the dogs, confident in their position but wary of the odds.

Javier had never seen wolf-dog hybrids before but it only took a minute to recognize these marauders as the predators that were pillaging the flocks all through the valley. Javier also recognized that these wolf-hybrids seemed immature and gaunt, not more than a year or so old. They looked like what had been described as the wolf-dogs that had been escaping from Spencer's place. Young,

James MacKrell

hungry, and inexperienced, he thought if he yelled at them he might scare them away.

"You! Get the hell out of here," He screamed, and his dogs started barking again. "Get away! Get gone!" He fired his 410 shotgun at them but the pellets fell short.

The young wolf-dogs didn't move. All of Javier's screaming and threats wouldn't budge them. Blu couldn't stand the tension anymore. He moved back to get a running start at the intruders and was passed over by nearly four hundred pounds of Pyrenees. Gabe and Mike had vaulted the fence and charged full steam up the hillside. Blu was right behind them with his eyes ablaze. Gabe reached the perimeter of the rock wall first to the right of the four wolf-dogs. Before they could react to one shaggy attacker, Mike rounded the top on their left and started barking in his loudest voice. The gray heads turned to face him, leaving a split second for Gabe to rush them. Blu bounded over the rocks and tore into the hind leg of the Malamute cross, burying his fangs deep in the muscle that ran down his back. A German shepherd cross wheeled to grab Blu, but was foiled by the instant vice-like grip of Mike's enormous jaws around the Shepherd's throat. With a shuddering bite he rendered the wolf-dog helpless. The brown and tan body slumped into a puddle, unable to move. Mike pounced on the neck of the other Shepherd-looking dog and with a twist of his head broke the wolf-dog's neck. The two remaining would-be killers fled in an instant into the inky blackness of the forest. Blu, with blood dripping from his fangs, started to pursue. Gabe headed him off and knocked Blu to the ground.

"No Blu, it could be a trap. We've won, we've protected our own. Believe me, those two won't be coming back tonight!"

Blu gasped for air and righted himself. He looked into the great dog's eyes, acknowledging the reprimand and thankful for saving his life.

Much to the amazement of Javier, the violence ended in only a matter of minutes. As the three dogs returned down the hillside, blooded and proudly victorious, each acted like a pup waiting for the warm hands of praise and congratulations. The Great Pyrenees', and the Aussies' hearts pumped extra beats of pride. Blu limped over to Javier, his leg torn by the fight. Mike's and Gabe's shaggy white coats were full of blood. The good part was it wasn't theirs. They were working dogs and tonight again proved to the Master their utter loyalty, even to the death.

* * *

The clouds thickened, covering the face of the moon and sinking the landscape into a blackout. The wolf-dogs that survived the onslaught of the attacking dogs stood bloodied and confused in the darkness. Slowly, one wolf-dog turned and silently slunk away, his tail tucked tightly between his legs. At no time did the other survivor make eye contact with the retreating animal. They weren't part of a pack; they were just two animals alone in the forest who decided that sheep would be much easier prey than the animals of the wild.

James MacKrell

Chapter 21
"Two different worlds..."

Bandit's belly didn't scrape the grass as much as it had to a few days ago. His legs grew up strong and sinewy and his coat had come in full and wavy black. The white chest hair appeared like a bib and the bright specks of copper over his eyes accentuated the blackness of his face. Now his fur, thick due to living in the freezing cold and ice, started thinning since spring had arrived. It had been a hard winter for the twosome. Bandit knew of nothing else, but Sheena believed this wasn't the way for them to live their lives, alone with no pack or mates.

Bandit had a lot of playmates. There were rabbits that offered sport by hopping out of reach and then diving down holes with Bandit close behind them, the birds soaring from the meadow floor moments before his jaws snapped upon them, leaving him staring at the sky wondering, *"Why can't I do that?"*

There were the insects singing and chirping from all directions and squirrels scampering high into trees he couldn't climb. More and more Bandit's playful games gave way to a more serious attitude. He was maturing and to Sheena he seemed to have left the puppy world behind.

His test of maturity came late one afternoon at the mouth of the den. Sheena was curled up in sleep, resting for what would be a full night of hunting. Bandit had found an old bone and sharpened his new adult teeth. The rhythm of Sheena's soft breathing let him know she had dozed off. Bandit played quietly, gnawing on the bone and picking up loose pieces of sticks to try his strong jaws.

At first, the stench drifted in on wisps of afternoon air. A gentle breeze carried the acrid odor and filled the portion of the den where Bandit lay. This strange reek caused him to put aside his toys and focus on discerning this disgusting odor's origin. He turned his head toward the opening of the den and the stink became more and more distasteful.

His keen nose detected the smell of urine and a musk he wasn't familiar with. Then a disturbance outside the den caught his attention. Bandit quieted, and lowered his head to the ground. His ears listened intently to detect a hostile noise.

The hackles rose on his withers and a strange metallic tang flooded his mouth. On high alert, his eyes could see farther and clearer than before and each sound was magnified. The threat had a face with hot eyes and long whiskers sprouting from its snout. The tops of its tufted ears stood erect. To the left of the den opening, the young bobcat's eyes met the furious eyes of Bandit. The cat, testing his abilities to hunt, awoke the instinct in Bandit to defend. He remembered the look of the cougar that threatened him and Sheena, and the fear of that attack heightened his defense against this aggressor. The stealthy cat crept closer to the mouth of the burrow, parting the grass on both sides. The bobcat inched ahead on padded paws that housed lethal weapons. The Aussie's first line of defense was his strong jaws coupled with his agility, but the narrowness of the den's aperture restricted Bandit's maneuverability, so any attack by Bandit had to be straight on and furious. The cat let out a brutal cry, reverberating off the den walls, causing Sheena's head to pop up behind Bandit. Before she issued a warning, Bandit launched himself right into the face of the young prowler. Surprised by the sudden attack, the wildcat fell back on his haunches, slightly off balance, nearly falling over. With all the ferocity he could muster, Bandit's jaws snapped shut just behind the young cat's ears, grabbing the trespasser by the nape of the neck. The bobcat squealed, slashing the air with his claws, but since he was no more schooled in warfare than Bandit, they both rolled on the ground amid sounds of great fury, Bandit hanging onto the cat's neck for dear life. Sheena watched as her pup's head twisted and turned slinging the immature cat from left to right. The young cat's weight proved too much for Bandit to hang onto for long, so the last fling sent the bewhiskered interloper rolling down the hill, bouncing off rocks and tree stumps, flipping about to get its feet back under it before dashing off. Bandit shook himself and proudly stood in the doorway furiously barking, *"And don't you come back! You leave us alone or the next time will be too bad for you."*

He felt Sheena's presence beside him so he didn't turn to face her; he kept his eyes trained on the fleeing feline. He had never experienced such a sensation. Warmth flooded his body, rolling in waves from his head to the tip of his tailless butt.

Sheena's tongue massaged and cleaned his wounds and reassured him of her pride and approval, her eyes half closed as she continued to minister to her hero. Soft whimpers of love filled his ears.

He had fought for their little family and won. This was his graduation day.

* * *

Bandit's sister, Falen, had never been threatened in her life. Oh, the scare the other night got her attention, but she relied on her mother to handle things like that. As

Bandit had grown, Falen, too, was filling out with her gorgeous array of color splashed over her coat. Her eyes were golden-colored due to the red pigment that dominated her fur. Those eyes could plead, question, and demand, depending on her mood at the moment, though of course that mood was subject to change in a matter of seconds. Her mother ambled over and gave little Falen a cursory lick, just a gentle touch to remind her all was well and safe.

A magpie stretched its white-striped wings and flew over the top of the cabin. Swooping down on an unsuspecting beetle, she lifted off like a rocket, winging effortlessly into the sky, a tiny disappearing dot.

Both Jenny and Falen followed the flight but with different thoughts. To Falen, it was just another day in her lessons on observation, and she had a world of things to observe. Her lessons began in the hole in the gully wall and continued with new experiences daily.

Jenny, on the other hand, had a mind full of memories. Her heart broke every time she looked up the rocky road to the high pastures, remembering the pup that didn't come home. She was sure he was dead, but that fact didn't keep her from hoping that someday they would be reunited. Jenny remembered her pleas to the Spirit of the Day and Night and flushed warm by the thought of her answered prayers. She offered up her hope that in some way her baby had been protected and remained alive. As the days turned into months her hopes of his return dimmed, but as much as she despaired, a voice from deep within reminded her of the feelings of hopelessness in the gully. Had she not been rescued after all?

Falen's red and copper butt brushed against her mother's leg. As she continued her gaze up the hillside, the touch of her baby girl renewed her belief in the Spirit of the

Day and Night to protect them and keep them full of the wonder of the life they had been given.

James MacKrell

Chapter 22
"What could have been…"

The sunlight filtering through the leaves and branches of the trees, created a dappled pattern outside the opening to Sheena's den. The wind caused the branches and limbs to gently sway, making black and gold splotches mixed with clear yellow-white, the perfect palette against the cobalt Montana sky. A canopy of jade-tinted needles fluttered in the breeze, casting a crisp and clean fragrance to the air. The buzz of living things provided the musical score for this perfect of days. Sheena lay fat and lazy. She and Bandit had eaten their fill on the remains of her hunt. Basking in the morning sun they let the gentle breezes lull them to sleep. Sheena's head rested on some tufts of grass, while Bandit played sleepily at her feet. The Aussie pup had grown so fast his black body was nearly as long as hers, yet he still thought of himself as a puppy.

As he bumped and rolled on her, the body of a maturing male aroused a deep desire in her. As she slept, visions of the great wolf, Stone, played across the panorama of her dreams. Bandit nipped her leg ever so gently, and all she could do was let out a sigh and let her sleeping eyelids flutter in time to the music of her dream.

An interesting sound reached her ears, soft thumping in the ear against the ground. Her exposed ear flipped up and swiveled, seeking the source of the noise like an aerial antenna. She picked her head up.

The rhythmic cadence of padded paws trotting in unison up the old deer trail adjacent to the mountain brook made soft sounds in the silent forest. A buck and a doe, sucking up the cool, sweet water in mid-stream, looked up to watch the parade; glad it was passing them by. Sheena remained hidden. The granite rocks piled and stacked as if by a master plan camouflaged the wolf pack, letting their gray coats meld into the surroundings. Even the touches of brown on Beauty's coat blended into the environs so well Sheena couldn't spot the wolves until they crested at the bend in the trail. Sheena held her breath. Bandit stood rock solid, sensing the importance of the moment.

Leading the pack, Stone slowed his trot and began sniffing the air, as he tried to locate a smell, something out of the ordinary that he was sensing.

Beauty inched up closer to her mate, her nose twitching from left to right.

The other lesser pack members all held back, careful not to interfere with the mighty leader. Stone stopped, his nose detecting something odd. His yellow eyes furtively searched for any sign of the animal that was the source of the smell. To Stone the scent seemed both familiar and strange.

Beauty slinked closer to the side of her mate. With the silence of a knife cut, Stone separated the branches on the bush and spotted Sheena and Bandit lying in the grass staring back at him. Beauty coughed, hoping to distract her mate from the striking wolf-dog.

Sheena's eyes grew soft and she panted in a slow rhythm so as not to disturb anything about this moment. One of the pack males inched along side to see what interrupted their progress. Beauty quickly snapped at his muzzle and let out a low menacing growl. The soldier wolf knew instantly he had done wrong and without showing the other pack wolves any sign of fear or humiliation, he back-peddled until he safely put distance between the alpha bitch and his sore nose.

138   James MacKrell

Stone never took his eyes from the sight of this sun-drenched beauty lifting her white face with eyes in worship of him.

"Where is the fear in your eyes?"

Sheena rose slowly to her full height and without moving any closer to the wolf pack, she stood tall and looked him straight in the eye.

"I have no fear, of you or anything I confront."

"Are you so strong and brave you engage me, the mighty Stone in mortal combat?"

"No, my Lord, I would only hope to stand with you in battle, and in the hunt, to be devoted to you, and place your needs above my own."

Stone took an incremental step forward, and Beauty inched up as well, careful to stay back of his loins. Sheena remained rock solid, not a muscle or a tendon moved in her body.

"How dare you address me with such familiarity. You do not know of me, and yet *you stand there as an equal to me, the leader?*

"I am alone. I have no master, no leader, and no reason to fear man or beast. I have earned my freedom from the jaws of oppression in a human-made hell."

She kept her eyes locked on his. The wolf bristled.

"I am Stone, the most feared. I rule everywhere my paws touch down, and I rule everything in my domain. Do I not rule you, female?"

"No one rules me except the sun and the stars. I answer to no master except the Spirit of the Day and Night."

Stone's eyes never drifted to Bandit, who had moved away from the back of Sheena toward the rocks where he could hide.

For what seemed at the time to be an eternity, no one spoke or moved. Even the birds and other animals in the vicinity were silenced by the tension. Beauty drew behind Stone and crept up on his other side, the side facing Sheena. Her eyes full of hate sought the eyes of Sheena, who only had eyes for Stone. One of the pack wolves standing behind shifted his position and inadvertently snapped a twig, the sudden noise piercing the stillness like a gunshot. The sound startled Beauty and Bandit; Sheena and Stone still didn't move.

In this dance, Stone made the first gesture. He turned ever so slowly and stepped a little to the left. Sheena responded by moving her head to the right, exposing her backside toward Stone's giant head.

One hundred-fifty seven pounds of timber wolf tensed every muscle in his body like a weight-lifter's well-oiled form posing before the judges. His powerful jaws and generously ruffed head and neck sat upon a lean and muscular body, carried on strong, straight legs, and long, arched feet. Sheena stretched to her full height, and tilted her head toward the alpha wolf with eyes beckoning like a courtesan.

The law of the pack insists power and authority tenuously hold every position. Stone overpowered the old leader to assume his place and he knew that someday one of the younger wolves would challenge his right to lead. The alpha female held her right to leadership by the same laws. She would continue to be his mate, unless deposed by another female through battle. Right now she faced a challenger for the first time in her short life. Sheena posed a threat, and Beauty didn't like threats.

James MacKrell

Chapter 23
"The fight of death…"

Beauty's yellow eyes darkened as the tension in her body mounted. Her lips parted and curled into a menacing snarl of hate. She rose to her full height, her ears pointed straight forward. She was ready to defend her authority or die trying.

A low guttural growl from the alpha female warned Sheena, whose gaze stayed steadily on Stone's face. As Beauty moved a little closer to Sheena, Stone retreated, stepping backward as if to clear the battlefield.

Beauty snarled, *"You dare challenge my place, you worthless excuse for a wolf?"*

The alpha bitch exposed her long and powerful fangs. Saliva dripped, and her eyes glowed red as fire, because of her excitement.

Sheena turned her head to face Beauty, making it clear she would not back down as the she-wolf, body lowered, her ears and eyes trained on Sheena, approached. A slow circle started as each of the females probed for an excuse to attack.

Out of the corner of her eye, Beauty glanced back at Stone, hoping for his blessing. He remained like granite.

Beauty feinted toward Sheena; Sheena tensed for a second, but then relaxed her muscles to be fully battle-ready. The ballet continued with each staying a safe distance from the other, but circling with eyes locked in a lethal stare.

Beauty made the first overt move, launching herself at Sheena in an attempt to take out her legs. Sheena dodged the wolf's snapping jaws and made a grab of her own, burying her teeth deep into the neck of her foe. Growls being exchanged with yelps of pain, the two canines tumbled over and over, fighting for that one position that would prove deadly to the other.

Thanks to her Malamute blood, Sheena had the weight advantage. The Malamute, bred for countless generations to haul heavy loads over long distances in frigid and punishing terrain, developed large, strong bones and a broad muscular body. Her sheer mass proved a worthy match for the skill of Beauty.

The wolf was an accomplished fighter and was used to intimidating any opposition. This battle with Sheena was something she thought she was equal to, but the brute strength of the wolf-dog proved too much for her to handle. Sheena pinned Beauty onto her back and transferred her bite from the neck to the throat. Beauty thrashed about, trying to force her release, but unable to escape the wolf-dog's jaws, her muscles relaxed and accepted defeat. With teeth still tight on the wolf's throat, Sheena growled a death threat. She had punctured the skin but had not taken a fatal bite. The conquered she-wolf remained reticent, her eyes averted from Sheena's angry gaze. Without shifting her stance, Sheena released her hold and raised her head, still staring at the she-wolf lying prostrate on the ground.

Stone lowered his head. He had just watched his mate vanquished in battle, something he had never witnessed before. The other pack wolves started muttering to themselves, worried and anxious about what would happen next. A change in leadership was disturbing to the entire pack and there was a feeling inside of each that the impending death of their Queen was a sad sight to behold.

James MacKrell

Sheena stood over the submissive form of Beauty, as she let out a howl of victory shattering the peace of the late afternoon's silence.

She addressed Stone and said, *"I grant this bitch life. She deserves to live with the knowledge that she faced me and lost."*

One foot at a time she removed herself from the defeated wolf, as she lay on the ground in complete humiliation.

As she stepped toward Stone, he raised his head high, and slowly looked away from Sheena. He didn't look at Beauty either. Sheena was devastated. She had fought bravely, and she had conquered her foe! She deserved her prize, her place by the side of the alpha male, and yet he ignored her. With a glance from Stone back to Beauty, and again back to Stone, Sheena's expression showed the confusion in her heart. This isn't how the tradition worked. She had been rebuked.

"What more do you want of me, Lord Stone?"

He didn't answer.

Beauty slowly got up from the ground, her neck bloody from Sheena's assault.

"Am I banished my Lord? Is my defeat to be the death of me?" She glanced at Sheena. *"Is this stranger to take my place?"*

Sheena stood quietly waiting. It wasn't her place to offer any suggestions or cause any further bloodshed.

Stone stepped away from the circle of conflict, positioning himself on a nearby bit of ledge, and looked down on both of the females.

All was silent. The pack wolves looked in the direction of their leader, waiting for his proclamation. Softly among themselves, the pack muttered, *"What's*

going to happen to Beauty?" "Is this our new queen?"
"What will Stone do, what will he say?"

Little Bandit watched warily, making sure to stay as inconspicuous as possible.

"Fair Beauty, you started a fight you could not finish". Without changing his gaze he continued, *"By the laws of the pack you should be dead."* He turned his attention to Sheena.

"And you, the victor, fought well. You challenged the alpha female and deposed her."

A smile creased Sheena's lips and her eyes glowed with pride and anticipation. Her heart swelled with affection for the mighty Stone.

"Yet Beauty, my faithful companion, you will not be sent from our pack." He turned to look at her. She avoided his gaze.

"You will live amongst us, always mindful of this defeat. It will make you stronger *and much, much wiser."*

The assembly heard the sigh of relief from her soul. She wouldn't be abandoned. There was mercy in the heart of Stone.

Sheena was now totally confused. She wondered almost aloud, *"If she stays, do I go, or do we stay as part of the pack together? Will Stone now be my mate, and Beauty banished from her place of honor?"* Her breath quickened, and she strained to make sure she heard everything Stone was about to say.

"You, the victor, what is your name?"

"I am called Sheena, my Lord." She looked over to the black and white form now rising slowly from the grass. *"My cub is called Bandit."*

The tension filled the air like a cold mist. Sheena counted her breaths waiting for Stone to continue.

"You are a worthy warrior, mighty in battle and gracious in triumph. You could have killed Beauty. That was your right. Yet you chose to let her live. That was your choice, and also your fate."

What was he talking about? She had won. She was ready to assume her throne, yet it sounded like she was to be the one banished. *"How could that be?"*

Not a whisper was heard. All the pack stood at attention. Sheena's tail drooped a little. Her eyes radiated the confusion engulfing her heart.

"You have the blood of our mortal enemy, the Dog. I wondered when I first saw you if you did not carry the heritage of the Dog. I now know that you do. The Dog is most hated among our kind."

Sheena couldn't believe her ears. Stone's eyes grew fierce as he continued.

"Dog has chosen to live with and aid our greatest adversary, Man."

He looked away for a moment, paused, then faced Sheena head on once again. *"Man has killed wolves for generations, not for food but out of hatred. Dogs are the same. They chose to live with and serve Man, and because of that, they are equally despised. I cannot let you and your dog pup live with us. It is against the rule of the pack."*

Stone lowered his head ever so slightly, as though in apology. He seemed sorry for the words as he said them.

"You and your dog cub may live in my territory in peace. We will not harm you or the cub. Yet since you carry with you the blood of the Dog, I cannot accept you as a wolf or a pack member." He turned and said, *"Come, Beauty, we must leave."*

As one, the pack resumed their journey. Sheena stood in the clearing, her heart broken. Bandit sensed her pain and edged up to her, licking the wounds on the side of her face. With one last look at the retreating pack, she turned and said, *"Let's go, Bandit. We are on our own again."*

James MacKrell

Chapter 24
"The turning of the leaves"

All during the hottest months of summer, Sheena had taken her fast-growing charge up to the higher and cooler elevations of the mountains, far away from humans.

Back in late July, Bandit expressed a curiosity about several people standing in a stream with long sticks in their hands. He wanted to approach them in a friendly manner, but Sheena stopped him with a fierce rebuke.

"Those are humans and they mean you harm. They can't be trusted. You must always flee from them." Sadly she remembered the pain that association with humans caused when Stone and the pack left without her.

Puzzled, Bandit didn't see a threat from the men laughing and playing in the water. He'd been in the same stream many times and knew what fun he had splashing and jumping in the cold mountain water. How much he enjoyed sticking his nose under, trying to catch the fish. In fact, he wanted to run down and meet them; maybe they would let him play, too.

Sheena snarled a growl of caution, deep and serious. Bandit turned his back on the fishermen, and only stole a glance as Sheena led them away from the chance of contact.

Bandit whined, *"What would it hurt to meet them? They seem less fierce than a lot of other animals we meet."*

Sheena stopped dead in her tracks. She whirled around to face Bandit with reproach in her eyes.

"Of all the things that prowl in these forests, Humans are the most dangerous. They kill for the sport,

*leaving the prey to rot where it falls. Humans use a method
we know nothing about or how to defend ourselves against.
It is called 'deceit' in their language; we have no word for
it. They will come at you smiling, and sometimes even
offering food, yet beat you with sticks and cage you and
deprive you of your freedom.   No, Bandit, never,
ever trust these humans. Only evil can come from an
involvement with them."*

He listened attentively, yet in the deepest recesses
of his heart he believed her wrong. For Bandit was dog,
and not just any dog but an Australian Shepherd. To live
and work with humans had been the prime duty of his
breed for generations.

* * *

The summer was passing at the Townsend Sheep
Ranch with plenty of work and play for all who resided
there. The long days drifted into nights with Javier reading,
after the TV weather reports, and the dogs playing 'gotcha'
in the front yard.

Lonnie's time with the animals grew short. He
enrolled in Montana State University on an FFA
scholarship he earned through hard work and exceptional
studies. He also turned out to be a pretty good Rodeo
cowboy, winning honors for calf roping at the Billings Fair.
He recommended his cousin, Jeremy Sanderson, to become
the new helper for Javier. Actually, Jeremy lived a mile or
two closer to Javier's place and could get there sooner and
stay later. He had a couple of months before school, which
was plenty of time to train Jeremy.

Different from Lonnie in appearance, he shared the
same work ethic and respect for animals.

The dogs loved Jeremy as they had Lonnie. He
took the time to pet and play with them all, especially little

Falen. Falen and Jeremy became nearly inseparable, with her nipping at his heels as he made his rounds. She pranced along to the barn, to the feed bin, and out into the sheep pens, making sure Jeremy had all the help he needed. The kid loved it, and the bond between the two grew daily.

"Jeremy, you're gonna have to stop playing with Falen until you get your chores done," Lonnie told him one day.

Lonnie exerted his new found authority over the younger boy since he was only 14, and Lonnie just celebrated his 18th birthday.

Resplendent in his blue FFA corduroy jacket, Lonnie's Montana State baseball cap gave him the look of a college man, he thought. It was something he'd been waiting for a long time. Lonnie had a date that night, so he hurried home and let Jeremy stay for supper at Javier's. Jeremy loved the Basque lamb stew, and thoroughly enjoyed listening to Javier chatter about his life as a youngster in California, and all the stories regarding Jim Townsend and their early years together. Falen had one paw on Jeremy's outstretched leg and her head placed in his lap. There was a time last spring when her whole body fit into the boy's lap, but not anymore.

"Mister Javier, have you heard anything about that survivalist who raises those wolf-dogs? My dad said he believes the man they call Spencer is up to no good."

Javier placed his cup of tea on the railing and paused before he answered. He didn't want to alarm the boy needlessly, nor bear witness to facts he couldn't verify. After a moment or two he said, "I believe your dad's right. However, there is always a lot of chatter about an unfriendly person, or one who keeps to himself, avoiding contact with his neighbors, so we will have to be patient."

He looked off into the night, trying to gain insight into how to counsel the young man.

"We must always be ready to take heed of threats and loose words spoken by men intending us harm, but until they make a threatening move, we've got to hold our peace." Javier turned to the boy and added, "I share your father's concern though. We both have a lot to lose from this renegade if he decides to do us harm."

Jeremy didn't take his eyes off the ageless face of Javier.

"Yes sir!!" he replied.

Jeremy worked out so well that as the months headed into fall, Jeremy was doing almost all of the work. The mountains of the range began to cool appreciably at night and the days were growing shorter. Almost a year since Jenny's ordeal, Falen was nearly full-grown and becoming a useful and talented stock dog. There were still mutterings about Spencer and his wolf-dogs, but now it was being marked off by most of the ranchers as just a lot of talk. Falen learned her craft well, under the tutelage of Blu, Mate, Brady, and her mother. Athletic and able to work all day without tiring, she still had plenty of energy to play with Jeremy in the evenings.

No wolf-dogs plagued the place since Gabe, Mike, and Blu ran off the skinny hybrids. Life stayed busy but normal around the ranch. The promise of a good winter seemed evident by the large amounts of hay Javier had stored in his barns.

James MacKrell

Chapter 25
"The movement of time…"

Falen jumped up on Javier's favorite easy chair with a piece of her throw blanket in the corner of her mouth. Any second she would fly off the recliner, ragged blanket in tow, and scamper through the house running into the furniture and generally making a mess, stopping to wet her front paws in the water dish, soaking the kitchen floor. Jenny curled up near the fireplace, warmed by the embers of the fire Javier had started earlier.

On this night Jenny's responsibility was to guard the house. Blu and Brady jumped into the truck for the ride into Big Timber on a grocery run. Still early in the evening, Jenny took every opportunity to store up some energy for the next day's work.

Something caught her attention. She heard crying, whimpering and snuffling from Javier's bedroom.

"I'd better check this out," she muttered and headed for the door, wondering if Little Falen had anything to do with this or someway was entangled in the blanket she dragged around like a cape.

"Falen, what are you doing? What is the matter?"

She used her nose to push aside the already opened door and step-by-step entered the room. The crying only grew louder. At first Jenny couldn't locate her puppy. Falen was covered by the blanket and wedged in between the bed and the wall. Moving around Javier's bed, Jenny saw the red, copper, and white coat of her baby, lying still in the gap. Falen whimpered loudly, her little heart broken.

Jenny started to speak but the sight of the blue merle coat in the corner next to the head of the bed shocked her. Falen's little nose pushed into the fur of the lifeless body of old Emma as she continued to whimper loudly. Jenny immediately joined in Falen's chorus of weeping. She never spent a day in her life without old Emma. She remained connected to the ancient old Aussie even when she and the puppies were lost. Then a thunderbolt shattered Jenny, *"What is the Master going to do?"*

Until Javier returned Falen and Jenny never left old Emma's body alone. She was precious to them, and they felt the need to stand guard over her lifeless form.

The minute Javier stepped from the truck he knew something was wrong. Brady and Blu vaulted out of the truck and ran toward the house. As they reached the porch, they all slowed their pace nearly to a stop.

Javier entered the house. "Jenny, where are you, girl? Falen, come! Emma, come in here, my girl."

Nothing happened. No one came. A shudder went through Javier's body as he entered the bedroom. His eyes flooded with tears at the sight. Old Emma, was lifeless, with her two faithful friends standing guard.

A memory flashed across the herdsman's mind. He thought back to the time long ago when Emma was on guard.

It was shortly after Jim Townsend's wife had lost her battle with cancer. Jim and Javier immersed themselves in work, too much work and not enough rest.

Jim Townsend's big heart gave out.

Emma, his loyal Aussie dog, found him lying in the loose hay on the barn floor. Javier came in to feed the cows, and found Emma curled up under Jim's lifeless arm, ever vigilant, ready to protect him from any and all intruders. Coronado knelt beside his friend; Emma crawled over to him whimpering, as if she'd been beaten.

From that moment on Emma and Javier shared the cabin, almost as equals. The herdsman thought of Jim Townsend daily, always thankful for his friendship and generosity.

Now dark times came to the household again. He picked up Emma, shaking as sobs racked his body. Jenny and the other dogs, with their heads drooping, filed out as Javier placed her tenderly in the barn and covered her with his favorite saddle blanket. As he walked back, a shooting star raced across the night sky. Javier knew that this light was the spirit of Emma running to the land of the Spirit of the Day and Night.

* * *

Darkness enveloped the pair on this moonless night. Sheena made sure her growing pup was safely in their den and fast asleep before she began her prowl for food. All through the summer prey had been plentiful. Bandit grew into a mature-looking dog; his black coat had lost all of its puppy hair and because of the rich diet Sheena provided, including trout from the streams, his coat was glossy and wavy. On nights as dark as this, he blended into the landscape, disappearing from sight.

As Sheena started off on her hunt she didn't notice that Bandit had woken up and begun following her at a discrete distance. He wasn't spying on her and he knew he would get scolded if caught, but as he aged, his need for sleep diminished. Wide awake and curious as to where Sheena went to find their food, he decided to tag along.

Her silver form moved with the grace of a ballet dancer, so quiet was her movement, with her ears primed for any sound and her nose probing the air for the scent of prey. To Sheena's mind, Bandit was growing all right and so was his appetite, which meant she needed to work twice as hard to keep them in food.

No matter what Sheena did, he figured as big as he was he could be some help. Tonight he risked her anger, but all for a good purpose. He did stay back, however, and kept to the darker areas of the forest, weaving in and out of the towering evergreens. At Alpine heights trees shoot up nearly straight from hillsides and under those trees the floor is paved with needles. It was easy for him to remain concealed. Sheena didn't know he trailed behind her. He had never disobeyed her before, and it would be a strange occurrence to her if he did now.

Just ahead and to the left of a pile of rocks jutting out from the ground, Bandit got a glimpse of something moving. He was sure Sheena saw it too.

He hung back, stopping by the trunk of a spruce tree. Sheena moved cat-like as she slowed her pace almost to a crawl and made her body slink close to the earth. Bandit feared she could hear him breathing so he remained motionless. Gradually she moved paw in front of paw, inching up to a pile of dead branches that would hide her from view. Oh, how Bandit wanted to follow. Good sense prevailed and he didn't advance, but he changed positions to get a better view of Sheena.

Through the bushes he spied what attracted Sheena's attention. A head with antlers firmly attached to the top of a slim and delicate face appeared above the bush line. Another animal, without antlers stepped just to the left of the first. The creature's large ears flitted to and fro, listening for disturbing sounds. Into a clearing strolled a smaller version of the two. Dappled with white spots against its fawn body, it was stretching its graceful neck to

James MacKrell

munch on some grass that had protruded through the spruce needle floor. Bandit's heart jumped for joy. He wanted to run up, barking to see if the little deer remembered him from their play several weeks ago. He would like to flop on his belly and bark joyously. What a time he and the playmate had as the deer family grazed nearby. Sheena shot up, and started to lunge at the fawn to take her legs out. Bandit, not watching Sheena, could conceal his joy no more and he barked, *"My friend, it is me, let's play again. We had such good times in the meadow when you ran and I chased you until we both fell down tired and happy."*

Sheena twisted in mid-air, shocked by Bandit's antics. She just missed an opportunity for a kill. The stag and doe bolted and ran, their fawn close behind. Over bushes and trees the trio leaped and in an instant they disappeared.

Bandit didn't need to be told Sheena would be mad. He felt it.

Most Australian Shepherds have no tails and Bandit was no exception. Where his tail would have grown he had a copper spot that looked like a golden target. That was all you could see as the Aussie high-tailed it for the den, hoping to get in and pretend to be asleep before Sheena returned.

Sheena watched the fleeing pup and as angry as she was, she knew she needed to continue the hunt for them to have food in the morning. After each kill she dismembered the carcass to change its looks from a living thing to a slab of red meat. She hoped Bandit never knew how she got their food or to what ends she must go to provide for them.

Turning from watching Bandit scamper away, she moved back, ready to stay the entire night if she must. The beginning of the colder weather meant she needed to store up food and fat for the Montana winter. This would be her second winter alone with her Bandit.

She hoped they were better equipped to handle the hardships this time around.

Chapter 26
"The beginning of the road home…"

The winds increased and the temperatures at night dropped into the lower 40s and flirted with the 30s. Sheena knew the time had come to head back down the mountainside toward the meadow. Bandit took in all the beauty as the pair descended, passing tree stands flaming in the color of changing leaves, bushes shedding their foliage and the sky turning from a crystal blue to shades of slate.

The clouds started to lose their fluffy texture and now raced from west to east in slim ribbons so high in the sky they looked like jet contrails.

Bandit learned the wolf trait of traveling single file from Sheena, and when on the move their march made little if any noise.

* * *

The rocky terrain gave way to denser trees and heavier bushes. Bandit watched as an eagle circled in the stratosphere and mountain birds darted in and out of the treetops. Ground squirrels and chipmunks were working as fast as they could to store up winter rations. Bunnies scurried across the trail and beavers plied their craft in the many fat streams that slipped down the mountainside.

Near a grove of trees that emptied into a clearing, a herd of elk moved slowly, grazing on the last stands of grass before the season ended.

No sign had been seen of the Absoraka wolf pack. Stone was fading from Sheena's memory. Her self-reliance allowed her to dismiss her broken heart and concentrate on the task of day-to-day survival. Simple existence in the wild is tough: doubly tough when you live a solitary life. Sure, she had Bandit, but deep in her understanding, as the puppy matured, Sheena knew that one day he would return to his own.

Sheena chose a warm, flat rock to rest in the sun. Bandit was growing past chasing butterflies and preferred to torment the local rabbit population. One particularly fast hare raced in a zigzag pattern, leading Bandit down through a draw and up the other side. At the crest, the wily rabbit leapt over the edge and disappeared down the hillside among the boulders strewn across the landscape. Bandit paused at the top, his tongue hanging loosely from the side of this mouth panting hard. He searched for any sign of the mysterious bunny but finally gave up. He turned to look back up the hill at where Sheena was resting, but out of the corner of his eye a sight grabbed his attention. He looked back down to the floor of the meadow, enraptured by what his eyes were beholding.

A large animal with a human growing out of its middle was leading another animal, a pack mule, along with a band of white animals up the hillside toward the pasture. Dogs were nipping at the animals to force them to follow the lead of the man-animal that was plodding along. He had never seen so many animals bunched together in one place.

He was so drawn to the event taking place before him that he started to climb down the hillside for a closer look. He noticed animals that looked a lot like him moving around and between the white, woolly creatures. Although they resembled him much more than wolves, they were colored differently. One of what Bandit took to be a dog, like Sheena had called him, was a blue shade mixed with

158   James MacKrell

the color of dirt and some patches on him, white as clouds. Another appeared to be about his size and age as she was running around with less purpose as the others and her coat was redder with patches of white and copper. Then he saw her. She moved with all the style and grace he had witnessed in deer. She was as black as he, with a collar of white and legs that were copper up to her shoulders. He had never seen an animal move with such ease. The woollies seemed to obey her every request as she drove them ever closer to the man-thing that was leading.

His heart beat in the cadence of a snare drum; he wanted to join them in the fun. Why chase rabbits when he could be playing with all these noisy white animals and chase that man up to the pasture with all the other dogs? His eyes were ablaze with desire.

His attention on the flock was interrupted by a howl up the side of the mountain. It was Sheena calling him, and he knew he must obey. Sadly he left the scene, looking back over his shoulder at the carnival of activity.

"I would love to play with them," he stopped for a moment. *"I could help them chase those odd looking animals. What fun we could have."*

Earlier that morning Javier had gotten an early start. The sun was yet to rise in the east and the morning chill hung in the air. By lantern light Javier was digging a hole near the strand of cottonwood trees. He had chosen this place because even in winter the sun always seemed to shine on this spot, and to the immediate left the chokecherry bushes protected it. From the porch looking straight into the front yard, you couldn't help but see the patch of ground that would be made sacred in a matter of moments.

The hole was sufficiently deep to protect the body from scavengers and wide enough for Emma's old bed to fit into the bottom. As the ground mounded up by the shovelful, Blu and Jenny lay to the side as if they were supervising. A heavy air hung all around the ranch. Even the sheep crowded up against the front of the pens as witnesses to the ceremony.

Jenny raced back into the barn and lie beside the body of old Emma. Emma was wrapped in a special cloth and was resting in her bed. Missy, the cat, was perched up on a stool nearby, purring softly. Javier entered the barn, and with salty tears running down his cheeks, he gently lifted the lifeless form into his strong arms and planted a kiss on the head of his trusted dog. He tried not to, but a sob from deep in his chest broke the stillness of the morning.

Slowly he walked around to the front yard to Emma's final resting place some fifty paces from the cabin's front door. Kneeling, he tenderly placed her body into the crypt. Blu was whimpering and Jenny had taken a place near Javier's knees where she could see down into the grave. Loud barking broke the mood. Falen was racing across the yard with her blanket in her mouth dashing for the site of burial. Jenny was so angry at her pup, *"How dare she play at a moment like this?"*

Javier looked up in horror and Blu jumped to his feet like something was attacking them. Falen ran all the harder and skidded to a stop near the open hole. She raised her head and flung the bottom of the blanket into the hole. She then took her nose and pushed the rest of the flannel cloth down on top of Emma. Then she looked up with a 'so there' expression, so proud of herself for being able to contribute. She moved over by her mother and plopped down, her part of the ritual over. Javier smiled for the first time since Emma died.   He ruffled up the head of the

James MacKrell

little Aussie and started the final covering of the gravesite. As Falen passed her uncle Blu, he whispered, *"Well done, little one."*

Chapter 27
"An awakening to his purpose…"

Bandit couldn't get the panorama that spread out on the hillside the day before out of his mind. As he slept, visions of sheep danced in his dreams. What fascinated him most was the dogs caring for the flock, and how much, to his eyes, they resembled him.

"I don't dare tell Sheena about this. This would really make her mad. She probably wants us to leave so I can't watch them again."

Sheena hated open spaces, even the meadowland around the gully where she found Bandit. Having been in cages much of her life, the tight, sheltered quarters gave her a feeling of security. Too much clearing posed a danger with nowhere to hide in case something or someone threatened them. The darker the forest and the more trees and bushes, the better she felt.

As the black dog matured, the need for companionship grew, and not the kind Sheena desired. He wanted freedom, a chance to be among people whom he believed offered no danger.

"If the man with the dogs likes them, wouldn't he like me?"

He vowed when morning came to try to get as close to the woollies as possible without being seen. If there was one thing Sheena taught him over the past year, it was how to move without being observed. He became as good as any wolf or coyote. He really wanted a closer look at the beautiful black dog every other dog seemed to admire. There was something about her that enthralled him.

                          * * *

     Sheena trotted down a rabbit trail and laced in and
out of the tree line, clinging to the underbrush and rocks as
cover. Bandit had been gone much of the morning. She
was more and more acceptant of his frequent absences
since, as he matured, he loved roaming the hillsides on his
own almost daily. He never strayed from the territory
Sheena had established, but he did like the solitude of his
jaunts through the landscape. To run in the meadows and
clearings thrilled him. The feel of the sun's warmth
beating down on his wavy black fur filled him with joy.
Streams posed a wonderful detour for him. To frolic in the
fast- moving, shallow creeks and try to catch the elusive
trout became one of his favorite pastimes. For a while
Sheena watched him from a distance, up the hill, fretting
and worrying. But the more he roamed and reliably
returned in the late afternoon, the more she let her guard
down.
     Yet, not only did Bandit's body grow, but his mind
was expanding as well. Now, when she wanted him to do
something, he would argue. His assertiveness pleased
Sheena, but also it gave her a source of concern. He was
becoming a full grown male, with all the needs and desires
of a grownup.
     Saddened by the differences emerging in his
personality, she knew he was a dog, pure and simple, and
she could not make him over into a wolf.
     Where Sheena was shy by nature, Bandit's
personality showed eagerness and social ability. Even
when he confronted others with his friendly ways, many of
the wild animals mistook his playfulness for aggression.
Sheena remembered all too well when Bandit decided that

the black and white animal that scurried away could be a subject of curiosity. The skunk used its most effective defense system and sprayed Bandit into submission. For weeks, he spent his nights alone outside the den. Sheena wanted none of that stink on her.

Several of the other animals, including weasels and badgers, mistook his advances as an invitation to battle. Bandit held his own, but came away disappointed with the fierceness of his neighbors.

"They are all so mean," he complained to Sheena. *"Nobody wants to play."*

"The forest isn't a place for play, Bandit." Sheena gave him her most disapproving stare. *"Life in the wild is hard. You have to find food, and protect yourself from other animals who would take it away. You must always be ready to fight and defend your territory. No, this is no place to play."*

He shook his head sorrowfully and muttered, *"Then this is no place for me."*

A knife went through her heart at the words she knew were inevitable. Bandit was a dog, and in her eyes a fine dog at that, but the ways of the wolves were demanding and she feared he would never be happy as he grew older.

It was the forth night Javier and the dogs stayed in the hills tending the flock. Javier spent his quiet hours mulling over the ruckus caused by the wolf-dogs and the troublesome man, Ronnie Spencer. As he surveyed the blanket of twinkling stars above in the clear sky, he wondered if his neighbors might lose sheep tonight to the hungry, desperate animals lost from Spencer's so-called kennel.

* * *

Gabe and Mike kept their nightly rounds of the perimeters watching for any predators endangering the sheep. Jenny slept peacefully under the stars, as did Blu and the rest of the Aussies. Only little Falen seemed restless as the noises of the night, the screeching of owls, and wolves howling their mournful tunes kept her a bit on edge. Each new frightening sound caused an eyelid to pop open. She nestled herself closer to her mother and finally dozed off.

The morning burst with all the brilliance an autumn sunrise can bring to the Montana mountains. The lemony dazzling light filled the hillside, announcing another day of perfect grazing weather. This time there were no troubling clouds building on the backside of the western mountains. The days proved restful for Javier; he tended his sheep, which lazily nipped at the grass, milling about without a care. They bedded down after filling their bellies and dozed in the warmth of the sunlight. Javier figured in a few more days he would head back down the hillside again to prepare for the coming winter months.

Suddenly Falen jumped up and ran toward the edge of the pastureland barking her head off. Javier looked, as did Jenny, to figure out what could be drawing her attention. Then they saw Lonnie and Jeremy coming up on ATVs, bringing some supplies. Jenny and Falen knew there would be some extra treats for them. Jeremy ruffled Falen's coat as she bounded about so happy to see him. Later, he took Falen aside and worked a few sheep on the fringes of the flock as he practiced his handling abilities and Falen's response to his orders. Javier watched Jeremy with pride. Falen could work sheep all by herself now. The signals for left or right spun her instantly in different directions.

James MacKrell

Two pairs of eyes were observing all of the activity in the meadow. Bandit stealthily positioned himself near an outcropping of rocks shaded on both ends by large spruce trees, and Sheena, about five hundred yards away up the hillside, observed from a flat rocky ledge. From her vantage point, the scene playing out before her was breaking her heart. She loved Bandit; many times in their travels she would have given her life for him. Now, in her soul, she knew it was time to give him her greatest gift, the freedom to live with his own kind. Being with family was important to Sheena, even if she had never enjoyed that security herself. She forced her eyes away from the pasture and focused on the upper part of the mountain. Her sadness caused a gripping pain in her stomach. She was leaving Bandit. Her heart told her it was best for her beloved cub, the little, black dog she had named, Bandit. Bandit never knew she was up there.

The sheep covered almost the entire meadow, and the Aussies positioned themselves where they could survey the band of sheep. Bandit crept closer to the rim of the clearing, careful to stay hidden. All of a sudden Gabe caught wind of a smell he knew all too well. The hackles rose on the Pyrenees's shaggy back. He barked a warning and Mike joined him on the western side of the pasture. Bandit instantly knew this was dangerous and as quietly as he could, he retreated back up the hillside.

Confused, his heart told him this was the group he belonged with. They were his destiny, and yet he feared for his life if the two terrible dogs caught him. As he scampered up the hillside, the yellow in the west started changing into gold and then into a deep orange. As he reached Sheena, darkness fell on the pasture below and the flames of Javier's campfire were all he could see.

James MacKrell

Chapter 28
"And you will be my son."

Jenny awoke from a troubling dream. All night she had tossed and turned, fitful in her sleep, never getting comfortable. Little Falen had rested her head on her mother's hind legs, cutting off the circulation and causing Jenny to wake with tingling and numbness in her back end. She shook off the cold morning air and stretched, arching her back to try to remove some of the lameness. Grass where she slept had stuck to her forehead, causing an almost mask-like covering to her eyes. She rolled to remove the debris and nudged Falen from her slumber to face a new day of work.

Jenny couldn't shake the feeling of her dreams. She knew it was only a mind sketch, but it seemed so real she could almost identify the smell of the dog in the dream.

"If it were only so," she sighed, letting warm breath out through her nostrils. *"It would be the most wonderful thing in the world, if only my dream would come true."*

In her dream she was running through multi-colored grass with gentle breezes blowing in her face. Suddenly the odor of warm milk filled her nose and the wind increased just enough to blur her vision. When she looked again the flowers in the meadow parted and a tiny black dog walked forward with the most beautiful eyes Jenny had ever seen. He came up to her and began to suckle her. The sensation thrilled her to the core. Life-giving milk was flowing from her body into the tiny puppy. As he drank he grew before her eyes. As he finished he looked into her eyes standing a little taller than she, and he was the exact replica of her own countenance.

"Oh, Spirit of the Day and Night, please, could it be a message from my little puppy? Could my baby be alive? Would you be so gracious as to bring him back to me?"

Her heart missed a beat, and turning to lick and nuzzle her precious daughter, she knew she had a lot to be thankful for. After all, she was working, and that was what pleased Aussies the most.

* * *

Bandit greeted the morning in shivers. At the entrance to the den lay a pile of old bones, with all the nourishment sucked dry. They were the remains of a meal several days old and chewed beyond recognition. Bits and pieces lay on the ground with some sinew, dried and tasteless. Bandit mouthed one of the leftovers and quickly discarded it as useless.

He missed Sheena. She wasn't in their den. In all of his remembrance he had never been alone. His memories of his mother had faded, not completely, but faded to where it strained his thinking to bring a scent or picture to mind.

"What was she like?" He dropped his head to his front paws and stretched out his hind legs as far as he could. *"I wonder if she remembers me?"* He raised his head, *"I wonder if she would like me now?"*

Listlessly he ambled out of the den, climbed the rocks, and poured himself on the sun-warmed rock ledge. Absently he looked in the direction where he had last seen the sheep and the shepherds. The sun had reached the pastureland before the high hills where he was shaded by the tall forest trees. There in the sunlight he saw a beautiful

James MacKrell

picture. The grass eaters were already up from their sleeping positions and the dogs he longed to play with were running to and fro tending to the needs of the sheep. It was perfect in Bandit's eyes; living beings working together for the good of all; no killing, no fear, just the Spirit of the Day and Night's creatures facing another day, together.

He put aside his hunger and trotted down to the edge of the forest, getting as close as he could without being seen. The morning brought warmer temperatures, and Bandit nibbled on some pieces of grass just to have something in his stomach.

He found a good hiding place and settled down to be audience for Javier, Jenny, Falen, and the sheep. If the truth were known he was a little afraid of the big, shaggy, white dogs. They were almost as terrifying as the grizzly bears who ruled the forest. Even Stone and the Absoraka wolf pack were afraid of the bears. Nothing he had seen since the giant grizzlies was as frightening as these massive dogs. Yet there were the other dogs, nimble and stylish, circling the flock and making sure that each animal wasn't disturbed, but protected and corralled.

These other dogs, like the one that Bandit thought looked like him, all had no tails. Bandit had long wondered if he was the only living thing without a tail, but much to his delight, here were five or six canines all running around, and none of them had a tail either. The lost dog never felt so good, so natural. If these dogs didn't have a tail, then it must be all right. He wasn't different; there were others just like him. The sense of belonging swelled in his mind.

Again he watched as the man in the midst of all these animals fed the dogs, and did a strange thing. With each of the dogs he fed, the human stopped and rubbed their heads with tender pats. All the way from across the grazing land Bandit could feel the warmth that existed between this human and the dogs.

"Oh , to be loved like that." He let out a tiny whimper. *"No wonder they work so hard for that human; he loves them and they love him."*

* * *

After licking the pan clean of kibble, Jenny and Falen moved to Javier's side. Blu was already on the far side of the flock with Mate and Brady. Little Falen flopped down by Javier's tent, and Jenny acted like she would love to help the herdsman cook his own breakfast.

Jenny's dream wouldn't leave her. She mulled it over and over in her mind, wondering if it had a meaning or if it was just the longing in her heart to find out what had happened to her little coal-black puppy. As they passed the gully that imprisoned her for so long, she trotted over to the side of the steep crevice to see if there was anything or any sign that would mean the puppy was still alive. She fought the urge to dash down to the bottom and look in the cave that had saved her life, but she sniffed the still air, remembering all the smells that were so familiar during her ordeal.

Falen barked at a passing rabbit and the sound of her barking snapped Jenny back from her despondency to the present. Jenny ran back to her job and kept her eyes on the movement of the sheep.

Chapter 29
"I will lay down my life…"

      The drama taking place in front of Bandit held his attention. The Aussies were moving around the sheep, keeping them together, but never attacking them as prey. It befuddled him, knowing what Sheena would have done; but somehow, deep down, he felt this was right, though he didn't know why. The man kept his distance from the action, every once in a while shouting something. Sometimes he would stick both fingers into his mouth, make a shrill sound, and without looking his way, the Aussies changed direction and drove the band the other way. The beautiful black dog he so admired circled, keeping the sheep in the middle between her and the man. If he went one direction, she would go the other. They worked like a team, a team Bandit wanted to join.

* * *

      To get a better view he raised up a little as a gentle breeze wafted over his head. It took a second to reach the nose of the black tri-colored female working on the west side of the pasture. She whirled and stared in the direction of Bandit. Her nose punched the air, her nostrils twitching. As fast as the scent wafted near her space it left.

      Bandit tucked his head back down behind the tall, browning grass and out of the direct line of the blowing wind. She studied the area for a moment and then swung her attention back to the sheep. They were now nibbling their way back to the main flock. She turned back for a minute. Bandit thought she looked straight at him, and then she returned to her duty.

His eyes didn't leave her as she trotted all the way across the pasture. Again he heard the whistling sound. The black dog's head popped up toward the whistle and in a split second she tore off in an opposite direction to the other side of the band of sheep. Two more shrill sounds and the dog colored like the meadow flowers joined her and seemed to be pushing the entire band of sheep over to the backside of the grassland. The giant shaggy white monsters walked calmly with the grass eaters, and Bandit lost sight of them in the mass of dirty white. The human pulled the big brown moose-like animal with no antlers, and climbed up on its back. He headed south, up higher into the hills, and all the woollies, much to Bandit's surprise, followed him. Behind were the dogs keeping their distance, but at constant attention.

As this scene unfolded, he followed them along, pulled by an invisible leash, as if hypnotized.

No one in the grassy field paid any attention to Bandit. Their tasks totally consumed them.

All day he followed, ducking deeper into the forest every time the wind changed so it wouldn't blow his scent toward the terrible twin beasts milling around the woollies. As the afternoon light faded, long shadows from the hillsides inked across the open area. Bandit stayed in the shadows of the tree line. He crossed a small mountain stream and drank his fill of the sweet water, washing away the dust that clouded the air from the plodding ewes. Never once did he think of Sheena. He didn't wonder where she was or what she was doing. Enraptured by the beautiful dance being staged, Bandit kept loping along to keep up. The sheep were pushed in from the edges of the flock. The two large Pyrenees drifted to the outside and began their

James MacKrell

nightly circle of protection. Gabe and Mike ventured toward the outer limits, and Bandit skirted the area and fled up into the hills onto the higher ground. As he raced upwards his thoughts finally returned to Sheena. He thought just maybe he had been wrong about her leaving. He hoped when he got back Sheena would have their supper waiting and he could eat his fill. He jumped over the rocks and made a semi-circle in the grass near the hidden opening of the den. Glancing up toward the ledge he half expected the gray form of his beloved Sheena to be lying peacefully waiting for him. She wasn't. He barked his greeting he knew would not be returned. He had to try. *"I'm here, I just arrived back, let's eat."* His greeting met only silence. He had to face the truth. Sheena wasn't coming back. Slowly he walked to the opening of the den and called again, *"Sheena, are you here? It's me, Bandit. I've been gone all day and I have a lot to tell you."* He knew sooner or later he must discuss with her the woollies and the dogs he'd seen. The news would slip out since he had never kept anything from her before. He wasn't a liar and if confronted he would spill the whole story. He called again, *"Sheena, where are you? I can't smell your scent. Are you here?"*

Again his pleas were met with silence. The darkness of the den seemed so empty. He panted deeply and hacked a cough from the dryness of his throat. With his eyes cast downward, he admitted the truth. Sheena was gone, and what hurt worse, he knew she wasn't coming back. He fell into a pitiful mound of flesh on the floor, whimpering like a beaten puppy. Bandit was alone now, and he hated it.

Early in the morning, Bandit woke with hunger pains still gripping his stomach and marched back toward his viewing stand to observe all the action in the pasture below.

As the sheep band slowly grazed, Bandit followed. Before he knew it he was standing out in the meadow in full view of the dogs and the man. Jenny saw him first, and cautiously approached, never taking her eyes off his face. The closer she got the more Bandit stood still. He didn't move a muscle. She stopped about five yards away. His heart beat in a strange rhythm. He knew this dog; he didn't know from where, but he knew her and wanted to get to know her a lot better.

* * *

When first he set foot on the pasture, Jenny spotted him. He resembled a dog, a dog in fact that favored her. There seemed to be an invisible line connecting her and this strange, new dog. She didn't know why, but something forced her toward him. Step by step her confidence grew. With each piece of ground covered, her heart beat faster. Despite the rhythmic thudding of hooves and the baaing sheep, Jenny heard only silence as her mind raced, the moment standing still in time.

Then from her heart the memory came back clearly. It was his eyes. Peering into his face, breathing in his scent, she was drawn forward, slowly at first, inch by inch. She let out whimpers of welcome as recognition poured over her.

"Are my prayers being answered? Is this my lost baby, alive and standing here before me, a handsome full-grown dog?"

Her eyes glistened, as she looked him over in loving amazement.

James MacKrell

Bandit responded to the sounds the beautiful dog made, the way her voice sounded, the softness in her eyes, and the gracefulness of her form. All of these things exploded in Bandit's mind. He started taking small steps toward her, slowly to make the moment last. Without fear, or awareness of the other dogs that now surrounded the pair, he only had eyes for her. A warm and loving aura filled the space between the two black dogs. Pictures in his mind flashed, feelings of a red and black cloth, the smell of milk and of devotion. Then he whispered the only word on his lips, *"Mother?"* At the same time Jenny said, *"My puppy?"*

The words unleashed a torrent of joy and happiness. Jenny's baby was found, and the mother that had been etched in Bandit's memory had reappeared. His tail-less butt wiggled with elation. Both came together with sniffs of joy and yips of thanksgiving.

Loving licks covered his face while he whined words of adoration.

Her heart poured praise to the Spirit of the Day and Night, her prayers were been answered, her baby was alive, and she would be forever grateful.

James MacKrell

Chapter 30
"The family circle…"

One at a time, the other dogs moved up and around Jenny and Bandit. As Jenny continued to pour affection out, Bandit busied himself returning the love. Blu joined in as well. He warily approached the two at first, reached out as far as his neck would allow, and drew in a breath of Bandit's scent. He recoiled; Bandit smelled of the wild. He smelled of earth, pine and vegetation, and the diet of raw wild meat he'd eaten all his short life, very different from the mingled scents of human, sheep, and the trappings of domesticated living that enveloped the sheepdogs. Even Mike and Gabe lumbered forward to get a scent of this new creature. They were calm because both assumed he posed no threat.

As the acceptance of the group grew, Bandit began frantically wagging his tailless back end. He understood he had at long last found his mother.

"Hey there, what's going on, who is that and what are you all doing?"

Falen burst into the circle grinning and looking from dogface to dogface. She stopped and got a good look at Bandit. She didn't stop smiling or talking. She stepped a little closer so her nose could explore his body. All the time wiggling, Falen looked up at her mother and licked the side of her face over and over.

"Falen, this is your brother. He was lost when we were found, and now he's found us again. Our family is once again complete."

Not one of the dogs looked up as the quiet presence of Javier joined the group.

"What's going on here, my dogs?" He stepped into the circle and knelt beside Jenny and Falen. Gingerly he reached out for Bandit. Bandit shrank back at first, not quite out of reach, but a year of being told to distrust humans had certainly taken its toll. As Javier's hand approached his back, Bandit's body shivered. He clenched his teeth and decided to let this human touch his body. Jenny leaned against Javier's kneeling leg, indicating a connection between the dogs and this man.

She kept her eyes on Bandit's face, softly whining, *"This is our master, he is a good and kindly person who loves each of us. We work for him, not from fear or reward, but in love, as we accomplish our lives together. He gives us food and shelter, and we give him our hearts."*

To Bandit nothing could describe the sensation of the man's hand softly patting his back. Javier eased his fingers up to Bandit's head, all the while whispering, "good dog, my good dog." He soothingly stroked the strange dog's head.

"This is what it feels like." The warm Montana sun in summer didn't feel as good to Bandit as Javier's caresses. He let the muscles in his neck relax, then his facial muscles, and soon the warm feeling of complete relaxation ran down his body like warm mud after an August rain. Jenny continued to lick and massage him all over as Javier continued gently stroking. Falen tried to nose out her mother but a small growl sent her scampering back. Bandit was surrounded with love and acceptance. He never felt so good.

As Javier petted Bandit he carefully examined the dog's body. Javier knew him to be an Australian Shepherd, but where he came from Javier could only guess; yet by the way Jenny acted he wondered how she could be so caring to a strange dog. His careful eye went over the dog. In body structure he seemed to be a replica of Jenny. In fact this dog resembled the great Warner. Strong across the chest, longer than tall and with hind legs built for driving, he pondered, "Could this be another of Jenny's puppies? Did I leave one behind?"

Looking first at Jenny, then Falen, and back to the black dog, he murmured aloud, "I wonder?"

He noticed how Jenny acted around this dog. She'd been around plenty of strange dogs, but she never carried on like this. Carefully, so as not to startle the new arrival, Javier stood up and moved deliberately outside of the circle. To his amazement Jenny stayed licking and pampering the black dog. Javier studied the dog's face and with his trained eye from judging livestock all his life, the characteristics were indistinguishable in both the female dog and the male. When Blu, Jenny's full brother, eased up along side the new dog, Javier could tell somewhere in the linage they must have shared ancestors. While all Aussies share a distinct appearance, family lines tend to throw the same body size and shape in most of their descendents. The only difference between Blu and the black Aussie seemed the color of their coats, and the new dog's ebony coat mirrored Jenny's. Even the tiny patches of copper over his eyes reflected the look of Jenny's face. "Yes." Javier had to admit; the more he looked, the more similarities he found in the dogs.

* * *

Blu, Jenny, and Falen, along with Mike and Gabe, needed to return to their tasks. Without calling him specifically, the herdsman turned back toward the flocks and gave a simple command, "Come, my dogs."

"Won't you come with us, my son? You would be welcomed, you would be cared far, and you would be loved."

She turned and deliberately started walking back toward the camp, glancing over her shoulder from time to time to see if her lost pup was following.

Javier strolled away, with Jenny and Blu at his heel. Mike and Gabe ran back to the center of the flock and little Falen walked behind, looking over her shoulder at this strange black dog, and wondered, *"Is this really my brother?"*

Bandit didn't know what happened. All the attention he was enjoying suddenly walked off.

"Why are you leaving me?" His eyes followed their retreat. It wasn't like they were fleeing from him, he hadn't done anything wrong. The Man and dogs just left him standing.

"What was the sound the human made?" With a tilt of the head, he continued, *"It sounded like he wanted the dogs to follow him. When he said it, they did. They left me and went after him straight away."*

Before he realized it he found himself about fifty paces behind the group, following along. Bandit overheard one of the white shaggy dogs refer to the human as Javier. Bandit didn't know what it meant but assumed that was his name.

No one had asked him what he was called by; they just referred to him as "Black Dog". Jenny, however, called him *"my son."*

As Bandit moved into Jenny's world he brought with him the only life he had known. He was raised wild, in a frightening environment where the law of kill or be killed is a way of life.

* * *

He followed the procession back to camp, careful to stay about fifty paces behind, always checking for an escape route if something should threaten him or if he had misjudged the pack of dogs and the human leading them. Following he had to walk among the woollies. He had never been this close to animals like this and his eyes flitted, always looking for a sign of attack. His breath came in short pants as he tried to relieve the tension and the fear that bubbled inside.

"Should I continue to follow this pack? Will they keep on accepting me like they did this morning? Or like wily wolves, are they luring me to a place where they can kill me and eat my flesh and bones?"

He decided to keep his eyes on the dog he loved. By looking at her and her only, could he make it through the strange surroundings? Step by step, the sounds of Jenny became more familiar in his ears. The little tri-colored female who trotted inches from his mother awoke memories deep in his soul. He could almost feel her tiny body rolling over him in a dark place a long time ago.

* * *

Javier thought long and hard on the walk back to the camp about just how to treat this dog and whether this was a stray that was lost from one of his fellow ranchers.

Mulling over all the possibilities, he came to the conclusion that it couldn't be a lost dog. A dog of this age would be trained. Bandit exhibited no human contact traits.

Javier could see and feel the wildness in his eyes, and while he was docile enough to allow petting, the rancher could feel the jumpiness right under the skin. The more he thought about it, the more convinced he was that, indeed, this was one of Jenny's puppies that had somehow, some way, survived on its own.

It didn't take many hours for Blu and the rest of the Aussies to ignore the strange dog and go on about their business. As they worked, Bandit lay in the grass, usually near cover, and observed. He never made any overt moves. He didn't get up to run away, nor did he try to join the others. He was a spectator, just with a much closer view than he had had before.

From the corner of his eye he saw the man called Javier moving toward him. He was carrying something, and Bandit wondered if he meant him harm. The grass was lush and comfortable, and if his experience with this human that morning was any indication, he believed he had nothing to worry about. Yet he kept his eyes fastened on Javier as he drew ever closer. Javier stopped a good five yards away and cooed softly to Bandit. "Here, my boy, here, good dog, here is something for you to eat."

When Bandit was looking straight at him, Javier put down the pan with some kibble and fresh lamb meat mixed together. Then without turning, he backed away to see what the dog would do.

The aroma of the food drifted toward Bandit, since Javier had placed the pan downwind from where he lay. Nothing ever smelled so good.

Bandit got up and inched, sniffing the air, toward the pan of food. The meat was fresh but didn't have that bloody smell Bandit was used to. Yet it filled his nostrils with a fragrance that caused his taste buds to jump alive. He watched Javier carefully. *"Is this a trap?"* He had seen

James MacKrell

the wolves put a dead carcass out in the open so when a buzzard or a hawk came down to feed they would leap on the unsuspecting bird and kill it.

Almost crawling, with his belly slunk nearly to the ground, he approached the delicious-smelling food. He grabbed a bite of the mixture and quickly pulled back, mouthing the meat and watching for any reaction from Javier. Along with the food the man brought a pan filled with cool water. Quickly, Bandit grabbed another mouthful and just as quick as before pulled back to face Javier, with the pan of food between them. This time he gulped the food down. In a great gasp he almost choked, getting mouthful after mouthful into his stomach. Confident that the man wasn't going to do him harm, he slowed his eating and relaxed. His sides heaved with each gulp. Having his fill, he drifted over to the water dish and lapped up the sweet water. Only after a good while did he, totally satisfied, return to where he was resting before.

Speaking in the softest of voices, Javier whispered, "You are a good dog, my Jenny's son." He reached out to pet him. At first Bandit pulled his head away, but remembering how good it felt this morning, he allowed this human to touch him again. He closed his eyes, for the first time in days, and relaxed under the gentle pressure of Javier's touch. Bandit was tired, bone tired, and full for the first time in days. He looked up at the man and sighed, *"It is good to be with you human. You are truly a good and kindly man.*

Book Three
My Home, My Heart

Chapter 31
"Getting to know you…"

Night fell and the bustle around the campsite grew in intensity. Bandit, still cautious, made sure he never got any closer than about twenty yards from the gathering around the fire, always looking for an escape route if he needed one. Javier placed oats out for the animal that Bandit had learned was called Horse and the mule named Sarah. The sheep bunched up, not only for protection but to keep warm from the cooling night air. All of the dogs had eaten their fill. Bandit was still full from his afternoon meal in the wild. He only ate every other day or so and since he retained the urge to gorge himself whenever he ate, his stomach pooched out and gave him a rotund appearance from the fresh lamb he had consumed that morning. He rarely slept in the open, except on warm nights, and then he would nestle in the grass and let the dew cool his body. The campfire, with its sparks dancing like lightning bugs invading the heavens, gave a red glow to everything it reflected on. Bandit stayed in the shadows just out of the circle of light, staring at the spectacle before him.

Jenny noticed him standing all alone and trotted over, nudging him in the side. She whimpered a low sound of affection. He responded in kind. She rubbed her body against his and licked his ears. Her baby, delivered to her again by the Spirit of the Day and Night. As her tongue massaged his lithe body she thought of the wisdom of old Emma. Motherhood proved to be a great gift indeed, especially when you got to experience it twice.

Down from the Mountain

The camp quieted as each dog found his or her sleeping place and settled down. Jenny moved outside her regular spot, closer to where Bandit lay. Knowing he would spend a restless night, she sensed he needed her. She lowered her body alongside his and nuzzled her face against his shoulder. He flinched at first, but the love for this wonderful dog overcame his shyness, and he snuggled quietly, almost as if in his mother's arms. When the two awoke, they found little Falen sprawled across their legs, three Aussies, one family.

* * *

The first night with Jenny ended. The next morning Bandit seemed to grow more used to the others and less fearful; however, he kept a distance, still a little wary. He respected the Pyrenees and marveled as they searched the perimeter, warning off predators. Once, on the far side of the pasture, Gabe and Mike dashed into the edge of the woods raging and growling at a prowler.

Quick as silver they returned to their flock convinced the assassin had fled. Bandit wondered if it could have been Sheena.

The day passed and the night fell, and again Javier brought rations to Bandit, and sat with him while he ate. Little by little Bandit seemed to have acquired a taste for the kibble, especially if Javier had mixed the raw lamb in it. After he had consumed the food, Javier spent some more time stroking his wavy coat and speaking in a soft, soothing voice. Bandit believed there was a place for him; the dogs accepted him and he began to meld into the security of Javier's pack.

One morning Javier rose early, fed the dogs and Bayo, and saddled the horse, attaching the small camp

James MacKrell

wagon that carried supplies. Bandit noticed a difference in Jenny and the other Aussies' attitudes. Moving around the side of the flock and standing at all corners of the grazing sheep, they appeared as guards. Even Falen seemed more serious and business-like. The tent where the man slept was collapsed, folded, and added to the utensils already packed and stored on the wagon. The flock was moving, but to where Bandit didn't know. He remained fixed, and for the first time since joining the group, he was lost and confused. He had no skills to help the other dogs, no talents to aid Javier.

"Why are they going? We are happy here, there is plenty of food and water, and we are protected from intruders. Why would they abandon all of this?" Then as his head drooped a little, he considered with a jolt, *"Are they going to leave me?"*

The ache in his heart grew until he nearly cried out. *"This isn't fair!"* He had been found and now he would be lost again.

From around a group of ewes Blu bounded in Bandit's direction. Grinning as only Aussies can, full of vitality and joy, he yapped, *"Hey, Black dog, you had better get ready, we are going home; down the mountain trail to our home at the ranch. You don't want to be left behind, so let's get a move on."* With that Blu spun on his heels and dashed in the direction of the back of the sheep band. Bandit was bewildered. He wasn't sure what Blu meant by "home."

Before his mind concocted any more questions Falen greeted him with, *"Better hurry up! Momma wants us moving with the flock. You don't want to be left behind."*

"Left behind?" Being left behind had been the story of Bandit's life. Left in the gully, then the Absoraka wolf

pack had left him and Sheena, and finally Sheena had left him, but now rather than being left he was urged to join. He belonged. This was his pack. What a joyous feeling.

* * *

Sheena was used to loneliness. She moved when she wanted, killed when and what she wanted, and searched for a mate without being encumbered by a dog. She missed Bandit but her wild urges reminded her of a life she knew Bandit could never share. She wondered about him, but as quickly as that thought appeared, she re-focused on an old deer that looked like supper.

The two lives, so intertwined for a year, parted. Each animal pursuing his destiny, the wolf in Sheena desired to live free and wild. Bandit, the dog, sought the comfort and caring of a domestic existence. Both had been thrown together for a short while and now each would trod a trail of their own choosing.

Jenny ran alongside Bandit down the path. *"What are you called? Do you have a name?"*

"The wolf named me Bandit." He looked at his mother. *"I am not sure what it means, but I like the sound of it."*

"Then that is who you shall be. Somehow I will convince the Master of your name before he starts calling you some silly name like Blackie or something just as bad." She told him, *"Blu hated his name at first, but got used to it. Imagine all of your life having to answer to Blu. Oh well, I've called him worse things."*

A group of ewes began to wander off the trail in search of another blade of grass. Jenny sprung and dispatched them back on down the hill with the others. Bandit trotted along noticing the lower they ascended, the

James MacKrell

more the foliage changed. Trees appeared to grow closer together and fewer large rocks stuck their heads up out of the Earth.

Bayo, having made this same journey time and time again, was of his own volition steadily clipping along toward home, allowing Javier's attention to focus only on his thoughts and the sheep and dogs that followed. The Aussies policed the back and sides of the flock, moving this mass of living wool down the hillside. It would be an all-day journey with the band of Suffolk scheduled to arrive past the setting of the sun. The parade bounded along, trotting to the rhythm of the bleating of the sheep. They blended their voices with the barking of the dogs, being led by an old Basque herdsman singing a folk song from his ancestors' native mountains of the Spanish Pyrenees. If it were possible the forest animals would have stood and clapped their approval. For thousands of years sheep had followed their shepherd, beside still waters and even past the Valley of the Shadow of Death. This ancient trade is repeated hundreds of times a year in these Montana mountains.

In faraway places people depended on farmers and ranchers to deliver the food needed for their table and the wool to make garments and blankets for their comfort. The world depended on farmers and these Montana sheep men depended on their dogs.

As Bandit passed over a rise in the road, he glimpsed a sight new to his understanding. Down the hill, nestled in a grove of trees, with fall berries bursting on the bushes surrounding the building, there was a cabin, with lights shining through windows to welcome them home. Jeremy had come over, not only to feed the stock left behind, but also to build a fire in the fireplace. Bandit saw that Jenny, Blu, Mate, and Falen seemed very excited about seeing the dwelling. He could hear their ecstatic barks, *"We are home. This is our home. We've returned. How good it is to be home!"*

For the first time on the trip, Bandit sprinted up to the head of the flock. He trotted alongside Bayo, still keeping a safe distance and looked up into the face of the Master. Without missing a step he barked, *"Thank you, I will live among you and learn to be helpful. You will be my Master and I will be your dog."*

He had no idea what the future would hold for this twosome, but the Spirit of the Day and Night knew that Javier and Bandit would have a long and fruitful life together. Jenny would be so proud.

Chapter 32
"And the prince came..."

    She peered into the underbrush. A sound like an animal in trouble caught Sheena's attention. On cat-like paws she moved closer to the pile of brush at the foot of some spruce trees. Dark shadows flickered with the wind. The sun behind her gave light to the area, but she had a hard time seeing any movement or hearing the distressing cries. Above her, on a ledge cropping out of the hillside, she spotted the slightest bit of motion. Her nerves were rattled; she didn't know if her jumpiness was due to being alone, missing the companionship of Bandit, or if something strange was happening in her body.

    A quick glimpse of movement upon the ledge grabbed her interest.

    "Did the wounded animal I seek escape the brush and make it up to the top of the ledge?"

    Fearing a trap Sheena stayed firmly planted below, gazing upward at the outcrop. She moved a bit toward the left where the branches thinned, giving her a better view. Right behind the shelf, higher than she could see, an animal rested, exhausted from pursuit of his victim. She inched a bit closer up the hill. Stepping on some dead branches, her weight cracked them like toothpicks. The creature on the ledge shot to its feet at the snapping sound. Sheena caught her breath. A full-grown male wolf with a silver-gray tint to his fur stood with a paw still pinning the body of the rabbit he had just killed.

    Sheena remained steady, returning the wolf's stare. It wasn't in any way threatening. She sensed no aggression in his eyes, but rather a sense of pride, confidence and, maybe, admiration? Not a muscle moved on the graceful wolf-dog, or in the body of the timber wolf still rooted to the ledge.

Where is his pack? Am I to be challenged again? Do I have to fight when I would much rather just leave this wolf behind, and any trouble following him? Sheena thought.

Ever so smoothly, the wolf placed one paw down the side of the ridge and started a descent toward Sheena. He never made any abrupt moves; he seemed to glide down the slope. No stones moved, no branches broke, and not a leaf rustled, as he drew closer to Sheena. Instead of approaching her, head down in an attack mode, he stood straight up to his impressive full height, his eyes trained on hers as he descended.

Her heartbeat sped up, yet she breathed slower. Each hair on her body stood as if standing at attention. Her eyes seemed to water and her nose dampened.

He came toward her, quietly and cautiously whispering a low murmur.

"You are beautiful, she-wolf. You are to me like a dream." He slid up to within a couple of feet. He panted heavily, each breath hot. She didn't move, even when he searched her body with his nose. Her tail switched from side to side, her breathing slowed even more.

As he looked into her yellow eyes he said, *"I am Steel."* A beam of sunlight broke through the branches of the cottonwoods, causing his entire body to shimmer. The shadows covered the ground in front and in back of him. The circle of light beamed as if just for him. Sheena lowered her head a bit to avoid the sun's glare.

"What are you called, female?"

James MacKrell

Sheena raised her head high and allowed Steel to approach her, expecting to be regarded as an equal. She would accept nothing less.

"I am Sheena, a lone warrior without fear or master."

"Do you not listen to the Spirit of the Day and Night?" he eased his head back to better hear her answer.

She turned to face this wolf of wolves and said, *"The blessed Spirit of the Day and Night has protected me since my birth. The Spirit leads me in light and darkness. Without the Spirit I am nothing, for He has determined my path long before my mother bore me."*

With pride in her voice she continued, *"I answer only to Him, for there is no one and no thing that can claim rights over me. I am Sheena, alone and proud. My freedom was won by the grace of the Spirit. For Him and Him only do I live."*

Quiet settled the air before she spoke again, *"And who are you, Steel? Do you live alone or do you have a pack leader who commands you?"*

"I, female, have no pack leader. I have no pack. I live for myself, and I do not fear or trust anyone."

As he spoke he walked even closer to Sheena. She could smell his musk and it excited her. He stood about three inches higher than she, muscles well defined and a bright sheen to his luxurious coat. Taken by her beauty, he combed her body with his deep yellow eyes.

"Steel, warrior of warriors, is there any way that I could assist you or be of service to you?" As he looked back into her face she turned her piercing gaze into his eyes and did not falter. Steel was a little taken aback by her directness, yet the assertiveness she exhibited strangely appealed to the wolf.

He turned his eyes away and moved to the left, turning up the hillside leading away from Sheena. She had experienced abandonment before; she knew the drill. Her eyes clouded over with disappointment.

The timber wolf walked about ten yards away and then suddenly stopped and picked up his rabbit. He looked back over his shoulder, and said, *"Well or not? I have things to do and miles to cover. If you are with me, are you coming, come now. If you decide to stay, that is your choice. I can take care of myself; but if you come, I will treat you like an equal and we can carve out our lives together."*

Sheena couldn't speak. She tried but the tightening in her throat nearly choked her. Her heart pounded in her gray chest. Steel edged back up to the trail, lingering in wait for Sheena to join him. She was part of a twosome again, and this time her life would be with her own kind.

* * *

The first night at the cabin confused Bandit. He was used to sleeping in a den. The kennels and the barrels, even filled with a comfortable straw bed, still disturbed him greatly. There were too many strange smells. He hated the feeling of being caged and pushed constantly against the chain link fence, trying to find an opening. Javier even put Jenny in with him, but that did not assuage his anxiety. All night he paced. All night he howled, all night he kept everyone within earshot awake. Even Bayo seemed perturbed and very little ever troubled Bayo.

Javier also missed Jenny's companionship. Since Emma's death Jenny and Falen had moved into the house and their warm bodies near to him had a calming effect on

James MacKrell

the old herdsman. Falen tried to sooth him, but she missed Jenny too and wasn't much help.

Morning came and when Javier approached the kennels he found a nearly exhausted Bandit and a Jenny who looked like she had been on a thirty-mile trek.

He placed the morning mixture of lamb meat and kibble down and to his surprise neither dog seemed very interested.

With the kennel door ajar, Jenny sped through his legs and dashed for the cabin. Bandit sprinted away to a hole he had found earlier in the side of the hill that rose from the barnyard behind the kennels. His copper-patched butt disappeared into the fissure he had discovered earlier and promptly curled up into a ball. Exhausted, he soon fell fast asleep.

Javier studied both dashes from the kennel and made a judicious decision. Jenny sleeps in the cabin and Bandit sleeps wherever he wants. Javier's face broke into a huge smile while watching the black dog hightail it back into the hillside.

"That black dog runs like an escaped burglar." Then from out of the blue he heard himself say, "That's why I should call that little thief, Bandit, he, with his black mask and all." He laughed, remembering the time Bandit grabbed his gloves and fled to under the porch and buried them in a pile of leaves. Bandit! It sounded good so he said it again, "Yeah, Bandit suits him perfectly. He came out of the night black as pitch with those copper markings on his face and over his eyes. Bandit it shall be."

When night fell again, Jenny dove into her own bed, flipped on her back, and gave thanks for the reprieve from the kennel. Falen appointed herself as Javier's personal protector and jumped up on the quilt at the foot of the bed, sleeping where no dog had slept before. Blu and Mate snug in their kennels, Mike and Gabe snoozing among the sheep, and Bandit, pleased that the Master had called him by name, curled up in his den.

Chapter 33
"Now act like a shepherd..."

Bandit lay in the shade by an old tractor, his eyes never leaving the sight of Jenny, Falen, and Blu scrambling around some sheep in the pen. Under the expert eyes of Javier and the eager eyes of Jeremy, they performed without a flaw, making sure each ewe and buck moved with minimum confusion or fear into the confines of a smaller pen. Each command spoken by Javier was instantly obeyed. Bandit heard the sounds the Master made but hadn't been around him long enough to figure out what each utterance meant. He learned "come" and "here." These terms must have been important, Bandit noted, because when Javier spoke them, the dogs perked up and responded. Bandit started to recognize the human word for his name. "Band-dit" became special to him. He figured that name was meant for him only. When Javier uttered "Jen-Eee" his mother responded, likewise the sound "Fal-Len" grabbed the attention of his sister.

When each expression was followed by the sound of "Here" or "Come" each dog went scampering to Javier's side. Mike and Gabe didn't seem to pay much attention to the commands; they just stayed out in the pen milling vigilantly around and through their sheep.

Bandit's keen eyes took in everything. From insects flickering around to the movement of the trees and the shadows cast by the swaying limbs, birds flying by and small animals on the ground; all were etched in Bandit's young mind.

In the wild, he and Sheena traveled so far and so often that the appearance and smells of a single locale flew by. Now he was a part of this land, this ranch, these sheep, these dogs and most of all, his mother and his Master. The knowledge of belonging demanded much more attention than the footloose life of the forest. Before, his main concern was eating and not being eaten. Here, now, at his home, as Blu referred to it, he felt a kinship with each living creature, and he knew they felt the same about him.

His sense of survival kept him attentively attuned to sounds of the night. Somehow, he knew it was his responsibility to make sure no one, man or beast, invaded the area around the kennels, barn, and house. From his den, which he carved out deeper into the side of the hillside, he could oversee the entire compound, well hidden from prying eyes.

* * *

He grew to know that his food would be placed at the same spot, just inside the kennel yard next to the watering trough, every day. Once Falen tried to grab a bite from Bandit's bowl, but with a growl and a quick snap of the air by Bandit, she quickly backed away, leaving her brother to his dish. She looked hurt as if she'd been denied her rightful fare, but as soon as Bandit finished eating, she made a beeline for the bowl, not so much to find any remaining food, but to prove to her brother she could eat wherever she pleased. Some mornings not a parcel of kibble was left, but she pretended to grab a morsel or two just to keep up appearances.

James MacKrell

Jeremy had finished his feeding chores and had started mucking the stalls in the barn when Javier rounded the door.

"Jeremy, hold down the place for me for a while, I've got to head into Big Timber for a meeting with Doc and Charlie. I shouldn't be too long. If you get hungry there's some leftover lamb stew in the fridge, and I made a jar of sun tea yesterday afternoon. It's on the railing of the back porch."

Falen had assumed her place next to Jeremy's left knee. Bandit had started following Falen and the boy around like a toddler, absorbing as many spoken sounds as he could and watching to see the reaction to them by Falen. "Over there" was a sound that caused his sister to move to a spot where the boy's arm seemed to be pointing. "Stay" was a strange sound, but every time Bandit heard it, Falen or the other dogs stopped moving and kept their eyes on Jeremy or Javier, whoever spoke the word-sound.

Jeremy finished his daily routine, putting the dogs up for the night, checking Bayo's stall and making sure the chickens had enough feed. The cows aimlessly wandered in their pasture with plenty of hay, the sheep were penned, and Jenny, Falen, and Bandit were in tow as the boy walked back to the cabin.

For the last several days Bandit had begun to be able to separate the man-made sounds from the cacophony of noise ever present around the ranch. The baaing of the sheep, the bawl of the cows, the constant chatter of the chickens, and the artificial sounds on the road just outside the ranch became easily discernable from the sounds of Jeremy's and Javier's voices.

* * *

He didn't hear the rush of the oncoming attack. Bandit let the afternoon sunshine lull his guard, and his attacker took every advantage. From across the front yard, Falen charged as hard as she could and rolled over the sleeping Bandit, jumped to her feet and grabbed him by the nape of the neck. He responded by ducking his head and grabbing her front foot, pulling it upward and flipping her on her red butt. She hit the ground and Bandit nipped her backside and pushed her down with all his might. The play fight went on for minutes with both out of breath and panting heavily. Bandit grinned with his tongue lolling out of the left side of his mouth; Falen had stretched out on her back and was a bundle of happiness. The puppy play had been missing in Bandit's young life, and as his and his sister's muscles continued to grow, the exercise proved helpful in keeping them fit and lean. Both youngsters collapsed. Falen gave Bandit's lips a lick and he responded with loving little nips on her neck.

Jenny watched from the porch, thankful to the Spirit of the Day and Night that her babies were healthy and well. What a contrast they were with Bandit's blackness radiating in the sunlight, and Falen's red body gleaming with ripples on her wavy coat.

High above the ranch yard eyes focused on the frolicking pair. Silently the watchers turned and moved back into the security of the forest.

"That's my Bandit," Sheena spoke to Steel.

He gave an approving look at the Aussie. *"You have raised him well. You, my mate, should be proud. I only hope we will be as fortunate with our own."*

Steel then led the way as Sheena's proud heart beat to the rhythm of the wolf trot.

* * *

From out in the sheep pens, Gabe and Mike stopped and took a hard long look in the direction of the hillside where Sheena and Steel were. Sniffing the air, each was satisfied that no threat existed, and lay back down among the sheep.

* * *

As night fell Javier returned from town, and Jeremy headed to his home, one ranch over. Everyone prepared for bedtime, with Mate and Blu nosing open the doors on their kennels, and Falen and Jenny heading up toward the cabin with Javier. For the first time, Bandit started to follow Jenny as she climbed the steps to the porch. Javier noticed but decided wisely not to make a big deal out of it. As Javier opened the door and held it for the dogs, Falen rushed inside and headed for the hearth near the fireplace. Jenny watched keenly to see what Bandit would do. He paused and sniffed the smells inside the open door. The warmth and the odor of food piqued his attention. His nose sniffed the air and his eyes surveyed all he could see of the inside while still standing with most of his body outside the door. He placed one paw inside the threshold. Jenny scooted inside between him and the doorframe and immediately turned to face him.

"Come Bandit, come on in. It's our home." Jenny looked around as she spoke. Javier stood stock still, making sure no sudden movement would spook the half-wild Aussie. Bandit's other front paw reached across the door jamb and he let his front ease into the room. Falen raised her head from the fire-heated hearth, looked at Bandit, and lay back down. *"He can come in or not, it makes no difference to me."*

"I am afraid, my mother. I've never been in a cave like this before. I am scared of the things I don't know." His eyes were wide and apprehensive. Javier knelt down and reached his hands out to Bandit.

"Here, my black beauty." He offered a small piece of dry bread to Bandit and said,. "You are welcome, my dog, welcome to our home and your home. You are safe here and you are loved." Javier didn't move toward the dog, who continued inching toward the piece of bread. Instead he just held his hand steady and spoke tenderly, urging the quivering dog on. Bandit's eyes darted between the outstretched hand and Javier's eyes; he reached with his head as far as he could without totally committing his body. With his eyes firmly planted on Javier's face he allowed the morsel to slip into his waiting mouth. The flavor of butter hit his taste buds, exploding so much his eyes nearly closed.

James MacKrell

Chapter 34
"Work goes on...."

As the months wore on, Bandit became more proficient in his work.

"Bandit, you are learning that we all have jobs here. We all work together for the good of the Master. It's our right and privilege to have valuable jobs. The more useful a dog is, the better it is for all of us."

Bandit listened attentively to his mother. His eyes riveted on her face as his mind sucked in each piece of advice. He had lost his initial fear after living in the house and being around Jenny and Javier. As the household got ready for bed, Bandit would leave the cabin to return to his den.

At dawn he outraced everyone to the breakfast bowl and jumped for joy when he got to join Javier on his early morning rounds. Several times late at night Javier awoke to the sound of Bandit's growl. He recognized his warning bark. Javier already sensed that Bandit couldn't be fooled and would investigate immediately.

Bandit knew not to make a mistake. A misstep might well mean becoming someone's supper. He heard Sheena voicing cautious reminders deep in his mind.

"Bandit, never take anything for granted. Your next step may possibly be your last. We survive by our wits and our attention to our surroundings."

Bandit knew death. As a member of Javier's pack he had assumed more responsibility. From his vantage point at the mouth of the den, he slept with one ear alert and an eye always awake. He had plenty of time to sneak a nap in the sunshine of the Montana afternoons.

* * *

The door vibrated with the heavy knock of a gloved hand. The muffled noise of the pounding didn't cover the boisterous sound of a drunken voice yelling at the top of his lungs.

"Spence, is your lazy ass up this time of night? Get up out of that sack, if that's where you are, and open this God-damned door. You got company, you useless piece of dreck." A hacking cough stopped the diatribe.

The hammering continued and after the coughing calmed down, the yelling grew in strength. The loud barking of the kenneled dogs and hybrids made him shout to be heard. The partially hung door vibrated each time the huge fist beat on the planks. No lights shown in the windows. Heat still radiated through the cracks in the siding, noting a fire had been burning in the grate several hours ago. Gerald "Hardcore" Harrison ripped off one of his motorcycle gloves and bellowed the name of the only buddy he had in the Mississippi National Guard.

Ronnie had joined the Guard when he worked in Biloxi on one of the gambling boats. The National Guard afforded him a chance to shoot some of the army's newest high-powered rifles. He and Hardcore loved shooting at things. Very rarely did they hit what they had aimed for. No sharpshooter's accommodation ever decorated their chests, nor any good conduct medals either.

Ronnie stumbled from the chair he had passed out in and tripped over partially empty bottles of whiskey littering the floor.

James MacKrell

"Just a minute, keep your britches on! I'll be right there." He pushed the torn curtain on the front window back to peer out to the porch. His bleary eyes barely focused, but he made out who was hollering by the guttural rasp of the voice. The dark image of the massive biker leaning against the door created a spark in Ronnie's dull memory. If Spencer hadn't been hung over, he probably wouldn't have opened the front door to Hardcore. He never did like him. Sober, Spencer would have recalled the many times Harrison's loud mouth got the pair thrown in some pretty lousy local jails.

He yanked open the door, causing Hardcore to fall into the house splaying out on the threshold. With spittle drooling from his chin he looked up at Spencer and slurred, "Waz up, me amigo? Let's rack um up and spend a little time terrorizing this one buffalo town. Get it? One buffalo instead of one hoss…"

His head lolled back against the cracked linoleum, his eyes walled back into his skull. Hardcore had passed out cold, so Ronnie pulled all 275 pounds into the living room and left him there to sleep it off. Spencer staggered into his bedroom and flopped on the bed. At no time did he or Hardcore pay any attention to the howling of the wolf-dogs penned in the dilapidated kennels. The ruckus stopped as quickly as it began. The snoring in the house drowned out any outside noise.

The bright Montana sun showed through the tattered curtains and blasted open the eyes of the two drunks. If headaches scored as natural disasters, these two had a whopper about 12 on the Richter scale.

* * *

Spring budded out as only it can in the south-central part of Big Sky country. The ranches in the area around McLeod flourished with activity. Shearing and lambing occupied most of the farmer's attention that time of year. Out-of-town farm workers filled each ranch, including Javier's. Specialized experts were hired and extra cowboys were taken on to help with the chores. That is why in the midst of all the sunup to sundown work, the call from Otis Millman, pleading with Javier to break away and meet Doc Williams and several of his neighbors, surprised him. This wasn't an idle call. The demand for his attention made him jump into the truck and head for Big Timber. All the dogs were up to their tailless butts in work, so for company, Javier loaded up Bandit for the ride into town.

Jeremy stayed behind to keep an eye on the place while the for-hire workers went about their tasks. For all of the ranches around the McLeod area, spring meant lambing and lambing demanded a lot of hands all working to get the ewes sheared and in the Jugs with the newborn. The sheep have to be moved from pen to pen and run through the chutes so sorting can be done. Lonnie was home from Montana State and his experience helped a lot. He had a way with the Aussies and they would work as well for him as for Javier. Shearing took a particular skill and the shearers that worked for the Combine Ranches were some of the best in the field. Javier's mind was on all the work left behind as the Tundra headed into town.

"This better be really important, my Bandit boy." His right hand gently rested on the neck of Bandit, who stared out the window. Bouncing around the cab, Bandit's legs were a little shaky as the truck moved through the winding mountain roads. His head swung left and right, trying to keep up as the scenery flew past his window.

Javier's eyes were strained from the glare off the windshield. Bandit stole a look up at the Master and his senses told him something was wrong. He had never seen the old herdsman so quiet, so introspective, so worried.

James MacKrell

Chapter 35
"In the face of a building threat..."

Bandit settled down after Javier parked the truck in front of the Pioneer Day Café in Big Timber. The parking spaces were slanted from the street to the curb. As he got out, Javier recognized both Charlie Millman's SUV and various other vehicles belonging to his friends and fellow ranchers. A green pickup with State of Montana logos on the doors nudged in between Doc Williams and a red sedan Javier had never seen. Across the street several sheriff's cars and some SUVs owned by the Fish, Wildlife, and Parks Department were parked.

The bell above the door jingled as Javier strode through.

"They're all out in our back room," the friendly waitress, who nearly spilled the pot of coffee in her hand, said. "You know your way."

Javier acknowledged the patrons Annie was serving. He had a 'waving acquaintance' with them as they all exited from church each Sunday morning. They smiled and returned the gesture as Javier doffed his Montana State ball cap and headed for the double glass doors separating the main dining room from the banquet room used by the Kiwanis, Lions, and other civic organizations. If you were going to schedule a meeting, the Pioneer or the school auditorium was the place. If the assembly moved to the county courthouse, it was serious.

As he passed by the counter and through the doors he exchanged greetings with several of the ranchers, and stopped to speak to Doc and Charlie and a man Javier had never met.

"Javier Coronado, I would like you to meet Mr. John Hawkfeather from the Crow Nation. He has some specialized information to share with us.

"I'm pleased to meet you, Mr. Hawkfeather."

"Likewise, I'm sure, Mr. Coronado."

Still holding a firm grip on the handshake, Javier added, "Please, call me Javier. Everyone else does."

"Then call me John," he smiled.

Doc urged them to take their seats around the big rectangular table with coffee cups and glasses of water stationed at each seat. Javier spied two open chairs and grabbed one and motioned for Charlie to take the other.

"What's this all about, Charlie?"

Charlie, absent his normal grin, replied solemnly.

"Javier, I got the notion from the sound of Doc's voice this could seriously affect all of us.

Why else would they pull us away from spring lambing?"

The podium at the end of the table still had the Big Timber Kiwanis's Club insignia on its front, leftover from yesterday's meeting. Sheriff Wade Thompson adjusted the gooseneck microphone to his speaking height and breathed into it to make sure it was on. Thompson stood tall behind the podium, and today he chose to array himself in his full official uniform.

"Gentlemen and ladies, if I could have your attention, we can get this hastily called meeting started so we can all get back to the things we're needing to do today."

The sheriff looked to his right at Franklin Jenkins, probably the oldest man in the room at 89, and teased, "I know Franklin here needs to rush back to that daybed on his back porch so he can drift off again in this Montana sunshine."

Everyone in the room laughed except the octogenarian, who leaned over to the man setting next to him and said, "What did he say?"

Even though the laughter in the room gave the appearance of another lighthearted meeting, tension boiled just under the surface.

The sheriff continued, "Today we have representatives of most of our county, state, and federal governments assembled to work out a plan to ease your burden over the predation of our county livestock."

As an agreeing murmur danced around the table, all eyes flicked from the sheriff to the other officials representing the National Forest Service, Fish, Wildlife, and Parks, and members of the local ranchers' association. Javier caught the eye of his new acquaintance, John Hawkfeather, who nodded.

The sheriff sipped a glass of water and continued, "I would like to introduce someone whom you all may know who has studied our problem and has some suggestions. Here is Dr. William Scanlin from the State's Agriculture Department"

Dr. Scanlin rose and thanked the sheriff and proceeded to outline the estimated cost to each rancher if the predation continued at the present rate. He then turned the podium over to Rusty Thorne from Montana Fish, Wildlife, and Parks. Warden Thorne greeted the assembly.

"Ranchers and citizens, thank you for coming today on such short notice, but due to the numerous complaints our department has recently received, we believe you people in the Big Timber area are suffering the loss of a lot of livestock, especially the sheep people near McLeod."

Javier shifted in his seat; he remembered the attacks in the mountains averted by Gabe and Mike, and the close call behind the outbuildings next to the large sheep pen. Charlie Millman had spoken of some six of his breeding ewes that had been slaughtered and Lonnie's uncle and Jeremy's family had lost quite a few weanling calves.

The warden went on, "As you all know we have some pretty strict guidelines for wolf management in this state. The federal government requires us here in Montana to maintain a minimum of 100 wolves and 10 breeding pairs. Today that population has grown to about 420 plus wolves and some 73 packs that we monitor. As the killings grew we monitored the known Absaroka-Beartooth packs in our area, especially the Absaroka pack, and found them fairly far from any ranch lands. The looks of the kills told us another story. Instead of being quick and efficient like most wolf pack kills are, these seem to have all the markings of dog killings where one or two animals ravage the stock.

Several comments erupted. "I just wish someone would allow us to shoot these varmints," came one angry shout.

In the back a rancher rose to say, "The state already allows us to protect our stock and kill any wolf that is harassing sheep."

From up front came the comment, "I would like to do nothing but sit on my butt with my rifle and shoot at any of the gray monsters that come near, but I have a lot of other things to keep up with."

From the left side of the table an attendee said, "I agree! I'm never around, nor any of my hands, until it's too late."

Another rancher near the speaker said, "Be sure you know what you're doing when you kill a wolf. You have to have proof of the killing and about a truckload of 'red tape' papers to fill out. The Feds will come down on you worse than them wolves. That's why I trust my protection to my guard dogs." Javier nodded in agreement.

"Gentlemen, let me continue." Warden Thorne grabbed both sides of the podium and frowned as he said, "Most of the predation is occurring near a mountain valley cut back into the hills where we have located a breeder of wolf-hybrids who is running an operation not registered with any state, county or federal agency. We've identified the man as Ronald Spencer, who has a past criminal record in several states. Since his lease backs up to national forest lands we've sent agents to scope out the surroundings and believe that he is in violation of both State and Federal laws. The disturbing factor is that his wolf-dogs are escaping regularly and disappearing into the forest. It's these dogs, we believe, who are causing all the livestock deaths in that region. We've also found carcasses of some of these dogs left to rot in grasslands behind his place."

The room was silent as Warden Thorne paused for a moment. Dr. Kainer has asked Mr. John Hawkfeather of the Crow Nation to join us. Mr. Hawkfeather had a similar problem on their grazing lands several years ago and is offering some suggestions that just might help us. He can answer any questions about the similarities of these sheep and cattle killings.

"We are asking you today to assist us in any data we can compile about this illegal wolf-hybrid breeding operation and any information you may have or can gain Ronald Spencer."

John Hawkfeather outlined the problem for the sheepherders on the reservation and suggested that the same way they ended the problem just might work here in this area.

The meeting ended with several of the men and women breaking into small groups to discuss the options. Javier heard the horn honk on his pickup and wondered who was blowing it. He bid good day to Charlie, Doc, and John, and headed back to the truck. As he exited the café and turned toward his Tundra he broke out in laughter. Bandit was sitting behind the steering wheel. His paw rested on the horn in the middle. Whether he meant to or not, Bandit had sent a message, *"Hey there, Master, you've been in that place too long. Get out here and let's go home."*

As the two drove back to the ranch, Javier mulled over the suggestions learned that day and was intrigued with the statements from John Hawkfeather. Never did he feel he was in any danger himself.

Chapter 36
"The lost cowboys..."

The gravel crunched under the tires of the worn pickup Spencer purchased from a used-car lot in Billings. Empty beer cans rattled around the rusty tools and other debris littering the bed of the F-150. Hardcore Harrison hung his multi-color, tattooed arm out the window, letting the smoke from his chewed cigar drift behind the vehicle. Spencer drove, his head in a fog because of the previous night's drinking. When the duo ran out of beer, they started on jug wine, which after finishing a bottle or two left them practically comatose.

"Hair of the dog, my man, hair of the dog." Hardcore mumbled.

Hardcore's breath smelled about eight days old. Spencer leaned his head out the truck window, trying to avoid the stench. Hardcore erupted in a coughing fit as he giggled about his joke. "Hair of the wolf, I meant to say, hair of the wolf, my man..." his words faded into a spasm of hacking.

Cars, motorcycles, and trucks crammed the parking lot of The Last Cowboy Outpost as afternoon drinkers and mill workers just off shift, packed the bar. Spencer picked an empty space near a large tree off the gravel drive. He slammed the door and headed toward the entrance of the bar, leaving Hardcore coughing and hanging onto the truck for balance. A drop of rain splashed in the dust, preceding a shower from a dark cloud directly overhead. Spencer barely made the porch before the skies opened up. Hardcore's heavy boots slipped on the wet planks of the steps that had already iced over, and the massive biker fell flat on his back. He jumped up and wiped the mud from his pants, laughing and coughing all the louder.

Ronnie paid no attention, opened the screen door that had a wad of cotton affixed to the middle, and pushed on the wooden door to enter a world of smoke, confusion, and noise. The place, to quote Hardcore, was rockin' and a rollin.' The area around the bar was three deep in drinkers of all kinds and sizes. Loggers stood shoulder to shoulder with bikers. Suit coat sleeves reached over vest clad bare arms grabbing cold bottles of America's Lager. Sonny, the bartender, kept things moving as he reached into the jam-packed ice containers grabbing two and three beers at a time. A waitress carrying a tray of drafts over her head barely missed running into Hardcore, who was engrossed by a half-clad woman leaning against a pool table. His eyes lit up at what promised to be an event-filled afternoon.

"Well, 'scuze-me, amigo, watch where in the hell you're going," said the waitress as she balanced her load and wiggled out of Harrison's way.

Hardcore didn't acknowledge her presence. He plowed straight ahead, looking at the pool table over his right shoulder. Spencer found an empty booth near the back, thankfully near a men's room.

A waitress took their orders and ignored the smirk from Hardcore. Ronnie headed for the men's room as the provocatively dressed woman from the pool table sauntered over.

"Hello, big man, what brings you into the Cowboy?"

Hardcore tossed a mouthful of the peanuts, shells and all, from the bucket in the middle of the table into his mouth and answered, spewing bits of husk over the surface.

"Jest blew in, my lady, riding these ranges with an old army buddy." The woman leaned down and rested both hands on the table in front of Harrison, giving him an ample glimpse of her open blouse. Hardcore stopped in mid-sentence, staring at her cleavage. He then looked up into her face grinning, and quizzed, "What's a couple of hombres to do round these parts to have a party?"

"Depends, sugar. Do you want to stay on this planet or get a little blow to send you to heaven?"

His large hand started to vibrate on the table in time with some imaginary tune. The thought of scoring some dope greatly appealed to the biker. After all, that is how he and Spencer made most of their spending money back in Mississippi.

"You holding?" Hardcore grinned, "Are you the drugstore?"

The woman stood up and with a suggestive wink said, "Let's just say I'm the map to the pharmacy."

Ronnie rejoined the table as the lady turned and wiggled her way back across the room.

Several drinkers at tables nearby stared as she ambled away. Two of the men, dressed like ranch hands, tuned their attention to the conversation between Spencer and Harrison.

* * *

"Shit." Hardcore leaned into the face of Spencer, "if we found us a stash of blow, man, we could take over the neighborhood from the local yokels in this Cowboy town."

Spencer immediately imagined the cold steel bars of jail, and how every time he got hooked up with Harrison, something bad happened.

"Beats the hell out of sellin' them mangy half-wild dogs."

Spencer looked away.

"You ain't doin' worth a good crap at that guard dog business. I don't think you've sold one of them worthless curs in the past month. If it wasn't for your disability payments from Uncle Sugar you'd be starving."

Ronnie knew that was true. This whole operation to sell wolf-dogs as protection certainly didn't turn out as he had expected.

"Spence, a little blow can make your troubles disappear. Then we just take target practice at your so-called 'Lobos of the West.' Hardcore hit Ronnie on the arm in a playful gesture that caused his friend to nearly fall out of the chair.

At the next table over, one of the men leaned over to his companion and said, "Do you think one of these two is the guy the sheriff was talking about?"

* * *

Deputy Sheriff Tommy Hampton's radio buzzed. The caller's voice was subdued. "Tommy, we may have a couple of guys of interest here."

"Where are you?" Hampton asked as he drove from Big Timber down alongside of the Boulder River toward McLeod.

"At the Last Cowboy Saloon two out-of-towners' strolled in looking up to no good. Both pretty rough, and they fit the bill for druggies. I approached the big one and he seemed interested in scoring."

Tommy reached for his notepad in case the DEA agent had some more information.

"I believe one of our off-duty guys stopped in there today to meet with an old friend. He was wearing a light-

James MacKrell

colored work shirt when he left the office about an hour ago. I could buzz him if you need him."

"Naw, that's all right. I snapped a photo of these two with my cell phone. I'll e-mail you the picture."

"Great, Ruth. Thanks a bunch, and thanks for the head's up."

* * *

Two ranch hands exited the bar and jumped the puddles left by the icy rain and headed toward their truck. Both men worked a spread near McLeod about four miles from the Townsend Ranch. Their boss had attended the meeting at the café with the sheriff and Warden Thorne.

"Look at the muddy old Ford over there by the tree. What is that sign painted on the door?"

The younger man walked over and wiped some of the mud from the driver's side. "It says 'Lobo Kennels'. Do you think that's the guy the sheriff was talking about who raises those renegade wolf-dogs?"

"I don't know but let's jot down the license plate number and mention it to the boss."

They left the parking lot and headed out on Highway 289 toward McLeod.

Chapter 37
"When the night comes..."

Most of this chilly April day, things remained pretty normal around the Townsend Ranch.

Spring had settled into a routine; a hard routine, but still a routine. All of those extra hands employed for the shearing had left a month earlier and now the two or three hired on for the lambing season were taking up the slack. Here in April they worked mostly on tagging. Tagging is cleaning up the wool around the ewe's milk bag so the baby lambs can nurse better. Both of the farm hands showed up at five o'clock each morning, which meant Javier and the dogs had to pile out bright and early. For one thing they had to relieve poor Lonnie, home from college, who took the graveyard shift so the others, Javier included, could get some rest. It seems the pregnant ewes didn't mind when the lambs were born; any time of the day or night was alright with them, so someone had to be with them 24 hours a day. It usually fell to Javier but with Lonnie's experience and willingness to stay up all night, he gave the old herdsman a chance for some needed rest.

Jenny always seemed to be first out of the cabin. Blu, so used to his kennel that no one bothered to lock the gate anymore, stood waiting for the group.

When all were assembled the work began in earnest. Each dog would assist in bringing the sheep into the tagging area, then the Aussies would help drive the tagged ewes into the jugs to lamb. Each new mother would remain in the jugs for a few days to make sure she had enough milk to nurse the babies. If she did, the newborn and the ewe would be driven back into the pasture to grow. The rainstorm that nearly turned into an ice storm halted work for a while, as man and dog alike looked for some cover and a little warmth.

Jenny walked back toward the house behind Javier with Bandit and Falen at her heels.

"Well, my pups, what did you learn today?" Falen hated when Jenny began quizzing her about what she did or didn't know.

She disliked being put on the spot and treated like an ignorant whelp. Bandit, his usual attentive self, viewed the questions as a chance to prove to his mother once again his love and acceptance. The black pup remembered all the lessons taught him in the wild by Sheena were matters of life and death; he looked upon his time at home with Jenny every bit as important.

"I learned not to bother Blu when he's trying to pen the sheep." Falen turned up her nose and trotted ahead confidant that her response was enough to make her point. If she had arms she would have crossed them.

Bandit slowed his pace and his amber eyes squinted into the sun, pondering what to say, knowing how important it was to his mother. Falen glanced back, waiting for her brother's answer. She dreaded it when he took so long to respond. The longer he took, the better his response.

"I rushed a ewe and her lambs this morning trying to get them into a jug pen and caused her to nearly knock over the little ones. Because of my hurry the lamb might have been seriously hurt. I will try to exercise more patience in the future."

"Well done, my son, you are maturing into a wise shepherd and a wonderful help to Javier."

James MacKrell

Falen snorted and plowed ahead down the path to the front porch.

A sheriff's patrol car swung into the drive and parked. Deputy Tommy Hampton blew the horn to let anyone know he was there and slipped on his hat as he marched toward the cabin.

"Tommy, come on up. I just made a fresh pot o' joe."

Javier turned back into the house to fetch the cups and coffee. Tommy took off his hat, used his handkerchief to wipe the nervous perspiration from his forehead, and followed Javier into the warmth of the living room. He settled into the rocker nearest the fireplace. Jenny and her puppies walked up, sniffed the deputy and decided he was all right. All three dogs plopped down on the side of the living room by the hearth. Falen stuck her face into a water dish and with her front paws splashed most out on the wooden floor. Her head dripping wet, she then trotted over to Hampton's freshly pressed uniform pants, and wiped her muzzle on the lap of her human napkin. "Falen, go over and lie down with Jenny and Bandit and get out of Tommy's face."

Tommy glanced down, knowing it wasn't his face she was in, and tried to wipe away the blot. The redheaded pup, well aware of what she had done, strolled over and lay down with her back propped up against the wall and acted like she was the only living thing there.

"What brings you out on an afternoon like this? Not that I don't welcome the company."

Javier extended the coffeepot full of his favorite brew, the one with cinnamon, toward his friend and pulled up the other rocker and sat down.

* * *

Hampton dreaded the news he brought. Being the main deputy in this area of McLeod, Tommy was well acquainted with the ranchers and took his job of keeping the area safe very personally. The ride down from Big Timber had been troubling. A visit to each of the ranches with an alarming message wasn't exactly what he had planned when he started his shift. Hampton grew up a ranch boy and knew all too well farming is tough enough without some outlaws trying lay waste to all of the sheep and cattlemen's hard work. The deputy had a keen nose for trouble and even the steady flow of the beautiful Boulder River couldn't calm his apprehension as he drove south.

Hampton stopped first at the Townsend Sheep Company and Javier. He trusted Javier and was confident the Basque's calm demeanor would make the message easier for the messenger.

The coffee went down smoothly and gave the deputy a chance to organize his thoughts. The off-duty officer at The Last Cowboy Outpost conferred with the undercover DEA agent and a quick check of Spencer's and Harrison's backgrounds proved that these guys could be dangerous.

Hampton added, "Earlier at the Cowboy, when those two goons overheard a couple of guys talking about the sheriff's town meeting, they freaked. The off-duty deputy said they both jumped straight up and cursed loudly, calling the sheriff and the townspeople all kinds of names. Both stormed out of the bar with Spencer yelling, "I will teach these yokels a lesson, messing with me." Hardcore let out a whoop.

Now, instead of worrying about the predation of the wolf-dogs there is a new concern dealing with the safety of persons and property.

"We are going to add another patrol to the area, but as you know that's a lot to cover. We just all have to watch out for one another."

That being said Hampton rose, shook hands, and headed back to the car. He had a lot of ranch owners to speak to this afternoon, and with the busy season of spring all of them needed this news like a hole in the head. Tonight most of the homes in the area would have plenty to think about.

James MacKrell

Chapter 38
"The beginning of the end..."

"Help me carry this thing. It must weigh a ton."

Spencer grabbed the left leg of the freshly killed sheep trying to maneuver the carcass out of the truck so the two of them could carry it to the inside of the lean-to he called his barn. Hardcore appeared in no condition to offer any assistance, his crimson face and bleary eyes were the signs of someone who still suffered the effects of a significant amount of booze poured down his gullet.

Before they started out last night to steal a sheep to butcher for his hybrid wolf-dogs, they fortified themselves with a gallon of cheap wine. Now in the early morning hours Hardcore had thrown up most of the sandwiches he had shoved down and nothing came up now except bile.

"Just a minute, hoss," Hardcore got out before he wretched again. "Keep yer' britches on! Don't you see I'm sicker than hell?"

Spencer continued to tug on the dead sheep, pulling it closer to the open tailgate until the carcass dropped to the ground.

"Let's cut this thing up where it is. I don't think it can make me much sicker."

"Hardcore, you're useless. Why don't you go ahead and get the hell out of here."

Spencer looked up at the disheveled biker who had spots of vomit on his woolen shirt and suggested, "Why don't you head back down to Mississippi and get out of my damn life?"

"Man, you need me," Hardcore wiped his mouth on his sleeve.

Ronnie sarcastically said, "Yeah, like a dose of the runs."

Hardcore didn't pay any attention, "These farm hicks are going to clean your plow without your amigo here to protect you." Hardcore began to wretch again, but this time there was nothing left to throw up.

"All the rednecks will think a wolf grabbed this sheep." Spencer glanced up and a slight grin creased his face as he realized Harrison might be on to something.

Hardcore said, "We may have found an unlimited supply of food for your mangy wolf-dogs."

Spencer started butchering the dead ewe in the dirt, cutting the body into chunks to throw into the kennels. Both he and Hardcore were becoming more afraid of the hungry animals. He had lost over half of his stock due to carelessness and the condition of the cages being in such disrepair.

Both of the men marveled over how easily they invaded the ranch where they rustled the sheep. Hardcore remarked, "We could have broken in an' grabbed all of that farmer's crap if nobody was home."

To use Harrison's favorite expression Spencer added, "It would've been a piece of cake." Then he laughed, wiping a smear of the ewe's blood on his jeans.

Dead weight is hard to move and Spencer groaned as he pulled on the body of the slain sheep. "We might've got our butts shot off if one of them farmers caught us."

Harrison went into the barn to get another knife to help with the butchering. "Are you kidding me? These hayseeds couldn't hit your wolves at fifty yards, let alone people as stealthy as me and you."

"Ya know," Hardcore went on, "if we were of a mind to, we could pester the hell out of the farmers, and rob them blind in the meantime. Think of it. A couple of hits to the sheep and cattle farms and we might well high-tail it back down south, and let your lazy wolf-dogs fend for themselves."

Spencer stopped sawing on the carcass. Staring up at Harrison, his face contorted, as his mind whirled with the possibilities.

* * *

The top of the steep hill behind Javier's barns glowed like a forest fire as the evening sun sprayed its golden lights into the sky. Across the pastures the deep purple of nightfall painted rich hues in the firmament to the east. Bandit lay near the opening to the main barn with his black head resting on his front paws, looking up as the first specks of twinkling stars began a nightly dance. His gaze took in the sheep pens and lower pastures. Gabe and Mike wandered through the ewes and newborns, assuring them they had no need worry about safety.

Neither dogs' eyes would close until the Pyrenees believed no predator might attack the flock.

From high up the mountain and deep in the upper forest the shrill howl of wolves trumpeted messages to one another, calling pack mates to congregate.

A lonesome hoot pierced the air from the spruce trees, giving evidence of the owls' readiness to begin a nightly flight to search for food.

Bandit rolled over on his side and breathed in deeply, satisfied that his work had pleased the Master.

He rested in the knowledge of how his understanding of his job grew daily.

A tiny field mouse scurried by Bandit's nose. He hardly remembered when a creature like this little guy might've been supper. Now, with his lean muscles arched beneath his coat, Bandit had become a fit specimen, filling out into a mature shepherd.

"What are you doing, Bandit?" Bandit jumped in surprise out of his doldrums. Blu had walked up behind him and plopped down in the dirt, giving the black dog a start.

"Blu, I thought you were on the other side of the barn yard. I was lying around, thanking the Spirit of the Day and Night for our good fortune."

Bandit pulled his front paws under him and sat up on his haunches.

"I see a troubled look on your face. Is anything the matter?"

The blue merle dog shifted his position and without looking directly into Bandit's eyes let out a sigh through his nose and seemed to drift off into deep thought. His back leg reached up to scratch at an imaginary bug. Bandit loved Blu. He reminded him so much of his mother, wise and introspective. Blu was all business all the time. Bandit wondered where Falen got all of her tendencies to be such a clown.

Blu stretched his legs and arched his back. His nervousness this evening deeply disturbed Bandit. Blu got up and started to walk toward his kennel; instead he stopped and returned to where Bandit sat. A mournful sigh escaped Blu's nostrils again as he tried to push himself further down into the dirt. Each muscle in his lean body appeared to twitch on its own.

"Uncle, what is upsetting you? You seem very uneasy."

Blu's eyes canted toward the black Aussie.

"Our human is restless and I don't know why." Rising up a little he continued, *"I don't believe it's anything we've done. No misbehaving or not minding commands. We didn't lose any sheep and we all, including Falen, did our work with speed and correctness, yet our Master seems to have a deep look of concern in his eyes. I didn't force eye contact with him, but all the same he appears to be brooding and guarded."*

Bandit started to answer, but Blu cut him off. Once Blu began talking it seemed he had a hard time stopping. His concern for Javier had welled up so, it was as if he had opened a faucet and all his worries were pouring out.

"Do humans get like this often?" Bandit knew he had only lived with people for a relatively short period. Maybe this condition affected them from time to time. He remembered that sometimes Sheena seemed to be far away in her mind, and Bandit, no matter how much he played or teased her, couldn't relieve her anxiety. He also remembered, now that Blu had mentioned it, that the Master's hands had felt different on his skin when Javier petted him. A subtle tension extended through the old herdsman's fingers. Tactile awareness is something dogs are born with.

"I think he is sensing danger, not only to himself, but all of us as well."

Bandit agreed with Blu.

He, too, had an ill feeling about his beloved Master. He started to mention it to his mother, but decided all of the dogs raised on the ranch were able to read Javier's moods much better than he. He didn't want to appear an alarmist and worry his mother as well. Bandit loved the farm and all it comprised. In the wild he would've given his life to protect Sheena and the den. Now he had a strong desire to be protective of everything about his new pack, even the chickens.

He intended to continue the conversation, but just then Blu let out a long, gravelly snore. Bandit decided to let the sleeping dog lie.

Chapter 39
"The plan is hatched..."

Jeremy trudged out of his last class of the day at the local high school, trying to make sense of a conversation he had just had with a classmate.

He mulled over what Richard Simpson had said. Richard Simpson had told him an account so incredulous, but followed it with "cross my heart and hope to die", so it certainly must be true. What's more, many other people backed the facts, so it was very difficult for Jeremy to discount it. If only Lonnie wasn't back at Montana State. Lonnie would be able to see through this yarn or confirm it.

Jeremy hated to fret. One of his worries included all the time he spent in his own head trying to sort things out.

His introspection gripped his mind and sometimes wouldn't let go. He enjoyed the work at both his father's farm and Javier's because it allowed him to clear his head.

"There is a healing from good, honest, hard work. It cleans the soul and refreshes the mind," his Grandfather had told him, and just about everyone else within earshot. Grandfather Johnson, his mother's father, loved to extol the virtues of labor, something he recommended for every person but himself.

"Honest to God, Jeremy, my uncle said a monster roamed this part of Montana years ago, devouring sheep, calves, and dogs."

Rich's eyes were huge and glassy over his excitement about this story. He believed it to be true. According to him and his family, it could explain all the missing ewes and lambs the ranchers were reporting. Plus, no one had really seen any wolves actually attack and kill a sheep. The strange beings some claimed to see appeared more like hyenas than anything else. But Jeremy wondered what would a hyena be doing in Montana?

"I am telling you, Jeremy, these are the same monsters like the old Mormon settler shot over a hundred years ago."

Jeremy listened, totally enraptured. Rich went on, "Heck, the old settler even stuffed the thing, and by the way, it's now on display in the Madison Valley museum. My pop and I are going to visit it this weekend." The Simpson boy glanced down at the floor. "If ma will let us, we will."

The thought of monsters was a lot for Jeremy to think about on the ride home. Wolves, cougars, and coyotes were bad enough, but monsters?

His dad sat on the rail of their porch talking to Javier as Jeremy walked into the house. All Jeremy heard was, "If this killing of lambs and ewes doesn't end, we'll lose half of our crop."

The boy's ears opened and his eyes widened. "Sheep-eating monsters?" thought Jeremy. He flopped across his bed with a full-length horror movie playing in his head.

His father, Gus Sanderson, was an even-tempered man, a third generation sheep rancher in the mountains near McLeod. The Sanderson spread included both sheep and cattle and abundant fields of alfalfa. At the county fairs the Sandersons usually took home the most ribbons due to the emphasis placed on a breeding program honed over decades.

"Javier, we've all been hit really hard by predators no matter what they are." He chuckled, "Someone is filling our neighbors' heads about some kind of monster who supposedly roamed these parts over a hundred years ago, but if you ask me, the culprits all come from that survivalist Spencer's kennels, where he's been breeding trouble for a couple of years now."

"Tommy Hampton told me the game wardens scoped out Spencer's place a couple of weeks back. It was in complete disarray and some of the wolf-dogs roamed the grounds freely. Tommy said they all looked hungry, and you know what hunger can do to an animal. The wardens couldn't find Spencer, but said they believed another person, a rather large, heavy-set guy, has been seen leaving the compound. A motorcycle was leaning against the side of the house. The license plates were from Mississippi."

Gus looked away over his pastures and watched the grazing sheep for several minutes.

"With the price of supplies going sky-high and the markets in such turmoil, the last thing we need is an outside disturbance to combat."

Javier passed his coffee cup to Gus. "I agree, my friend." He slid off the rail. "I'd better head back. I just came over to give Jeremy a lift and save him the walk over." Jeremy strolled out on the porch ready to go. The evening's chores lay ahead and all of the work would give him plenty of time to excise the monsters from his thoughts.

* * *

"This dog is sick, Spence. Just look at him! All covered with sores and half his skin's all festered." Hardcore still had a mouth full of biscuit from breakfast. The night had passed quietly for Spencer and Harrison; they were getting ready for a possible customer first thing this morning, and a sick or dying dog could really throw a hitch in the plans.

The Malamute-wolf cross could hardly raise his head from the dirt floor of the cage he had been in for almost ten weeks. Mites and other parasites had invaded his skin to the point that open sores nearly covered his neck and back. At one time this wolf-dog's appearance would have drawn praise from anyone. Now he lay in his own excrement ready to give up and die.

"What's gonna happen when the dude from Washington State comes over to buy one of these worthless critters?"

Ronnie walked over and peered through the chain-link fence at the sick wolf-dog. The animal barely moved. His water dish was bone dry and the food dish had been licked clean.

"Hell, I don't know. Most of these dogs look like crap. I would like to get a few dollars for um' before I have to shoot the whole bunch. I'm tired of this. I'm tired of Montana and the hillbillies who live here. This operation looked good at the beginning, but the more I try to make ends meet the further I get behind."

Hardcore fingered the 38-caliber pistol he was cleaning. The weapon hadn't been fired in a long time and grime clogged the hammer. A pile of cans would provide some target practice this morning, target practice Harrison needed since he, more than likely, wouldn't hit any of the cans at any distance.

A car drove up in front. Spencer and Hardcore assumed the customer from Washington State had arrived. Ronnie went around to greet him while Hardcore threw a blanket of sorts over the sick dog.

A tall man in a gray-green uniform got out of the sedan that was clearly marked *Montana State Department of Fish, Wildlife and Parks*. Ronnie's heart sank. His shoulders drooped along with his mouth. "I have to keep Hardcore out of sight," he thought with a little panic. He tried to paste a sickly smile on his face, but his eyes hardened as the officer walked toward him, clipboard in hand.

Good morning, Mr. Spencer. I am Officer Waynewright from Fish, Wildlife, and Parks.

"Has somebody complained? I ain't done nothin' wrong. I run an up-and-up outfit here, and if any of the damn neighbors issued a complaint I can assure you they are out of their minds!"

The diatribe spilling out of Ronnie Spencer's mouth certainly wasn't what he had in mind. Fear has a strange way of controlling speech. Emotions can wreck the best-laid plans. Ronnie glanced at the drive and the road leading to the highway. This would be a terrible time for that guy who wanted to buy a wolf-dog to show up.

"I'm not here to hassle you, Mr. Spencer. We haven't gotten any complaints about your kennel, so you can relax. I am here to let you know we will be back for a full inspection of your operation toward the end of this month.. I wanted to give you a head's up since we've never met. I am sure Lobo Kennels falls into the specifications we require for a commercial kennels here in Montana. We will be checking over your sanitation, treatment of animals, and your first aid facilities. By the way, you aren't holding any pure wolves are you?" Ronnie looked shocked. He didn't know if he'd checked out if you could keep wolves or not. He was sure he didn't have any permits.

Waynewright knew full well Lobo wouldn't pass inspection. It was his way of letting Spencer know they were on to him and would be back with a fist full of citations to begin what the agent hoped would be the end of Lobo Kennels and Spencer in particular.

Chapter 40
"Sleep well my trusted friend..."

The bite felt to Bandit like a flea just behind his right ear. His back right foot whipped at the offender, trying to loosen him from his perch in the soft hair at the opening of the dog's ear canal.

When you're outdoors most of the time, in ground littered with spruce needles, fallen leaves, dirt, and debris, you're bound to pick up a flea or so. Fleas weren't new to Bandit; he hated the pesky things from puppy-hood. The tiny invaders bedeviled even the mighty Sheena, and she tried to relieve her itching by assuming the most undignified positions in an effort to scratch or rub them out of existence. At the beginning of the evening, Bandit seemed overly plagued by the parasites when all he wanted to do was curl up and doze, pondering the things he and Blu had talked about earlier.

A small rock jabbed into his left hip. He rolled over on the den floor trying to find a more comfortable position, but another flea attacked his midsection.

Bandit had way too much on his mind as evening fell. From his perch in his den halfway up the hillside, behind the main buildings on the Townsend Sheep Ranch, the moonlight played among the shadows from the outbuildings and trees. The Aussie loved this view. It gave him a sense of purpose to believe he offered an outpost of safety for the entire operation. His mother and sister were asleep peacefully in the cabin with Javier, and his uncle Blu and the other working dogs were snoring in the sleeping barrels inside their kennels. Bandit remained on guard, always vigilant and ready to alert his pack to any trouble.

Yet with all the peacefulness of this early evening, his restless soul kept him awake. Bandit's core joined with the nerve center of the Spirit of the Day and Night. Not for a millisecond did the heart of Bandit beat out of sorts with the mind of the Spirit, nor did the beautiful dog ever entertain an idea contrary to his faith in the Spirit's purpose. Selfishness and avarice were as foreign to Bandit's make-up as his ability to fly. And he had actually thought about flying while watching a bald eagle soar in the high Montana skies; but his foundation was as innate as his breathing. Bandit's happiness during his time with Sheena came from knowing somehow, some way, the Spirit of the Day and Night meant for him to return to his mother, whose love remained embedded in his heart. Now, all this apprehension he experienced on this early nightfall was conflicting to his being. The fact that his uncle Blu acted troubled seemed alien to his understanding of the dog's nature. Fright and fear were things dogs looked on as necessary for their survival, but both feelings were viewed more as tools than unavoidable conditions.

To Bandit's mind the unrest might break the cord of understanding between the dog and his Spirit. Bandit felt alone more than ever before. Even when abandoned by Sheena his nature seemed still connected to the universal mind, yet now everything was disjointed and broken, and he hoped the circumstances wouldn't last for very long.

"Bandit, be at peace." The Aussie's eyes popped open and his heart quickened. Who had spoken? Did the words come from inside or outside of his being? He stirred and started to rise to his feet, but a heavy cover unfurled over him, forcing him to lie still without movement. He

tried to answer, but it was like the soft bark forming in his throat lodged without a sound coming forth.

Again the voice spoke, *"Bandit, be at peace and listen to my words."*

Bandit's eyes softened and he felt the slow rhythmic beating of his heart.

"Whoever is there, whatever you want, speak, for I, Bandit, will listen and obey."

A cool mist poured into the den from the outside night air. Refreshing to the troubled dog and electrifying to his soul, it settled over his entire body. From deep within the mantle a spark began to grow until it felt like hundreds of loving hands all petting and stroking him at the same time.

He never wanted this sensation to end. If only what he experienced could be felt by his whole family. As he lay on the floor of the den he imagined all of his loved ones, Javier included, floating in this spring of love.

"Bandit, no matter what happens, no matter where you go or what is asked of you, rest assured that I will be with you, both day and night. Have no fear. I will always be there."

And just as suddenly as it came the sensation left. All Bandit heard was a small rush of wind coming from the back of the den into the night air. Then his eyes closed and he slept.

No one slept at Lobo Kennels that Friday night. Hardcore plunged into another drinking binge and the phone call Spencer got about nine o'clock informing him that his future customer from Washington State was coming on Sunday instead of tomorrow set his mind awhirl. To Spencer the good news was that the customer wanted two hybrids instead of one. This made the cash register in Ronnie's mind ring twice. The bad news plaguing him concerned the future run-in with the State officers. Ron Spencer was tired of trying to make it on the straight and narrow. He began to think about Hardcore's plan to rob the ranchers and head out of this, as Harrison put it, "God forsaken place."

Spencer would leave tonight if there weren't the possibility of picking up a couple of thousand dollars from the sale of two wolf-dog hybrids. After all, two thousand isn't something to leave on the table. He really could care less about the rest of the dogs; he would just as soon shoot them as not. Plus, the big drawback to the customer coming was how much work it would take to clean the place up and get rid of the castoffs that were sick or too mean to sell. At least he had a day and a half to get things in order. Hardcore Harrison had passed out, snoring deeply and pissing Spencer off to no end. Hell, Spencer thought, if you can't whip them, join them and he reached for the rest of the liquor jug Hardcore was holding in his arms. A half a bottle later Spencer faded into a drink-induced sleep, falling out of the chair in front of the TV. The last lucid thought in Ron Spencer's mind concerned the State officers and the misery they could cause him.

Chapter 41
"Nowhere to run...."

Thirteen-year-old Anthony Keske kicked a discarded pop can on the side of the two-lane dirt road that was a short five-mile hike between his father's place and his uncle Jimmy's. He still had stains on the front of his Dallas Cowboys tee-shirt from the homemade peach freeze his aunt Pat had churned up that Saturday afternoon. The familiarity of the fire road offered chances to pitch rocks at busy squirrels and chipmunks, and pester birds hanging on to cottonwood limbs in the early evening breezes. All of his family and friends called him Tony since his father, a pro-football fan, named him after his favorite old time player, Tony Dorsett. Due to a childhood injury Anthony Keske would never play football; the wreck on the tractor at his father's farm left his right leg mangled, which resulted in that leg being shorter than his left. He walked with a limp but it didn't seem to impair him. It certainly didn't hinder his abilities. He was fast in everything but running.

The woodland path was a favorite hiking destination for area residents. It skirted the mountains and climbed up into the hills, dipping through mountain streams and cascading down into the valleys. Anthony used it often as a short-cut home that kept him off the busy highway. The woods gave him a peaceful feeling and the loneliness of the terrain allowed him to forget his physical disabilities as compared with other young men his age. Anthony Keske was a happy boy who made good grades in school, an outstanding member of the Future Farmers of America, and a sports fan who held more facts in his head than most books. The quietness of the stroll through the woods allowed young Keske to play all kinds of imaginary games. Sometimes it was fierce Indians behind every tree; at other times desperate outlaws skulked around every bend. Anthony's mind stayed vigilant because of the rumors circulating around school about the half-wolf monster roaming the forest, preying on dogs and sheep.

Shadows have a strange way of adding to the intrigue of a teenage mind. The more Tony thought about the so-called monster, the more he saw unusual movement in the woods. His ears were on high alert and his eyes darted from tree to tree, from rock to grass following the beam of the flashlight he carried, searching for anything that might resemble a dangerous monster. He stepped gingerly across the rocks that made a footbridge of sorts over the stream that ran down from the mountainside. Tiny fish played among the round stones and a grass snake slithered away before getting stepped on by Tony's heavy boot. The first stars were shining through the slate gray sky and darkness piled up on the eastern horizon. The evening was idyllic; gentle breezes wafted with the scent of wildflowers and wet spruce needles from a recent shower. He didn't remember when Seth Anderson's boy had been shot at while walking down the same path, but that was nearly a year ago. As Tony topped a hill on the road, the kennels of Ron Spencer lay out before him, wedged between two hillsides. The outbuildings were in disrepair. The general seediness of the place, with old cans and trash barrels overflowing, gave the impression of abandonment. There wasn't even a sound from the loathsome collection of wolf-dogs, some chained to trees, others crowded behind double wire fences. Young Keske stooped to pick up a flat rock and thought about hurling it at the kennels just to see

James MacKrell

if he could set the wolves off howling. He started to, but thought better of it.

He pitied the wretched creatures in their condition and squalor. What would be gained by trying to arouse them? He tossed the brown stone at a nearby tree trunk.

No lights were visible in the house near the kennels. The old truck was missing and a motorcycle still leaned against the side of the barn like it had that morning when Tony had passed by.

A sound up the road caught Tony's attention, but as soon as it sounded the air was quiet and still again. A low howl came from one of the wolves back at Spencer's place; it had a mournful cry, sounding like the wail of an animal in severe pain. Goosebumps rose in ripples over the boy's skin. Even with his bad leg he hastened his step.

Night was falling fast and he shivered as he thought of how much farther he had to go to get home. Keske started whistling an old song his grandmother used to sing. It took his mind off the building shadows deep in the trees and the sounds of accompanying nightfall in the forest. His right leg began to tire as he tried to force the gimpy leg to match the long stride of his left. His arms started swinging in time with the song he whistled, but his eyes never ceased darting from one imagined apparition to another. The slightest puff of breeze could turn a stand of small spruce trees into a group of malevolent warriors plodding to kidnap the boy.

About a mile past Spencer's Lobo Kennels the two-lane path swung hard to the right and plunged down a steep embankment to the shore of a fast-moving stream strewn with sharp rocks and fallen logs. The night stars were playing peek-a-boo behind the cover of black rain-bearing clouds. Anthony decided to hurry across the stream and head for home, nearly two miles away. A giant lighting bolt illuminated the ebony sky and the crash of thunder startled the Keske boy as he reached out with his bad leg for a firm footing in the stream. With flaying arms he tried to right himself before falling into the icy mountain water. Reflex caused him to twist in the air, protecting his crippled leg. The off-balance movement sent him crashing into a submerged piece of an abandoned stove whose jagged edge hid just below the surface of the water. His flashlight flew out of his hand and sank beneath the surface of the stream. The ghostly light floated away and then went dark, carried by the swift current. The rusty iron dug into his thigh, ripping his leg open and impaling him on the piece of metal. He screamed with all his might, but apparently on this night nothing but the forest animals heard him. Sitting down in the waist-deep water he tried to stop the bleeding. Blood was fanning out into the stream and it seemed like it wouldn't stop. Without being able to fully raise himself out of the water, he inched off his belt and tied a makeshift tourniquet on his damaged leg. With both arms he pushed himself off the metal sheet with its jagged edges and slowly inched his way toward the shore.

"Help, can anyone hear me? Help me! I'm hurt! Please, somebody help me!"

Anthony Keske couldn't restrain the big salty tears running down his cheeks. His leg throbbed as much as it had when the tractor turned over on him. Even though his cut leg was almost useless it still quivered, and the severed muscles jumped out of control.

The Keske boy continued to scream into the blackness, wiping his face on the ice cream-sticky tee-shirt. His body temperature started falling fast in the icy water, and shivers racked his body. Again he screamed, "Please help me. Please, God, help me."

James MacKrell

A sound from behind him up on the bank startled him and he stopped screaming. He swirled his head at the noise and seeing nothing at first he started to again cry out for help. Then the sight of two amber eyes staring at him from beneath a bush caused the yell to catch in his throat. The pain in his leg disappeared as his heart raced with terror. A low guttural growl came from the underbrush. A black snout poked out, sniffing at the air in search of the source of the metallic smell of blood. Keske tried to shriek, but his vocal cords were frozen. With hackles up and head lowered, a black monster with fangs bared inched its way closer and closer to the stricken boy.

James MacKrell

Chapter 42
"Danger in the night…"

Old habits are hard to lose, especially if there is still pleasure associated with the trait. All the time Bandit spent with Sheena, he enjoyed the freedom to range from the den on outings. Sheena trained him correctly and trusted his instincts completely.

Once Javier allowed Bandit to live in his earthen den on the hill near the center of the outbuildings, Bandit took leave of the area at will, once again enjoying the liberty he loved so much in the wild.

Saturday evening offered such an opportunity. Bandit's work had been successfully done; the twilight hours were upon the ranch, and most of the dogs headed to a place of rest and sleep, refreshing them for the next day of their seven-days-a-week work schedule.

Aussies are strong and tireless by nature, and Bandit proved to be no exception. From his time in the wild his ability to imitate Sheena's wolf trot, covering large areas of land in short periods of time without any evidence of exhaustion, stayed with him.

The bond between Sheena and Bandit had now been transferred to Javier. Though Javier was alpha in Bandit's pack, he came to rely on Bandit's loyalty and skills as he did his other dogs. Trust is a two-way street and Bandit, in turn, trusted Javier. The bond between man and dog grew strong.

The stars began to break through the darkening heavens, and Bandit got the urge to explore and stretch his legs a little.

The cool evening air ruffled his heavy black coat and the gentle wind of the cooling night seemed to cleanse his tired eyes. As he settled into the wolf trot he had enjoyed with his foster-mother Sheena, his mind lapsed into a state of near meditation. Calmness covered him like his own coat and the feel of the warm earth on the pads of his feet reassured him of his uniqueness. Bandit was a dog, but in many ways he was also a product of his upbringing by Sheena. The call to be wild reverberated in his soul as deep as the copper coloring on his leggings.

With his mind free of responsibility, he relaxed and let the sounds of the night soothe his spirit. His serenity was shattered by a distant sound. A call of distress; he recognized it not by the words, but by the tenor of the screams. He skidded to a stop; both ears trained toward the faint wail coming from down the road. Bandit's antenna picked up the calls of fear, and he burst forward down the fire road, zigzagging around fallen timber and heading full steam ahead toward the origin of the cries. There is a universal sound to the fear of death, whether it's from the smallest of creatures or the most advanced of the animal family, man.

Bandit ran as speedily as his legs would carry him without a thought of danger to himself.

Young Keske had no idea a four-legged rescuer was rushing to his aid. All Keske could see was the fanged black monster inching ever closer and death looming in its presence. The moonlight splashing through the rain clouds reflected in the marauder's eyes, giving them a reflection of fire. The creature filled his nostrils with the bloody smell covering the helpless boy like a shroud. Gaunt from malnourishment, the predator had never faced a foe as large or as menacing as a human. Humans only caused him pain and mistreatment, so he circled the stricken child cautiously, in fear of what a person could do. The boy's cries softened into a steady whimper, his eyes frozen with fright. The animal parried forward with a growl, and then retreated a few steps just out of reach of the boy. Tony's blood-soaked pant legs gave evidence to the fact the blood draining from his body was making him weaker by the moment. The animal sensed death was near, and considered waiting for the boy to die rather than go in for the kill. The animal had never killed anything before. He had been raised in captivity, and was used to having his food brought to him. The art of fending for himself demanded skills he hadn't acquired. Skinny from lack of food, the black animal resembled a wolf but seemed broader across his chest than any wolf Tony had seen before. His tail curled up over his back and his coloring didn't resemble the silver of the Montana timber wolves. His coat had a dull black tint and his ears didn't have the sharp points a wolf's had but appeared more rounded with the right one flopping over.

The beast never took his eyes off the boy, challenging the child to make a move. Any sudden or forced action from the boy would be all it would take for the killer to attack. His black head was hung low and his attention riveted on his prey.

The Keske boy reached under the water for a large rock he could hurl at his attacker, but he didn't have the strength to pry it loose from the streambed. For the first time in his young life he believed he would die.

The wolf-dog stirred a little to his left nearer to the stream bank, putting the road at his back. His tail uncurled for a moment as he bared his fangs again to announce he was ready to commit to a kill. He never saw Bandit coming. The sudden sting he felt was from the sharp teeth of the Aussie as they plunged deeply into his neck. The sheer weight of Bandit hurling himself against him slammed the beast into the bank of the stream. With a loud yelp the wolf-dog tried to fight Bandit off, kicking furiously with his hind legs, trying to free himself from the death grip on his neck. Tony Keske was frozen, his eyes wide as adrenaline surged into every vein and muscle of the exhausted boy's body. He threw up his arms in front of his face, trying to ward off the fury of the fight taking place only a few feet away. For an instant the wolf-dog shook Bandit from his neck, and slashed back at the Aussie trying to rip his side open. Bandit's strength was more than enough to hold the immature dog off. Bandit latched onto the front leg of his foe and as he clamped down he could feel the bone snap under the crushing pressure of his jaw. The scream from the would-be killer expelled most of the air in his lungs, and he seemed to collapse on himself. Bandit, skilled in the ways of warfare, knew to ignore this for fear the animal could suddenly turn and catch Bandit in a death grip. That didn't happen. All the time with Sheena, and the many life-and-death struggles he had observed made him fully aware of the fact that the fight wasn't over until the foe submitted or was vanquished.

Bandit never let up. He ripped into the side of the wolf-dog tearing a large gash down its side. The animal, bleeding profusely, started to lose the will to fight. Bandit, sensing he had won, carefully and cautiously freed himself from the death struggle and backed away, keeping his body between the fallen wolf-dog and the stricken boy. Without taking his eyes off the pile of bloodied fur lying helplessly on the embankment, Bandit redirected his ears backward to hear any sounds being made by the youngster.

Keske's cries had turned into sighs. The beaten dog slowly righted himself and limped off into the night without a glance at Bandit or the injured young man.

James MacKrell

Bandit threw back his head and howled a song of victory to the night.

James MacKrell

Chapter 43
"A hero's welcome..."

"It's getting late, where do you think Anthony is?"

Gloria Keske slid the plate of fried potatoes near the dish containing meatloaf in the middle of the Keske's kitchen table and returned to the counter for the salad.

Anthony's father dismissed her question with a wave of his hand while reading a report on sheep husbandry in the local paper. "He's probably doddering along. You know him. He's got to explore everything on the road, even if he's seen it two thousand times. This isn't the first time he's been late." Ivyn Keske went back to reading, assuming his wife would serve his plate.

Most of dinner was consumed in silence, Gloria hashing over fears regarding her son's lateness. She tried not to let her imagination run away by conjuring up pictures in her mind. Ever since the accident had left Tony crippled, Gloria had developed a sixth sense about him and the harm that might befall him. Like the time he became trapped in the barn by falling bales of hay. The hay pinned him to the floor of the hayloft. An unexplainable anxiety drove her to head to the barn where she found him and quickly pulled him out and soothed his pain. She had the same fearful insight tonight. She knew Ivyn might mark it off to a mother's worry, but deep in her soul she believed something was terribly wrong. This feeling stayed with her and consumed her thinking throughout the evening meal. Finally, when Ivyn was blowing in his coffee cup to cool the liquid down to a drinkable temperature, she couldn't hold it in any longer.

Wringing her hands on her apron she sat back down beside her husband and, reaching for his arm, pleaded, "Ivyn, we must do something. The boy is late, I tell you, and I can't help but believe something is wrong."

Her husband looked up, turned and glanced at the clock showing half-past eight, and grimaced. Looking back up at his wife, he patted her hand, adding, "I'll get the ATV and run back down the road until I find him." Then a smile broke across his face as he tried to hide his growing fears about his boy from her. "He's probably gotten a late start. You know that kid. He can take care of himself. That's the way we've raised him. He's probably fine. This isn't his first trip down that road."

He stood and headed to the garage, slipped the key from the rack, and fired up the machine. He yelled back over his shoulder, "Honey, it's going to be just fine. Trust me. Our boy is on his way home right now." Oh, how he hoped his words were true.

* . * . *

The pain in Anthony's leg started to subside. He faced the dog that had saved his life. The bleeding from his leg tapered off, and some of his strength began returning now that he wasn't so frightened. Bandit looked at the injured child for a moment and slowly crept in the direction of him, wagging his tailless butt and trying not to alarm the human any further. Tony had squirmed his way out of the water and rested on the bank.

Tony sensed the black dog's good intentions and even reached out a little for Bandit. Gently, Bandit licked Tony's cheek as if to wipe away his tears. A low-soothing whimper came from the dog saying, *"There, strange boy. It's all right. You are safe. I will stay with you until your people come. The Spirit of the Day and Night is protecting us. We must stick together and wait this out."*

* * *

No one at the Townsend Sheep Company had any idea of the drama taking place several miles down the fire road. Rest soothed the working pains for both Javier and the dogs. The evening was calm, and even though the black clouds portended rain, all remained peaceful around the ranch. Jenny quickly jerked her head up from her sleeping blanket as if poked with a stick. She rolled over to an upright position, trying to shake the awful feeling she had awakened with. She couldn't hear anything or detect any strange smells to have given her alarm. Suddenly her mind's eye pictured her Bandit. She visualized him lost and alone as when he had been a puppy. A tremor ran over her body and her hair seemed to stand on end. Jenny glanced at Falen asleep at the end of the bed, and could hear the deep slumber of Javier.

"I must be mistaken. I think everything is all right. Nothing is amiss. It's just the same old nightmare I've had for so long."

She curled up again on her side and returned to sleep.

* * *

The ATV couldn't run fast enough for Ivyn Keske. His confident manner around his wife segued into near panic as he headed up the fire road looking for his crippled son. Ivyn had always been a strong person. He was an individual capable of keeping his emotions under a cheerful façade. He never seemed to worry and had a ready smile for everyone. This night, as it grew darker, there was no evidence of a smile. His lips moved constantly as he raced over the rocks and fallen tree limbs with a prayer of pleading for the safety of his boy.

The headlight on the all-terrain vehicle threw a beam only about 25 yards down the rocky road. With a death grip on the handlebars, Keske seemed to float above the seat of the motorized off-road vehicle, his eyes straining to see into the darkness for the missing boy.

With each bump or pothole, the machine would lurch and buck, nearly throwing the elder Keske off. Still he kept the throttle wide open, rushing to relieve his fears over the whereabouts of young Tony.

Many of the Keske's friends wondered why Ivyn seemed to ignore the handicap his son suffered. Some even spoke ill of his blasé attitude, negating the fact that Ivyn had grown up with such pain and misery as a child that he shielded himself in a veil of silence. Such was the case when Tony's accident had left him disabled. It just wasn't something Ivyn talked about. But at his core, the Montana rancher harbored resentment for the ill that had befallen his only child. Now all the hurt and pain rose to the surface. He silently mouthed, "Hang on son, I'm coming," over and over again.

The winding of the old fire road further limited the ability to see ahead. The bright beam would point skyward as the ATV climbed a hill only to plunge into darkness on the other side. Each second seemed like an hour to Ivyn. His heartbeat sounded like a rat-tat-a-tat of a machine gun. In the stillness of the night from time to time his cry of "Tony" was the only voice to pierce the forest. Down in the valley, lights flickered in the farm and ranch houses he was passing. The fact that his brother had informed him on his cell phone, that Tony had departed his place quite a few hours ago, didn't calm any frayed nerves. "Tony! Tony!" His screams were muffled by the noise of the whirling engine.

No one appeared on the road. No four-wheelers, no bikes nor horseback riders. The stricken father looked for any signs of activity or clues to where Tony might be, but there were none.

Tears threatened to stain the cheeks of the stoic rancher. His breath came in short, deliberate pants. Ivyn searched the night for any sign or sight of his beloved, missing son. He pushed himself and the four-wheel motorcycle on at reckless speeds.

James MacKrell

Chapter 44
"The light at the end of the road..."

The shivering prompted Bandit to lie as close as possible to the injured child in an effort to keep him warm. Even in severe pain young Tony's hand massaged the neck of his hero. Bandit's head rested across the wounded legs and his back pressed against the boy's side, holding him up out of the water. Keske's fingers played with the soft black fur around Bandit's ears. After the savagery of the life-and-death struggle with the wolf-dog, the pleasing strokes were welcome. A sigh escaped Bandit's nose as he nestled even closer to his new friend. The moonless night offered little in the way of illumination. The stars were beautiful, but they didn't throw enough light for Bandit to clearly survey the surroundings. The night air was still, the sounds of the forest seemed muted. Bandit couldn't leave the child; the thought didn't enter his mind.

From the eastern tip of the sky, red and green lights flickered as they headed in a straight line toward the Aussie and the boy.

"It might be a helicopter coming to get us. Yep, that might be just what it is." Keske's grip loosened on Bandit's neck as his whole body tensed at the idea of rescue.

"My dad would do something like that, dog. He would send in the National Guard if he thought I was in trouble." He scratched between Bandit's ears, adding, "My dad really loves me. He's going to make this all right. I bet he'll track down the monster and kill him, I betcha."

Bandit had no idea what the boy was saying; he only sensed by the tone of his voice he was feeling stronger. It pleased the Aussie since his inner voice tracked the condition of the human and his welfare. Bandit just knew. Canine intuition and a desire to work, protect, and please their humans has been part of their character for eons.

Bandit heard the whining drone of the motor long before the bright light split the heavens like a beacon searching the skies. The Aussie jumped without toppling his charge. So brilliant was the beam it resembled a laser show at a carnival. Tony's hand tightened and fear once again surged through his system. It was momentary but terrifying all the same. The noise reached them, sounding in the still air like a caravan of trucks all racing their engines. Bandit jumped up to be ready to protect the youngster. Every fiber of his black body was on guard. His head dropped to an attack position and his back legs set for a lunge if necessary. Then the words reached the ears of Tony and Bandit. "Tony, where are you? Tony, it's Dad!"

The stream flowed just off the road, and due to the darkness and the position where the boy and the dog huddled they might be hidden from view. Bandit started barking with all his might. His barks were both a warning to anything that could harm the duo, and a vocal alert to their presence. As the machine crested the hill the shaft of light illuminated the scene below. The brightness played like a theater spotlight upon the fallen boy and the black dog. The ATV's tires screeched as the brakes locked, causing Ivyn and the four-wheeler to skid to the side of the fire road. Rocks spewed in every direction as the elder Keske jumped from the vehicle and tumbled headlong down the steep embankment toward his son.

James MacKrell

Bandit, startled by the size of the person plunging toward them, couldn't make up his mind whether he needed to defend them or let the individual pass. He made a decision and squared his body, stepping in a direct line to the man tumbling down the bank.

"Dad! Dad! I'm over here. I knew you'd come find me! I just knew it."

Bandit sensed in the sound of the child's voice that the person was familiar and wasn't going to hurt them. He moved a little to the side, making sure a clear path existed so the father could reach his son. The barks turned from threats and warnings to chirps of joy.

"You've come, just like my friend said you would." He barked in the Australian Shepherd yip of happiness.

"All thanks be to the Spirit of the Day and Night, your lost boy is found."

If anything on this earth knew from first-hand experience the feelings that flowed when something lost is found, it was Bandit.

"Tony, I am here, my son. It's all right. You're going to be all right." The crack in Ivyn's voice released a flood of tears as the man gently knelt in the river rocks and held his son.

"Oh, dad. Oh, dad." Tony repeated over and over. His arms reached up to encircle his father's neck. Tears poured down the shirt his dad wore. Both seemed to collapse into one another with sobs of relief. Bandit stood by and even backed up a little, leaving the stage to the family.

The usual "what happened?" didn't seem necessary. Ivyn Keske straightened the bloody leg and adjusted the makeshift tourniquet. Tony continued to rest his head on the broad shoulder of his father, still weeping as a release of tension washed over him like a warm blanket.

Bandit watched the love flow between the boy and his dad. His heart swelled with pride and knowledge of how important love is to everyone's wellbeing. Slowly at first, Bandit's rear end started a rhythmic rocking of ecstasy. Dogs wag their tails like people smile. It's an act of pleasure and gratitude, signifying a bond built on mutual needs. Some Aussies, like Bandit, are born tailless and tend to wag their entire back ends in expressing boundless joy.

Bandit couldn't help it, his yaps and chirps filled the night air.

"Oh, I am so happy, I am so glad; I am thrilled with your love of each other."

As the Aussie's exuberance quelled, a silent prayer of thanksgiving continued in his heart.

"All thanks to you Mighty Spirit of the Day and Night. Once again you've shed your love and protection on your creatures. Tonight my soul bears witness to your greatness, oh Master of Masters."

Bandit stood at the edge of the circle, reaching to his full height. The Aussie had matured into quite a specimen. He topped the breed standard standing nearly 23 inches at his withers, and weighing a bit over 60 pounds. His first year of life set the tone for his muscular structure. If Bandit were human he would look like a bodybuilder. His coat shone like it had been oiled. On this night with the refraction of the ATV's headlamp Bandit stood like a star on stage. Ivyn turned to look at the strange dog standing by his son. Before he could ask, Tony uttered exclamations of near giddiness. "Dad, that dog saved my life. He is the reason that I am still here and alive." Keske looked at his son and words started to form on his lips when Tony bubbled on.

"There was this monster wolf-looking animal that was going to attack me. And all of a sudden this black dog jumped on the thing and beat him into the ground."

Bandit could sense they were talking about him and turned almost shyly to avoid the widening eyes of the man.

"Look, over there on the ground. You see all that blood? This very dog drove that wolf-lookin' creature into the ground and nearly killed him. I'm telling you, it was the worst fight I've ever seen. Thank God he came along or that wolf monster would have eaten me."

Tony's dad stared into his son's eyes and drank in every word the boy was saying. His hand reached up and stroked his beloved child's head. Tony nearly lost his breath due to the words of his rescue spilling out like water from a fire hose. Both of the Keskes looked up at the same time to see this wonder-dog of dogs. He was gone though, nowhere to be seen. Bandit had slipped into the darkness and headed for his home and some rest. All the way back down the fire road his mind whirled, thinking of the fate of the boy if he hadn't answered the call.

"It all works out for the best." His feet slipped into the ease of the wolf trot. *"Sheena would have been proud of me. I hope she knows."*

Chapter 45
"Tales of monsters..."

Bandit had just curled up in the den to get some well-needed rest when the roosters began crowing and the Townsend Sheep Company sprang to life. Bandit rolled over and lifted his tired head, looked over all the activity and whimpered; *"I guess I have to join the pack for another day of work."*

To the Australian Shepherd one day melded into the next, none had a difference, but if he had realized this was a Sunday morning he might've snuggled up with his blanket and gotten some much needed shuteye. Javier walked toward the barn with Falen close at heel. Jenny sprawled on the porch and Blu hadn't stirred in his kennel. The other dogs, Mate and Brady, paced near their feed bowls, ready to devour any food offerings Javier cared to make.

Stretching his battle-weary bones Bandit made a slow effort to join the rest of the group in the barnyard. He stumbled down the hillside and once again extended his body and legs to loosen his bunched-up muscles.

Blu sniffed a strange smell as he neared Bandit. The stink was acrid and coppery, with a heavy dose of the smell of fear, something Blu wasn't used to. As he got closer to the black dog he saw that Bandit's side was covered in blood. Alarmed Blu sniffed Bandit from head to tail and licked his face.

Blu barked, *"Where have you been? Has something hurt you? Why do you have so much blood on you?"*

Before Bandit could answer Javier joined the group, knelt by Bandit, and stroked his head. Javier, concerned about Bandit's bloody side, jumped up and fetched a bucket of warm water from the house. He returned with the bucket in hand along with several clean towels.

"There, there, my dog. Let's get you cleaned up and so we can see how bad you're hurt." His experienced hands dipped the cloth in the warm water and slowly combed and stroked Bandit's fur, removing the caked blood. The more he cleaned, the more he realized Bandit wasn't hurt at all. No cuts or puncture wounds and no gashes. Bandit held rock still as Javier washed him all over. The warm towels eased his sore body. As Javier swept his hands down the dog's legs, Bandit let out a sigh of pleasure.

"Well, if this isn't your blood, then who does it belong to?" Blu moved around so he could see Bandit's eyes. *"Did you kill something? If you look this bad the other animal must look like death."*

Bandit's lips started to draw back into a grin, but when he thought of the young boy he saved his eyes took on a far-away stare of contemplation.

"It's really nothing, Blu. I did what I had to do like you would or any of our dogs. I helped a helpless boy, and my reward is the peace of knowing the child is safe."

Blu realized Bandit wasn't going to say any more and flopped down in the dirt to watch Javier continue to clean and tend to Jenny's pup.

"I am puzzled, my dog. Where did this happen to you? There is no evidence of a fight here in the yard." Javier got up to full height and placed the towels back into the bucket of warm water and headed back into the cabin to return the pail and soaked rags.

As he walked away he said over his shoulder, "Bandit, whatever you did and whomever you fought, I certainly believe you were the winner."

Pride burst from his eyes as a smile spread across the herdsman's face.

Bandit stood there. Blu added, *"It might be all right with the Master, but when your Mother finds out about this, you are going to be in trouble."* Blu turned his back as if to end the conversation and walked away, stopping to pick up a much-used bone in need of some more gnawing.

* * *

"I am telling you Dad, the monster was huge and black and very scary. He hid in the bushes, and when I fell down in the creek he started to stalk me. He moved first this a-way and his terrible eyes always stared at me. I was really scared!"

Ivyn listened carefully this Sunday morning, constantly patting his son's shoulder, and from time to time tussling his blond hair. Before the older Keske could ask a question, words continued to tumble out of the boy's mouth.

"I know it's the monster everyone in school talks about. He's been seen around here, and everyone says it eats sheep and young children. I swear it's true. You just gotta believe me, Dad! The thing could kill us all."

"What is he talking about?" Gloria entered the den with a plate of breakfast food for Anthony. "What is this about a monster?

"Child, you know better than to believe in things like that."

Ivyn stayed quiet. He knew that just getting over an extremely frightening incident the imagination could run wild, especially since Tony had all night to think about his brush with death. Before he corrected or downplayed the boy's tale he took into consideration that he, too, had heard the story about a wolf-like monster. Too many of his friends and neighbors all of a sudden started losing lambs, calves, and pets not to give some credence to this rumor spreading so quickly up and down the valley.

Tony launched in again, relating the story of his hero, the black dog, who jumped out of the night to save him.

"I've never seen anything like it before. He never barked or growled; he just flew into the monster and took him head on. They rolled on the ground with fierce noises with the big black dog holding on for dear life and the monster yelping with pain. When it was over, the black dog moved closer to me and stayed next to me until you came."

The elder Keske never stopped rubbing and consoling his son.

"I know, son. From what I saw the dog was a magnificent specimen. I think I've seen him before, but I can't place where. I only got a glimpse of him. You saw him much better. Can you describe him a little more for me?"

"Well, he was an Aussie, that's for sure. He didn't have a tail and he was strong like all our Aussies are. You know Aussies, Dad, they ain't afraid of anything, monsters or not."

A picture flashed through Ivyn's mind of an Aussie riding in the front seat of a truck in Big Timber. To the best of his memory he thought it might have been Javier Coronado's truck. He wasn't sure. But he knew he found his boy not far from Javier's place. The next time he saw him he would ask about the black Aussie.

Last night the wounded hybrid wolfdog had crawled back to the only home he knew, Spencer's Lobo Kennels.

His broken front leg had swollen and the gaping wound to his side had collected a lot of dirt and debris, which mingled with the dried blood. Extremely weak once he reached the kennel area, the wolf-dog pulled himself along the ground to reach the water pan. Even though the water dish had algae and the water was stale and filthy, the wetness soothed his tired body. The dog lay for what seemed to him an eternity in the soggy dirt. A fever had already set in, causing the animal to have difficulty breathing. His eyes bulged with pain, and even after drinking water, his mouth felt hot and dry.

He changed positions and tried to roll over, but his side with the huge gash proved too painful to touch. Now that Sunday morning had dawned the wounded wolf-dog's breathing had slowed greatly, and the swelling in his leg had distorted the size of the limb.

Hardcore stumbled out of the house and headed for the pump to splash some cold water on his face. He didn't want to wake Spencer in case the argument last night that had nearly come to blows started to fester up again. He didn't see the dog lying on the ground and tripped over him, sprawling out in the water-soaked dirt. He kicked out at the wounded beast so viciously the limp body moved only about two feet. The wolf-dog probably didn't feel the abuse since he was so near death. It wasn't so much the severity of Bandit's attack as it was the horribly malnourished condition the dog had already been in. Hardcore Harrison pulled himself up to a standing position and kicked the dog one more time. The spirit of the mistreated animal took leave of the bloodied body. As brutal as the strike was, the lifeless body didn't move. Mangled, beaten, and starved, the skinny half-malamute, half-timber wolf had died. Hardcore returned to the watering trough and drenched his head and shoulders with the icy water, then headed back into the cabin, hoping not to disturb Spencer, so he could crawl back into the disheveled bed and sleep off another of his tremendous hangovers.

James MacKrell

Chapter 46
"The myth begins…"

When Spencer finally rolled out of bed and stumbled outside to the kennel yard, the sun's strong rays had begun their work on the flesh of the dead Malamute-wolf. Flies swirled around the lifeless dog.

"Hardcore, what the hell happened to this dog?" Spencer bellowed at the ramshackle cabin. "Did you kill this dog? Get your lazy butt out here and tell me what's going on."

The conversation quickly turned to how to dispose of the remains. Since the wolf-dog's body had been so mangled in the fight with Bandit, flies settled in on the bloody wounds and were swarming around the eyes and in and out of the gaping mouth.

"Let's just throw this thing away".

"Where?" Spencer knelt down to see how stiff the body had become.

"Where?" The biker wiped his mouth, "How about anywhere in this wide-open, God-forsaken place."

The smell of death wafted up as the wind gently blew. Hardcore lurched back up to rid his nose of the odor before it reached his already churning stomach. "Whatever we're going to do with this thing, we better do it soon or else the stench is going to run us out of the county."

* * *

Several miles away at the Townsend Sheep Company, Javier took a break from the morning chores for a cup of coffee. He reached the house just in time to answer the ringing phone.

"I am so sorry." Javier's expression grew grim as he talked to Jeremy's father, Gus Sanderson.

"You know Javier, on a spread like mine we work on such a small margin, the loss of several of my young bull calves hurts the old pocket book."

"How many did you lose?" Javier sipped his coffee, moving around to stare out his kitchen window at the sheep contentedly grazing while the Great Pyrenees milled throughout the flock.

"We found another one dead this morning, which makes four in the last several weeks. We have to do something. Have you talked to Doc Kainer again?"

"Yesterday, for a minute or two.

He's still working with Mr. Hawkfeather on a plan to bring up a trapper from Texas who is skilled in these matters. Out around San Angelo they had a huge problem with foxes and coyotes, and he's been successful in relocating several hundred into St. Francis Wolf Sanctuary in Montgomery, Texas. The wolves aren't releasable and live their lives out in safety and peace."

Gus Sanderson was a prudent man whose farm skills had been honed by generations of Sandersons, who had plied their living from the abundant soil of Montana.

"I spoke with three of our friends this morning," he said, "and they all reported calves or lambs slaughtered. Frank Robinson raised an issue. He said to his best recollection wolves aren't bold enough to come into the pastures near the main buildings. Secondly, the kills looked more like a pack of wild dogs. I don't know much about those things, but Frank swore he believed it had to be feral dogs."

James MacKrell

"I'm going to talk to Doc again this morning. I've got a lamb that could use some of his attention. I'll phone you back after I find out what he's up to."

He replaced the receiver and continued to gaze out the window. In his heart of hearts he knew the cause of all the troubles came from Lobo Kennels, and the drunken guy raising those wolf-dogs.

* * *

Hardcore struggled, trying to keep his nose away from the stench of the dead dog as the carcass was lifted into the bed of Spencer's truck. Once the dog was loaded Spencer headed out on the back roads, looking for a place to dump it.

They drove up into the forest on a dirt road skirting the farmlands in the valley. As the miles rolled by they couldn't seem to find an area suitably isolated to toss the dead body away without being discovered.

"Look down there, at that field. No one's around and we could pitch this thing out in the middle."

The way the hay field was laid out, mountain fingers cradled three sides, leaving an opening of a few hundred yards. The 75-acre field resembled a bowl with the hillside to the left much higher, obstructing the view from the highway. From the right rise a small road led down to a gate left unlocked, which gave access to Spencer's truck. The pair inched their way down the steep incline.

"Keep a watch out for anyone. If you see something let me know, and we'll hightail it out of here."

Hardcore Harrison's eyes scanned the woods opposite and the flat land in between. Nothing was seen moving. A lone dog, which resembled someone's Border

Collie, scampered across the barren field and quickly exited under the barb wire fence near the locked gate. Otherwise, on this Sunday morning the area seemed deserted. As the sun beat down Spencer parked the truck near the open back gate.

"We've got to carry this thing so we don't leave any tire tracks the local fuzz might identify."

Packing the dead dog wasn't a thrilling option for either man, but the one thing they couldn't risk was being tied to the dog, and therefore attached to the sheep killings up and down the valley.

"Slide the dog on this old blanket and we can carry it a lot easier in a sling," said Spencer. Hardcore nodded, trying to keep his face away from the dead dog's head; he struggled getting the bedspread under the corpse.

"Why don't we just leave this son of a bitch here by this gate and be done with this," fumed Hardcore. Spencer stopped dragging the blanket serving as a funeral coach. He wiped his forehead and lit a cigarette. Hardcore's eyes scanned the hillsides and the front of the massive field for anyone who might recognize them on this dumping mission. From right behind them a buck deer stepped up from the mountain stream, startling Spencer so much he dropped his smoke and nearly tripped over the dog.

"Man, you sure are jumpy," said Hardcore. The deer bolted back up the hillside so fast his hooves kicked up a shower of dirt.

"Let's just get this over with and get back to the house. I've got to feed them no-count dogs. I'm running out of kibble anyway and the son-of-a-bitch who was supposed to come over from Washington never showed."

"I know that. The damn State game warden didn't do you any good either, him wanting proof of them breedin's." Hardcore picked up a small stone and pitched it in the general direction of the creek.

"I think we ought to just shoot the whole bunch and let Montana kiss our butts as we get the hell out of here."

After all, thought Spencer, he had nothing to tie him to this place, and his idea of selling wolf-dogs as protection never caught on. It might have worked in an urban setting, but here in Montana the folks were too wise and savvy about animals to fall for a guise like that.

The two misfits continued to pull the dead wolf-dog in the blanket to the middle of the field. There they dumped him and gathered up the blanket and any other clue that would give them away. Hardcore even stopped to pick up the cigarette butt Spencer left by the gate. Convinced they had rid themselves of a problem, they bounded back into the truck and headed back on the forest road toward Lobo.

James MacKrell

Chapter 47
"Caught in a whirlwind of myth…"

Almost a week had passed since Spencer and Hardcore had dumped the body of the maltreated hybrid dog in the hay field. In that time, more calves and lambs were destroyed and the anxiety level of the ranchers steadily rose. At a meeting one night at the Pioneer Day Café all of the farmers agreed to pool their resources and hire a professional trapper from San Angelo, Texas to rid the valley of the feral wolf-dogs. Folks at Montana Fish, Wildlife and Parks approved since the traps were to be placed on private land and the captured would be hauled completely out-of-state. The trapper had connections in the panhandle of Texas with a group who ran a sanctuary for injured and maltreated animals, specializing in wolves. No one wanted to just shoot these animals since there was a chance a stray dog might be mistaken for one of the hybrids and killed.

So far the trapping had been fairly successful. Each night the trapper's men placed live traps around the ranches and each morning they retrieved tired, hungry, and pitiful specimens. They fed them and loaded them up on a truck bound for North Texas. In this time, 12 hybrid dogs had been caught and sent south.

No one had checked the hay field where Spencer and Hardcore had dumped the body of the Malamute wolf-dog.

Two days later a teenager, Walt Simpson, decided to cut across the field to get to the mountain stream that bordered the backside of the acreage to cast a line at some of the huge trout that called the waterway home. As the Simpson boy walked along through the tall grass, he was overcome by the stink of a dead animal. The closer he got, the stronger the smell. As he parted the hay stalks using his fly rod as a prod, he stared down on the disfigured body of the hybrid dog, which now resembled nothing he had ever seen before. The flesh was almost all gone due to carrion feeding; the eye sockets were nearly shut, leaving only slits around the swollen face, which gave it an otherworldly look. The lips were pulled back into a permanent grimace, giving the appearance of a snarling monster. What muscle was left was void of hair. The skin was pulled tight, resembling pigskin much more than a fur-bearing animal.

The Simpson boy dropped his fly rod and tackle box and jumped back in horror. He never smelled anything so vile nor had he witnessed anything quite as frightening.

"Good God Almighty, that's got to be the damn monster!"

His cousin, Richard, had spoken to everyone who would listen about the fabled monster and had even begun to reinforce his argument with little lies about having seen it himself. Now, Walt had confirmed it, for sure, and the boy couldn't wait to run home and get his cousin to come back to the field and verify the find.

Walter got his cousin on the phone with his tale of the monster's death and before he could hang up Richard was dialing everyone he knew to come see the famed monster. In a couple of hours the field was trampled with the curious. All who saw it testified to the fact this was indeed the Monster of Montana.

James MacKrell

* * *

Javier's phone rang. "Javier, this is Gus, are you watching the news?"

"No, but I can turn it on. What's up?"

Javier clicked on the set and eased into the overstuffed chair next to the table with the remains of the snack he had devoured earlier. The screen quickly gave off its silvery glow and the picture snapped into place.

"The crowds are building around this hay field as people pour in to get a close-up view of the body of the famed Montana Monster. My cameraman and I have never seen anything quite like this before."

The TV reporter was pushed a little out of the way while several people, mostly teenagers and some folks just off the road, wormed their way in for a better view. The journalist continued, "This young man was one of the first on the scene. Let's get his reaction."

The newsman turned and stuck his microphone into the face of a man about 20 years old.

"Are you from around here?" The reporter put on his best serious face.

"Nope."

"How did you hear of the discovery?"

"I stopped at the gas station back in Big Timber and some kids were talking about it. They told me how to find this place."

"Have you ever seen anything like this before?"

"Nope."

"What is your name?"

"Randolph Jenkins. I live over in Idaho. I was just riding through on my bike. This is a hellava thing, ain't it?"

"Yes sir, it certainly is. Back to you, David, in the studio. As we get more information we'll keep you posted. This is Mike Crew, live from McLeod Montana for Channel 11 News."

Javier clicked off the TV remote button and said to Gus, "What the hell is all that commotion?"

A chuckle came from the phone as Gus said, "Beat's me." It takes all kinds doesn't it?"

* * *

The subject of the Monster of Montana found interest all over the south central area of Big Sky country. The morning newspapers carried a front-page story and compared the finding to the wolf-like creature shot by a pioneer over 12 years ago. Javier had to admit the similarities were great.

As morning papers were unfolded across the many breakfast places in the wide area, talk centered around the monster.

"I seen it in person," offered one of the Pioneer Day's regular customers. The old one is stuffed and on display at the Madison Valley History Museum, and I swear to God, it looks just like that thing they rooted up in the hay field."

The eyes of the kids in the cafe brimmed with part fright and part curiosity. To hear their grownups talking about monsters was something they delighted in. If grownups believed, then it must be true.

"I believe it's this wild thing and maybe some more just like it that's feeding on all the lambs and calves."

Murmurs all around agreed. Very few risked the chance of debunking the story. After all, it had been on TV and in this morning's paper.

James MacKrell

That made it true, right?

Deputy Sheriff Tommy Hampton walked in and most of the conversation paused. Tommy ordered a coffee with cream to go and leaned on the counter, glancing at the headlines of the paper.

"What do you think of all that, Tommy?" The deputy frowned and gave a short answer, "I really don't know. We'll just have to wait and see when the State veterinarians get their lab work back." A small grin creased his lips, "Personally, I think it's a dead, lost dog that swelled up due to rotting." He tipped his hat, grabbed his coffee and headed back to the patrol car.

* * *

"Good God Almighty, come here, Spencer, and take a look at this picture in this morning's paper."

Ron Spencer moved over to the cluttered kitchen table and shoved away some two-day-old dirty dishes so he could read the front page.

"Damn, Hardcore, they're talking about that dog we threw away."

"You betcha. Damn, these hillbillies are dumb. They think they've gone and found them a for-real sheep-eatin' monster."

Both of them doubled up with laughter. Hardcore fell into a chair and Spencer fell down on the floor.

"If that gives them a thrill, just wait until we spring our little red hot surprises on these rubes."

James MacKrell

Chapter 48
"The burning storm of fear..."

Fear eats at the human psyche like ocean waves erode a beach. Nothing is noticeable in the short term, but over the weeks or months or years the constant, pounding surf wears down everything it touches.

In south central Montana the tide of fear was coming like wild surf. Innuendos and rumors surfaced daily with each story held by the pronouncement of certitude by an eye witness who supposedly saw an event or creature or swore the person who told him the tale witnessed it "with their own eyes."

Machinery, livestock, tools, and the like disappeared from farmyards and barns. Malicious damage cropped, up affecting a good number of the ranches. Fencing was torn down. Feeding bins were found ransacked. People were beginning to be afraid to go out at night. Kids stayed close to home. Phone lines buzzed with troubled calls. Shotguns and rifles were loaded in farm homes up and down the valley for protection, yet no one could identify the culprits. No one saw the damage being done. The atmosphere of peace had been ripped apart like a tissue paper dress.

* * *

All the animals at the Townsend Sheep Company seemed more restless than usual. The Great Pyrenees, Mike and Gabe, circled the sheep pasture with eyes darting about the surrounding countryside. Even trusty Bayo nervously kicked at his stall, after being fed and brushed down for the night. Bandit, Blu, Brady, and Jenny sniffed the evening air, trying to discover the origin of the odd reek. They recognized the acrid odor, having been around burning wood, but there was an element that seemed out of the ordinary, and perilous. Javier paced the yard as if driven by some inner force to make sure everything was in its place and nothing was amiss.

Earlier in the afternoon, Ivyn Keske had called.

"I tell you I couldn't believe the old barn went up so fast." Keske's stable had caught fire in the wee morning hours and due to some fuel oil he stored in the junk room near the big doors, the building exploded like a roman candle.

"What do you think set it off?" Javier eased down into his chair as he listened to Keske's panicked voice.

"Damn if I know, Javier. The fire chief said he noted strong traces of gasoline, but, of course, that could have come from those fuel cans inside. He looked for any electrical evidence of an igniter, but said to his eye, nothing seemed amiss. We saved most of the back side of the old structure, and I detected the smoke in time for Tony and me to get the animals out before it went up in flames."

Javier gazed out of the window at his old wooden barn and wondered how long it would take for it to burn completely down

Falen had entered the back door, the one she could open with her front paws.

She would just twist the knob and let herself in. She strolled into the living room with her eyes pinned on Javier's face as she brushed against his leg, sensing worry.

Absently he stroked the Aussie's back and let his fingers play through the wavy red hair on the nape of her neck. Ivyn Keske's voice betrayed the fear in his heart.

Several fires had broken out in the valley recently, and he wondered if the blaze at his place could have been deliberately set.

"That's certainly something to think about. What did Deputy Hampton say? Do we have an arsonist on the loose?"

"Tommy didn't know, but he said this many fires all occurring within a week's time sure looks suspicious."

Now, as Javier wandered through his property, the nagging thought of a fire destroying all he had worked so hard to maintain rocketed through his mind like electric arcs. He stopped for a moment at the pump of the deep well by the back door and pulled a dipper from the post. His hand had a noticeable tremble as he filled the drinking cup with the icy liquid from deep beneath the Montana soil. He tossed out the remaining water and stared at the puddle on the ground.

Blu and Bandit eased up along side, neither dog making any kind of fuss so they would not add to his distress.

As the evening shadows began to envelop the ranch yard, darkening movements demanded a watchful glance from the old herdsman. Each silhouette seemed more threatening after the call from Ivyn Keske.

* * *

One foot still had on a dirty sock, as Hardcore Harrison lay sprawled across a bed that hadn't been made in weeks. The sheets reeked of sweat and booze and were such a mess, Harrison had a difficult time trying to extradite his right foot from the tangled covers. Spencer slammed the back screen door as he marched into the main room, which appeared in as much of a mess as the bedroom where Hardcore still tried to pry open his eyes.

"God Almighty, damn, you old reprobate, we nearly had time to burn that son-of-a-bitch's house along with that raggedy-assed barn."

Spencer's speech was slurred from the constant drink he and Hardcore had been on since they started pillaging the farms around the area.

"Yeah, but we didn't get no loot. If we're just going to burn crap down and not get anything of value, we're going to be stuck here in cowboy heaven for a long time. Let's grab something worth stealing tonight. Maybe a car or a truck or something we can take with us and sell when we get back down south."

Spencer fingered a chrome-plated revolver and started to stick it into his belt when Hardcore let out a howl.

"Dumbass, don't be taking no guns. These hillbilly cops find a gun on us, we're going to go away for a long time. You just be cool, you hear. I've got my knife, and it's done me right for a coon's age. I can sell the fact that it's just a huntin' blade, but we ain't got no story for no gun."

Spencer thought about it, pointed the gun out the window, and pulled the trigger. The hammer fell on the open cylinder with a heavy click. "Bang, I gotcha!"

Chapter 49
"Heightened awareness..."

The radio crackled and buzzed during Deputy Tommy Hampton's entire shift. Never before had so much traffic rattled from the police speakers. Fire, State troopers and Emergency medical services battled for air space. Tommy sped toward another suspicious fire with the red lights and siren of the Fire Department's major engine pushing through the early evening's fading sunlight.

"T12, this is dispatch. If there is a chance this is a false alarm, double back and interview Keske."

"Roger, will do, and if this is a burner I'll stand by until Fred arrives. Is the arson inspector still headed out to the ruins at Watson's place?"

"Roger that. Keep us informed."

"Ten-four." Deputy Hampton's right hand ached from squeezing the microphone so tightly.

Just then the sheriff broke in on his secure band.

"Hamp, if you get a chance swing by the Lobo wolf-dog kennels and see what those two hard cases are up to."

Before Tommy could answer, the radio went silent. He reached for the window button on the Crown Vic to let a little night air into the cab of the patrol car pushing out the tang of human tension.

This week had been hard on everyone involved. At last report the wolf-dog trapper from Texas had relocated eleven animals, all in dire shape and near death. Tommy thought a stricken or sick animal, especially one starving, is more dangerous than a well-fed wolf. The basic problem was that although the Department of Wildlife knew how to predict the movements and actions of most of the wolf population, these wolf-dogs were another matter entirely.

The fire truck's turn signals blasted a deep yellow into the night, already filled with the glow of red emergency lights. Hampton slowed the cruiser and radioed.

"At the scene. We've got a burner. I'll be back on the air in a moment or two."

The Sheriff's patrol car skidded to a stop about twenty yards behind the fire apparatus, giving plenty of room for the first responders. Tommy's heart sank; this was certainly no false alarm. The flames from the hay barn reached high in the sky, each finger licking the blackness in savage bursts.

* * *

The right front tire of Spencer's old truck slammed into a pothole on a deserted asphalt road that wound through the back woods behind Watson's acreage and up into the National Forest. Both men were in a state of ecstasy, wiping the fuel oil from their hands.

"Boy, that bastard exploded like the bombs in Iraq."

"How the hell would you know, you 4-F slacker? The only war me and you saw was in a Gulf Port Mississippi strip joint," Spencer smirked.

Spencer's dirty hand tried to wipe the dirt and mud from the bottleneck of the eight-dollar pint they were pulling on. He lifted the bottle in the air and said, "Cheers, let's light up some more!"

* * *

Smoke travels fast in the forest and the light night winds spread the smell of burnt wood all over the valley. Extra state police had arrived, giving the Sheriff some needed help. The volunteer fire fighters were taxed beyond their limits. Yet the smoke trails in the evening air around the Townsend Sheep Company grounds seemed to hover quietly like phantoms in a ghastly black and white horror show.

Bandit's eyes watered and he sneezed repeatedly. He climbed the hill to his den, hoping for a night of rest. Blu had pushed the latch on his wire door up to let himself in. Jeremy had kenneled the rest of the dogs, and Mike and Gabe took up their nightly vigil around the flock.

Falen snuggled next to her mother, Jenny, who dozed by the hearth. Javier fell into bed with most of his clothes still on, prepared for another restless attempt at sleep. As his eyes began to droop his mind buzzed with the fear that some of his neighbors would be suffering events tonight that could financially ruin them.

* * *

This was no false alarm. Another tanker truck was needed to contain the flames to the out structures and keep them from wasting the main ranch house at Watson's. Tommy Hampton plus the other sheriff's officers, state troopers, and arson investigators remained with the firefighters until the last ember was out.

"I didn't see or hear anything. The only thing that grabbed my attention was the red glow on my back window. When I went out the barn was completely engulfed. I didn't have time to free the cows or my old mare. Damn, all that stock, and what breaks my heart, we had them all named. They were like family." A tear rolled down the old rancher's cheek. Watson's sheepdog sat at his heels and whimpered little noises of empathy. It was after midnight before Deputy Hampton could exit the scene, and true to his promise he rolled by Lobo Kennels to check on its occupants.

* * *

One light illuminated the backside of the trashy cabin Spencer called home. Most of the area was in darkness and when Hampton sounded the siren for a moment to announce his presence no one seemed to notice. The air was quiet. Only about three of the hybrid wolf-dogs remained in the kennels and all of them were too sick to notice the police officer's presence.

Armed with a patrolman's flashlight, Tommy loosened the safety tab on his holster so he had access to his sidearm in case of trouble.

The moon went behind some large clouds, casting darkened shadows over the area. Moaning came from the wolf-dog kennels, but that was the only sound that caught the deputy's attention. The yellow flashlight beam played over the yard, stopping at the place Spencer's truck had been parked. The tarp hastily thrown over the Harley exposed most of the bike to the weather.

Tommy stretched up to look into the window before flashing his light around the interior. As the beams cut the darkness he observed a messy but empty cabin.

No other noise was heard until the squawk of the police radio sounded in the cruiser.

"T-12, what's your 20." Again, "T-12, what's your 20?"

Deputy Hampton sprinted back to the patrol car and slid behind the wheel, reaching for the microphone.

James MacKrell

"At Lobo, dispatch, nothing here, no one on premises..."

"T-12, get back in service as soon as you can. I'll report your observations to the duty sergeant. Move back down the highway toward the Keske place, is that a 10-4?"

"Roger that.

James MacKrell

Chapter 50
"Threatened...."

"Over, Javier, let's keep in touch on the two-way and keep the system up this evening. You never know. Over."

"I hear and understand. I talked on the radio earlier to Sanderson and he thinks it's a good idea as well. I know that Deputy Hampton can monitor this channel. Let's try not to worry and get a good night's sleep. Good night, Ivyn, I am going to keep the receiver on ready in case you call, ten-four?"

"Got it, my friend. Give an extra rub on that black beauty of yours and thank him again for saving my kid's life."

Javier peered out of the kitchen window and looked up the hill toward Bandit's den. Pride swelled in his heart for the black Aussie and his ability to sense danger and help protect the ranch.

Javier ambled into the bedroom and rubbed Jenny's head as she lay in the exact spot old Emma used to. Falen was on the foot of the bed with her paws pointing toward the ceiling, fast asleep with her tongue poking out of her lips. Falen had no problem sleeping. Jenny was a little more restless.

Javier dozed off listening to the steady hum of the two-way radio. Because of the rugged terrain cell phones were virtually useless; the area was nearly devoid of cell towers. Each group of ranchers or families depended on radio communication to stay connected to each other in case of danger or accidents. Once Ivyn Keske had been trapped by a fallen tree and used his portable radio to summon help. Now each rancher feared the news a receiver could bring as the nights filled with terror.

* * *

"You're not saying much. Cat got your tongue?" Hardcore Harrison leaned out of the pickup's window and spit a wad of chewing tobacco toward the ditch. Ron Spencer stared straight ahead as his tired and bloodshot eyes strained to make out any rocks or craters on the forest's dirt road. His truck banged and rattled over the terrain and the constant jiggling churned up the stomach bile he was trying to hold down. Hardcore never stopped talking except when he needed to spit out the window. Both men had started adding some cocaine to their indulgences, washing down the high with booze. Their false sense of security caused them to blindly strike out in their two-man crime wave of arson and looting. The drugs in their bodies lent them a sense of invincibility. As they neared the turn-off down the mountain toward Lobo Kennels, Hardcore shouted out, "Hey Spence, look a-yonder. Is that someone driving out of your place?" Spencer strained to see out of the passenger-side window, but only caught a glimpse of what looked like headlight beams knifing through the trees.

"I guess it weren't nothing. Just my old brain playing tricks on me," Hardcore chuckled, as he reached for the almost empty bottle of whiskey left on the seat.

He stumbled as he followed Spencer into the shack.

Neither man paid any attention to the dogs in the kennel, most of which hadn't been fed for days.

* * *

James MacKrell

"I will bet a month's salary it's those two losers at that kennel." Hampton laid his hat on Captain Walters's desk and walked over to the coffee pot for the last dregs of the day's java.

"You say no one was there? Could you tell about what time they departed the premises?"

"No Sir, Captain. It looked pretty deserted and when I flashed my light through the windows the house was in such a disheveled mess that if you wanted to you could swear no one had been there in quite a while."

Captain Walters picked up a couple of papers off his desk and stared at them. He sipped from his coffee cup and gagged, as he spit out the cold coffee. "Damn, Hamp, how do you drink this stuff?"

A grin creased the deputy's face. "At least mine is still warm. I bet that cup of coffee has been on your desk since this morning." He rocked back in his chair.

"These police reports are pretty interesting about these two. Harrison has done hard time down in Arkansas. A two-year stint for battery and six months for burglary is all his jacket shows, but he was in the brig most of his time in the National Guard, mostly from stealing from the Company's stores."

"What about the other one, that Spencer?'. He looks a lot more dangerous to me than that overgrown biker."

"Spencer is another matter all together." Walters passed the rap sheet to his deputy. "Take a look at the second page. It's about an arson charge down in Houston. . They had the goods on him, but the courts let me him slide due to some trumped up defense allegation about the arrest. The lawyer created just enough doubt that the judge let him go. There is no record of his sticking around in Texas after that." Captain Walters pointed to a paragraph in the second page. "This gets my interest. You notice the police report says he was caught with low grade flammables that once ignited wouldn't leave a trace."

"That might explain why the Fire Marshall can't find any evidence of any accelerants around any of our fire scenes."

"You betcha." The captain leaned back in his desk chair and added, "Hamp, at roll call in the morning we need to post a 24/7 detail to keep an eye on this duo."

* * *

The eastern sky turned a slate shade of gray- pink as the dawn broke over south central Montana. The mountain peaks were bathed in black with just the outline tinged with color as the Big Sky yawned its arrival for another day. Javier had been up for at least an hour as the morning light seeped through the eastern windows of the ranch house of the Townsend Sheep Company. Jenny was first up and had sufficiently licked Javier's face with good morning kisses. Falen still slumbered at the foot of the bed. As was his habit, Javier exited the back door to splash cold well water in his face. It was always shockingly cold but a habit avoided only in coldest winter. This morning he needed the refreshing dose of icy water to jump-start his brain after another squirming night of sleep.

The phone in the kitchen started ringing. Javier bounced up the stairs and grabbed the receiver from its cradle just inside the kitchen.

"Hello," Javier reached with his other hand for a chair nearby.

"Javier, bad news, said Ivyn. The Simpson Ranch was burned out last night. The sheriff and the fire marshall

James MacKrell

are over there now." The line went silent for a moment as if neither man had words to express their feelings.

"How bad?" Again silence, then Keske spoke. "This was the worst of all. They got the house as well as the ranch buildings. Thanks to God Warner and Judy weren't home when it caught fire."

Javier silently shook his head. Finally he spoke, "Ivyn, we are really going to have to pray for our neighbors."

Keske added, "Yeah, and a lot of prayers for ourselves, too."

As Javier's eyes played across the ranch yard he noticed his dog Bandit staring off into the hillside as if on sentry patrol. Javier had spent enough time over the years to believe in the intuition of his dogs. Other people may look at them as just animals who operated by instinct, but Javier knew, especially as far as Australian Shepherds were concerned, their minds were whirling each and every minute. You can trust a dog, Javier said to himself, as soon as the dog learns to trust you.

James MacKrell

Chapter 51
"The watchman keeps the gate..."

Dawn's rays cast as many ominous shadows as the evening's light. The early morning's breaking sun created silhouettes confusing to the eye. Bandit's heightened sense of smell helped sift fact from what the eye perceived. His keen sense of smell kept him focused on the hillscape behind the ranch buildings still blackened by the lingering night.

Smoke is a fearsome thing to animals of all kinds, especially those whose lives depend on the ability to flee. Bayo nervously stomped and pranced in his stall. The cows, cooped in a safe pen, milled as the acrid odor of lingering ash drifted through the air. The nervous baaing of the sheep troubled the two guard dogs, Mike and Gabe. On edge, they constantly searched for the source of fear among their wooly charges.

Bandit's consistently prayerful mind sought help from the Spirit of the Day and Night. What he felt in return was a heightened sense of alertness, and a calming sensation of peace. Bandit was grounded in the pursuit of protection for his pack and his master, and was willing to do anything needed to keep his family safe. This morning his scrutiny of the darkened, forested, hillsides was constant and acute crowded out all of his other thinking. He could feel it in his bones. Something was going to happen and he knew he had to be prepared.

* * *

Roll call at the sheriff's office had none of the devil-may-care attitude of mornings past. No one passed any jokes or smart sayings. The events of the last two weeks had the members of the morning patrol shift on edge. Eyes were firm and hearts pulsed with extra anticipation. Calm was the order of the day as the sheriff, himself, approached the duty podium instead of Captain Walters. Walters took his place back and just to the left of the Sheriff, Wade Thompson, and cleared his throat repeatedly while clutching the folders he held in front of him as he stood at parade rest.

"Good morning, troops."

"Good morning, Sheriff," they answered in unison.

"Each of you is aware of how we in this valley have been confronted with a wave of terror reeking havoc on our residents."

Silence fell across the room. Furtive glances and nodding heads affirmed the sheriff's words.

"Captain Walters is going to pass out some duty sheets for each of you. We have to be on heightened awareness until this or these culprits are apprehended. All of your duty sheets for the day give instructions about the surveillance we want you to perform during the course of your shift. The pictures of the two individuals of interest are several years old, but according to Deputy Hampton, men resembling the pictures have been noticed around some local bars and are assumed to be the same who are operating the so-called kennel. I believe it's called the Lobo Kennels, where they allegedly breed those wolf-dogs."

Each patrol officer received the material and immediately set about to commit to memory the faces on the rap sheets.

James MacKrell

One hand shot up in the room after the information was passed out.

"Yes, Deputy Sloper." Thompson pointed to a young man standing at the back of the crowded room.

"Sir, if we come across these two what are our instructions? Should we approach and apprehend?"

"Good question, Deputy. At this time, here's what we want you to do. If you think you've identified either one of these two, please use caution and follow them at a discreet distance so as not to spook them. Ask for backup and we will coordinate a response that will keep a visual on them 24/7. Is that understood by all?"

Heads nodded in agreement. Captain Walters stepped up to the desk and added, "Folks, Deputy Hampton is going to hang around for a while to discuss with you and answer any questions you may have about those in question and the Kennels called Lobo. Don't keep him too long. Remember, he's on the late shift and probably needs a little sleep."

The last line brought chuckles from the group.

The cool, early morning hours seemed just the ticket for Greta Hanson and Jerry Lynch, two young hikers out discovering the uniqueness of Montana's untamed lands. Neither were experts in hiking so the dirt road running along the side of the National forest pleased them no end. Earlier they had left U.S. 90 at Big Timber, and followed Boulder Road as it meandered along the river through the beautiful valley. Once they found a turnoff leading into the mountains, they parked at the first Forestry road and set out on foot. They had been walking about two hours when the road dipped, curved, and paralleled the property owned by Ron Spencer. As they drew closer they were almost overcome by the stench of decaying flesh coming from down the hillside.

"Good God," Greta yelled, reaching for a bandana in an effort to cover her nose and mouth. "What in the world is that smell?"

Jerry coughed and said, "I don't know but it smells like a field of dead bodies."

"How would you know what a dead body smelled like?"

"I dunno, but this crap sure smells like something awful, worse than rotten eggs. This is the most horrible crap I've ever smelled."

"Look over there. Those two men are hauling something that looks like dead dogs."

Greta strained to see through the trees. "Yeah, they are dragging something and piling it on a fire. Is that what is making all this horrible smell?"

"I believe so. Let's get back to the car. I don't think my stomach can stand much more of this 'togetherness' with nature."

Greta and Jerry stopped by a mountain stream that crossed the road to wash off the stench clinging to their clothes. Greta scrubbed her arms nearly raw trying to relieve herself of the reek. After a couple of hours they returned to their car and found a sheriff's deputy standing next to it.

"Hello folks. Out for a walk?"

"Yes sir. Seemed like a good day for it," said Jerry.

"Until we came upon all that dead smell," Greta added. Jerry gave her a dirty glare, implying he didn't want to get involved with any police business. Greta continued anyway. We came upon a couple of guys who looked like they were burning dead dogs. My gosh! The smell was dreadful!" She pulled her handkerchief up to cover her mouth trying to keep from gagging again.

James MacKrell

The deputy's attention heightened and he pulled his notebook from the front seat of the cruiser. "Could you describe these two?" Before Jerry could answer, Greta blurted, "Oh yes, they were rather seedy looking, I guess you could say that. One was really big and fat and the other looked slimmer. I think that's right, a little slimmer. Well, I mean, standing next to the fat one anyone would look slimmer."

Jerry interrupted, "Really, officer, we didn't get a good look at them. It's pretty much like Greta says, one was fat, and the other fairly slim."

"Are you sure it was dogs they were burning?"

"I wouldn't swear to it, but it sure looked like that from where we were standing."

"Thanks folks, you've been a big help."

Greta chimed in, "Are those people dangerous or anything. I mean, are they criminals, and were we in danger?"

The deputy grinned, "No, you weren't in any danger. It's just that we have ordinances against burning animals and we like to know who is violating those restrictions. Good day to you both."

With that the hikers piled into their car and the sheriff's officer reached for the microphone on his radio.

"Dispatch this is T- 20, come in please."

The dispatcher answered and the young deputy urged back-up be sent so they could investigate. He assured dispatch they just might find something interesting.

James MacKrell

Chapter 52
"Slowly, the fuse burns..."

The deputies took turns with the binoculars, peering into the backyard of Lobo Kennels, taking notes. By the time Deputy Oliver joined the first deputy on the scene, a rookie named Jimmy Stillwell, the fire had burned down, leaving only the lingering stench to fill the air. The kennels were deserted. Stillwell had been on the detail with the trapper from San Angelo and was convinced most of the marauding wolf-dogs had been captured and shipped to a refuge out of state. According to Jimmy, "If those other hybrids only knew how lucky they were to get caught and transported. They would have suffered a fate like the poor pooches them two just burned up."

Stakeout is a lonely and tedious business, and the morning hours slowly drifted into noon and beyond without much movement from the suspects, who apparently were holed up in the cabin.

"What are we supposed to do?" the young deputy asked.

"Is this your first 'sit and observe?" The more seasoned lawman didn't put down the binoculars he held to his eyes.

"Yeah, why?" Oliver grinned through the toothpick he held between his teeth. "Cause this is it. This is what we do, sit on our butts and hope for some action. So far, this is about as exciting as it gets."

"Oh." Jimmy leaned back against the Department's four-wheeler, content to 'wait' away his shift hours.

The hours slowly drifted by, with still no sign of the two suspects or any sign of life around the shack.

"Hey, you two, what's up at the kennels?" Stillwell and Oliver turned to see the rusty face of Tommy Hampton, who was relieving them from the morning shift.

"Are you by yourself?" "Yep." Hampton grinned, "There's only two suspects, so the Sheriff needed only one good deputy."

"Right, Mister One-man-show." He turned to get into the four-wheeler, "The reason Hamp's so good at this is he's so used to sitting on his ass." They all laughed.

"Hey, Butch and Sundance, give me a ride back to the turnoff, and one of you can drive my patrol car back to the office. I'll keep this dune buggy."

"Works for me. Stillwell, let's head for the house."

As the three deputies bounced down the rocky road away from the Lobo, Ron and Hardcore ambled out of the front door.

* * *

"I've got a hellava idea, Spencer. Let's burn this place down tonight, and that'll draw all these big, bad lawmen out here, while we take the old forest road down to where it meets 289, hightail it over them mountains, and leave all these cowboys to kiss our asses."

Spencer rubbed his forehead, surveyed what little was left of his property, and nodded. "Not bad, not bad at all for a worn out cycle jockey."

Hardcore slapped him on the back a little too exuberantly, almost knocking Spencer down. "We should wait 'til dark and then leave with the lights off."

Both headed back into the cabin to have a drink on their good idea.

312   James MacKrell

* * *

"Javier!" Sergio Gonzales yelled above the noise of his honking horn on his pickup. He rolled into the front drive of Townsend Sheep Company and hollered out for his old friend. "Coronado, get your lazy butt out here and let me tell you my good news."

As Javier's smiling face appeared on the porch, Sergio became so excited he finished the greeting in his native Spanish.

"Le digo que mi amigo, éste es el día más grande. Mi hijo, Rick ha vuelto a casa de Iraq." Sergio continued gushing his joy in Spanish until a bemused Javier held up his hand.

"Whoa, ease back a little my friend." His hand was extended to grip the warm handshake of his dearest friend Sergio Gonzales. "I know your son is now home and I share your joy. If Isabel has been cooking all day, I can't wait to join you."

They had been boyhood companions and when Javier moved to Montana with Jim Townsend, Sergio followed a few years later. They were close, and this news about the Gonzales boy's return from the war zone was good news, indeed. Ricardo, or Rick as he was called, had been wounded in Iraq and had just been discharged from the hospital in Germany. His sudden arrival thrilled Javier immensely.

"He's been home all day, and you don't have him working? What's the matter, Amigo, you slippin'?"

Javier held the front door open and the beaming Sergio entered the ranch house.

"Let me pour you some tea. I just made a fresh Jar." Two glasses were brought down from the cupboard and the two old friends sat down to reminisce about young Rick's life. An IED had exploded under his Humvee, and Rick had lost his right leg. Javier's eyes welled with pride at the opportunity to see this fine young man again.

An hour went by and Sergio finally got up. "I will tell Isabel to pile on some extra frijoles for you. You know how much of her Ranchero beans you usually eat."

Coronado patted his stomach and added, "I wouldn't miss it for the world. See you at about six. You know I can't stay too late, too much to do."

"To hear you say it, you've never gotten through all your work in your life. Relax; there is plenty of work when you get back. Let's fiesta! My Ricky is home." With that Sergio tossed his hat back on his head and headed for his truck. Javier stood on the porch and smiled. He had never seen his friend so happy since the birth of that boy 23 years ago.

The old Basque rancher swung down from the porch and headed back toward the sheep pens. If he was going to go out tonight there was a lot of work to be done first.

* * *

In another part of the valley the afternoon sun filled the yard of Lobo Kennels, but Deputy Tom Hampton observed no movement, no action. Several times he was tempted to radio in and accept a call just out of boredom. After all, how long could the Sheriff expect him to sit on a vacant house and yard?

The long afternoon dragged on. The radio was pretty silent, just a call about a wreck or a minor disturbance. One of the advantages to patrolling this end of the county was that most times the calls were of a positive nature instead of being plunged into crime or violence. The past weeks' crime wave shook up the entire region.

Tommy glanced at his watch. It was already 5:30, the sun was moving westward, and the shadows were getting a little longer.

* * *

In the shack of a house occupied by Ron Spencer and Hardcore Harrison, a match lit a fuse placed on a table in the kitchen. With a hiss the fuse burned across the wooden table at an extremely slow rate. "There, that's good, that's damn good. As long as that wick don't burn any faster, we can be the hell out a here before the big bang..."

Both laughed and took another gulp of the whiskey and seven in their glasses.

Chapter 53
"On my honor I will do my best...."

Little by little the leaves ceased to rattle on the branches of the cottonwoods beside Javier's house. No spruce needles waved as the breeze died down to a hush. Bandit's ears stood nearly erect and his nose constantly probed for any scent out of the ordinary. The hair on his back rustled. His hearing seemed to have increased eighty-fold, and his eyes surveyed the outlying areas with the intensity of lasers. Blu eased up so as not to distract Bandit.

"What are you looking for, my son?" Blu peered toward where Bandit was looking.

Just a feeling, my uncle." Bandit didn't turn in Blu's direction. *"Just a feeling."*

Blu sniffed the air, looking for any sign of unrest. He moved to the other side of the stoic Aussie as if a change in position would give him a better view. As the wind began to pick up, Bandit spotted a piece of paper blowing across the trail leading from Javier's yard up the hill to the forest road. Bandit watched the paper flutter across the small trail and lodge in a small chokeberry bush near the top of the hill. Blu soon tired of this game and sauntered back to see if any of the other dogs had left any kibble in their bowls.

"I don't see anything, and I am more interested in looking for a soft place to stretch out my bones."

Bandit didn't move. He was riveted to his position so that if evil came down the trail he would be the first to greet it.

Falen jumped from the porch and dashed after a butterfly flittering around a late flower in the yard. Her red coat glistened in the late afternoon sunlight, and her devil-may-care attitude was as refreshing as the cool breeze that drifted across the yard again, stirring up leaves and the sweet smell of evergreen needles. She attacked imaginary foes and rolled in some dust to soothe a little itch on her back.

Bandit looked at his sister. His heart filled with love. She was like her mother in all ways except wisdom. Bandit wondered what she would have been like if it were her instead of him who had been raised by Sheena.

* * *

As the late afternoon shadows lengthened a German Shepherd-wolf mix raised his head from the dirt floor of the kennel for a final time. His eyes had clouded over and his belly was extended due to hunger. His head flopped back to the ground and his life faded away. He was the last living thing at Lobo Kennels since Hardcore and Spencer had lit the long fuse that sizzled toward the explosives crammed under the broken-down back porch of the shack. The fire was set to ignite some 30 minutes or so after the pair fled the scene in the old truck loaded down with Harrison's motorcycle. The little they were moving was piled in boxes in the bed of the truck. They didn't take much. Both wanted to put miles behind them before the fire department arrived at the scene of what they hoped would be a four-alarm fire. The diversion should give them time even over the bumpy forest roads to hit the highway and double back toward Big Timber to join U.S. Highway 90, and then hightail it down to the lower half of the United States. Ron had been careful to try to disguise his truck in case any of the Sweet Grass County Deputies were to spot them. It was risky, but both felt that if they moved far enough south on the forest roads and then swung to the north, they could avoid being spotted leaving the kennels, and hopefully be mistaken for tourists passing through town. Hardcore had even stolen some license plates off of a trailer from Idaho to further throw off any lawmen. The evening light was fading fast, and they wanted to make sure they were several miles into the woods before the flames announced their departure.

The truck was full of gas and they had plenty of liquor to hold them over. They set out to kick the dust of Montana off their boots. As the fuse smoked toward the piles of flammable rags and gasoline, Hardcore had a look back at the place and spit, just to say good riddance. Their escape plan might be flawed but in the condition they were in, it seemed brilliant. The dirt road was curtained on both sides by stately evergreens and other huge and brushy trees, which made the area a lot darker. Heavy growth obscured their view of the valley, but from time to time they would get a break in the underbrush and have a clear view of a ranch spread lying peaceful, awaiting the night.

* * *

One such ranch, the one belonging to Javier Coronado, buzzed with activity. Javier had decided to let Jenny and Falen go with him to the Gonzales' celebration. Rick had fallen in love with Jenny on his last leave, and Javier had realized that anything that resembled the old way of life would be a welcome sight for the boy.

Javier wondered how he personally would react to the young man's wounds. Young Gonzales had served his country well and his welcome home was something Javier wouldn't miss. Jenny didn't realize the importance of the visit. She just knew she was going for a ride and getting to go was one of the highlights of her life. Falen just always wanted to be included.

* * *

Tommy Hampton had left the area in back of the Lobo Kennels for a short time to answer an emergency call near the highway. A wreck had left two teenagers injured, and Tommy was the nearest Sweet Grass County emergency vehicle to the crash. He pulled away back down the dirt road quietly, and when he got far enough away from the location, he fired up his red light and ran hot to the scene of the traffic accident. Neither Hardcore nor Ron saw the police vehicle when they left. Tommy, set on the urgency of the call, didn't look over his shoulder to see the pickup slowly pull away from the front of the kennels.

* * *

As the rickety Ford F-150 bounced along on their escape path, the scene was quite different at Sergio Gonzales' joyful reunion of his war-veteran son's party. Isabel had prepared every dish Rick loved, including all sorts of delicacies she pulled from an old cookbook that had belonged to her mother. Falen was happy sitting next to Rick's wheelchair;, in fact Falen was happy anywhere if someone fiddled with her. She plopped her red head into Rick's lap and sopped up all his petting. Jenny played matron and allowed her little girl to garner all the attention.
Sergio and Javier seemed relaxed for the first time since all the troubles had started. Javier crammed goodies into his mouth like he hadn't eaten for weeks. Sergio

320   James MacKrell

served a rare Spanish wine hidden away for just such an occasion. The whole family had gathered along with friends like Javier, and the mood was very festive.

All of a sudden Jenny's mood changed. She moved toward a window and started whining in a low guttural tone. She seemed agitated. Javier couldn't figure out the cause.

"Here, my Jenny," he stroked her wavy hair. "Aren't you having fun, aren't you enjoying the tortillas Rick has been feeding you and Falen?" The more he soothed her the more she seemed to fret.

"Oh Master, she whined, *please try hard to understand dog talk."*

She rose up on her back paws and placed her front paws on the windowsill. She stared out through the glass and acted like she needed to go outside. Javier took the hint and excused himself to allow her to relieve herself. As soon as they were outside Jenny ran toward the truck and jumped up over and over, trying to make Javier understand they needed to leave.

Jenny barked over and over, *"Oh Master, we must leave. Something is terribly wrong. Let's go home. Bandit needs us. We need to go home. Please, please understand."*

Sergio came outside to see what the matter was. Falen pried herself away from Rick's attention, and once she heard her Mother's pleas, she joined in the chorus of distress.

"Javier, what's the matter? I've never seen Jenny act like this." Gonzales moved out into the yard next to the truck. "Is she hurt?"

Javier's mood darkened. "Only once did she act like this and it was when old Emma died."

He stroked the head of his Aussie, trying to sooth her feelings. "Please tell the others I must run home. If things are fine I will come back, but I know Jenny too well not to listen to her warnings."

As the pickup door opened Jenny bounded into the front seat. Falen jumped in beside her. It was about a 30-minute drive back to his house, but Javier believed in his heart Jenny's warnings must be heeded.

Chapter 54
"The descent into hell…"

By the time the first responders reached Lobo Kennels the shack smoldered like a long-used campfire. All of the outbuildings were charred and the embers glowed with the intensity of a coal fire. The stench of burned flesh filled the air.

"This place is so isolated if it hadn't been for the guy turning off on the dirt road and spotting the flames we would never have located the fire."

"Yeah, Captain. And if the blaze had spread to the woods and brush, we'd had a hellava time keeping it from spiraling into a full-fledged forest fire."

The fire captain glanced up at the sky and wiped the soot off his face. "If the winds had kept picking up this blaze might have gotten out of control real fast."

As the firemen put the equipment back on the truck, a Sweet Grass Sheriff's department patrol car pulled up. Tom Hampton exited the cruiser and waved to a couple of the volunteers he knew well as he approached the ladder commander.

"Evening, Captain." Captain Oscar Wentworth turned to greet Deputy Hampton, removing his glove and offering his hand.

"Hello, Deputy, you got here a little late to be able to help pull these hoses, but the boys might need a bit of help picking all of this up."

Hampton grinned, and reached into his back pocket to get out his notebook. "Arson again?"

"Could be. Silvestre found some smoldering rags, but we couldn't find any traces of accelerant. A lot like some of the others."

The pencil poised over the paper as Hampton tried to think of what to write. Just like the others wasn't going to cut it. The puzzle was did an arsonist target the Kennels or was the Kennels the home of the arsonist?" "No sign of life?"

The fire captain walked over to the smoldering remains of the shack and pointed out, "I think the place was pretty much cleaned out."

Hampton thought a minute at the possibilities and debated with himself about just how to report this information to the office. He didn't want to sound a needless alarm but on the other hand, he wanted to make sure everyone in the department was up to speed on the two hard cases who occupied these burned out kennels.

Back in the patrol car, Tommy carefully worded his report and suggested all units be on the alert for an old green F-150 Ford pickup. He described the vehicle as battered and added it might have dog crates in the bed.

* * *

Miles from the well-cooked remains of what was the wolf-dog breeding compound, Ron Spencer took another pull on the whiskey bottle, passed it to Harrison, and glanced through the underbrush at the darkening setting of the Townsend Sheep Company ranch house and buildings.

"Hey, lookee there… ain't that where that old wetback lives?"

Harrison lowered the bottle from his face and peered out the front windshield. "Yeah, I think so. What's that old illegal doing up here in All America country?" He laughed and put the container to his lips again.

Spencer slowed the truck and shut off the lights. "I gotta take a piss. Don't drink all the hooch while I'm gone."

"Hell, Spence, you can barely make it to the rear tires in the condition your in." Hardcore laughed so hard he started coughing and nearly threw up.

No lights were on at Javier's place. Even the dogs were quiet. To Spencer's eyes the ranch seemed deserted. Earlier when Javier had left for the Gonzales', party he forgot to leave any lights on. He didn't expect to return very late and darkness had little effect on his eyesight after spending so many years in the mountain pastures with only moonlight and stars for illumination. In the hour since he had left, a cloud cover had darkened the area.

Spencer stood by the left rear tire looking down on the valley. Hardcore piled out of the passenger's side and joined him around the back of the truck.

"Turn the damn light off you asshole," said Spencer. "Sorry." Hardcore snapped the mini flashlight off, and his eyes adjusted to the darkness again. "I think nobody's home."

"Yeah, sure looks like it." Spencer didn't take his gaze off the ranch yard. "What do you suppose that old Mexican has down there? Any Mexican gold?"

"I don't know, but I do know this, that old illegal alien doesn't need all that good American money he probably has stashed in there. We need to get rid of some of it for him. Maybe he'll head back over the Rio Grande where he belongs." Hardcore staggered back to the cab of the pickup and brought the whiskey bottle back with him.

* * *

There is nothing louder than drunks trying to whisper. Bandit heard the truck's tires on the gravel road and edged out of his den halfway up the hill. His nose scented the sweat and sour smell of the men. The wind blowing down the hill from the road made the intruders easier to locate. Bandit's alarm system worked overtime. From his years in the wild he knew stillness was the best defense, and not being seen was also a great offense.

What to human ears would have been muffled voices stood out in Bandit's mind. He read not the words but the intent behind the sounds. He knew they meant harm, and the Aussie was determined to protect that which was his. He looked over the ranch yard and saw Mike and Gabe on the other side of the pasture, looking in an opposite direction from the hillside.

"Boys, I wish I could bark and warn you, but I think we are going to have our hands full before this night is over." Bandit hoped his thoughts would somehow alert his fellow dogs. He scooted down and focused all of his energy up the hill toward the sounds of danger.

* * *

"We got any of that 'burn-um-up' left?"

Hardcore looked in the back seat of the pickup and announced, "A little. I'm a thinking just enough to warm up some tortillas if you know what I mean."

Both men stifled giggles and made their decision. "Shit, we're far enough away from the kennels. We ain't seen nobody on this God-forsaken train so let's leave these yahoos with one more callin' card."

Ron grinned an almost maniacal grin, sucked back some saliva that dripped from his lips, and said, "Old

James MacKrell

pardner, let's burn that wetback out like Sam Houston did to Santa Ana." With that they started their descent down the trail toward Coronado's place.

James MacKrell

Chapter 55
"Death in the darkness..."

The sound of stones tumbling and colliding down the hillside brought to mind the short retort of gunfire piercing the stillness of the night air.

A grunt or a cough added to the vibrations assaulting Bandit's alert ears.

Bandit had inched his way out of the den and was hidden behind some low bushes about twenty feet left of the path. The hillside rose out of the valley floor at a nearly a forty-five degree angle, which in good light made the trail hard to navigate. In the darkness both the tiredness and the alcohol in their systems already limited Hardcore's and Spencer's vision. Plus, exposure to manufactured luminosity over time limits one's ability to adjust to the absence of light. Impaired night vision isn't the case with animals. Dogs' night vision, while not as good as cats, still allows them to see very well in the dark. From his hiding place the men moving about were clearly visible to Bandit. It's a dog's nature to bark and warn strangers the animal considers a threat. But in the case of this dog, this Aussie raised in the wild by a wolf, his reaction was to be still, wary, and silent, hiding until the menace was completely ascertained. Wolf-like, Bandit continued to watch while his mind whirled, calculating strategies of attack and battle.

From the road to ground, the ranch yard was a distance of about 125 yards. The path wound around outcroppings of rock imbedded in the Montana mountains for hundreds of thousands of years. Sometimes the trail would drop a foot or so. At different places the incline widened and leveled out. The winding nature of the course led over timber that had fallen across the pathway. At other spots the track ran between overgrown bushes that made a person stoop to avoid branches. All of this caused the drunken intruders problems, which made them lose their cool, cursing or shouting when an errant branch slapped them across the face or arms. All the while the patient Bandit waited and planned his attack.

Out of breath, Spencer and Harrison plopped down on the trail. They didn't see the black figure stealthily shifting vantage points ahead of their descent. Bandit, like other great warriors, searched for an attack position but never lost contact with the threatening strangers.

From behind a large rock with spruce saplings branching from the forest floor providing a perfect canopy of camouflage, Bandit lowered his head in case he had to attack, and remained noiseless. Spencer and Hardcore never at any time in their climb down the hillside thought their lives were in danger. Bandit wasn't just any dog out to protect his home; Bandit had all the cunning of Sheena, and had witnessed fights to the death among fierce adversaries, combatants who made these drunks look like pushovers. Humans spend their lives in relative safety and security. Even those who are outside the law have a difficult time dealing with their own demise. Bulletproof is a description of those like Spencer and Harrison, who believe most of the peril is to others. Bandit on the other hand grew up in the kill or be killed struggle of the wild. Untamed and on guard, animals in their natural habitat never take their lives for granted. Well aware of the seriousness of this encounter, Bandit was ready. He knew he was in danger, as well as all he loved and cared for.

"Damn, if I had thought this was going to be this hard, we'd of stayed at the truck," complained Spencer.

James MacKrell

"Hell yes, we could have been miles away by now," muttered Hardcore.

"Yeah, but the climb back up is probably just as hard as our climb down."

"Right, let's make sure we twist some of these bushes out of the way, 'cause when we set this fire we sure as hell want to get out of here."

The crack of the broken branch made Bandit flinch, but he never gave away his position.

"I hope the other dogs don't wake up and start barking. I don't know what these two would do if warned."

The last time he saw Gabe and Mike they were about 300 yards away on the other side of the sheep pasture. The wind had shifted to the east and the scent of these two would be blown in the opposite direction from the Great Pyrenees guard dogs. Bandit assumed Blu and Mate were safely asleep in their kennels. Blu's kennel doors were never latched so in a time of need, the older Aussie could come to Bandit's aid.

"If the other dogs start barking I will attack before these two know what hit them." Bandit's mind kept a running conversation about the looming battle and his tactics.

With the exception of the mumblings of the intruders the night remained still. As the pair continued their downward climb, the materials they carried caused a misstep, sending stones rolling down the hillside. One rock bounced off a water pail, the noise sounding like a rifle shot. Harrison jumped at the noise, his foot slipping on the loose gravel.

He fell backward into Spencer. The two grumbled and complained but reached a section of the trail that leveled off just before reaching the ranch yard. Bandit had moved again so now he was hidden by one of the outbuildings and had a clear view of both men as they came nearer to the house.

"Here, help me tote this shit," Spencer handed a roll of fuse to Hardcore and shifted the gasoline can into his right hand. Harrison had stuffed some rags down his shirt to make them easier to carry.

"Where should we set this firecracker?"

"I don't think it makes a good God damn where, let's just get this done and get out of here. This is turning into a really bad idea. I don't think there is anything worth stealing that we could carry back up that bloody track."

Spencer stood up for a minute and continued, "Let's just light this place up and beat it back to the truck. By the time the locals find this we'll be turned around and halfway back to Big Timber."

Squatting like they had seen pictures of soldiers doing, they duck-walked across the yard toward the ranch house's back porch. Bandit slipped, again unseen, around the back of them to some shadows created by the haystack. Ron knelt down and fiddled in his pocket for his lighter. Harrison had piled the gasoline soaked rags dipped in gunpowder in a pile near the foundation post that held up the deck. The fuse was laid out running from under the floor to the spot where Spencer knelt about two feet away and just to the left of the stairs. The back porch was only about three feet from the ground so Hardcore had to wiggle on his belly to get out. He came around Spencer and crouched down on his heel just inches away from Spencer as he struck the lighters. The cigarette lighter had run out of fluid and the more Spencer cranked on the lighter the more sparks jumped into the air. Harrison fumbled through his front pockets for a book of matches he had picked up in a local bar. Both intently stared into the low light of their

James MacKrell

mini flashlight. They never saw the black fury descending on them.

Chapter 56
"A la muerte…"

The scream shattered the night like broken glass. In the darkness the furious Aussie leapt, landing square in the middle of the crouching Hardcore Harrison's shoulders, knocking him into the kneeling Ron Spencer and causing the mini flashlight to be flung from his hands. The dog's fangs dug deep into the nape of Hardcore's neck, causing him to freeze with fear and pain. He screamed. The scream was terrifying and woke all the animals at the ranch with a jolt. Blu started to bark furiously and with his paws lashed at the latch holding him prisoner. Mate threw his body at the kennel door in vain, trying to escape to rush toward the sounds of the fracas. Blood poured down Harrison's neck and filled the front of his shirt. Bandit's weight knocked him forward and he lay across the legs of Spencer. Bandit tore at his neck, twisting and turning, opening new gashes. Hardcore's screams didn't stop and Spencer started yelling at the top of his lungs.

"What is it for God's sake? I can't see. What's got a hold of you?"

The blood from Hardcore's neck ran into his mouth as he lay face down. Bandit's weight held him in place for a few moments, and while the dog was on top he tore at the man's back with his hind legs. The growling was fierce and the intruder's movements were frantic. In the darkness Spencer tried to knock the attacking dog from Harrison's back and missed. As his arm swung back Bandit loosened his death grip on the injured man and in a single bite clamped down on Spencer's arm. With a yank of his head with the man's arm still in a vise grip, the flesh on Spencer's forearm pulled away from the bone. Bandit spit out the arm flesh and grabbed again for Harrison. He sank his teeth deep into the back of the wounded man's arm. Both Spencer and Hardcore were struggling to get up. The ferocity of the attack kept knocking both men back to their knees.

Spencer's hand fell on a stick lying on the ground and in one swipe he struck Bandit across the head. It jarred Bandit loose and the dog fell headlong back to the ground. He jumped up and righted himself, lowering his head and showing his fangs. He swerved a bit to the right before plunging in at Spencer's kneecap. As his jaws closed on the man's leg Spencer swatted again with the stick but this time hit only his own leg as Bandit dodged the weapon. Hardcore struggled to his knees and punched the side of Bandit as the dog sought to charge for a new grip on Spencer. Across the yard, Blu fought with the latch on his kennel. Using his front paws as a human would use his hands, Blu placed his nose under the bolt and pushed up with both paws. The sound of the lock falling away thrilled the Aussie. The door on the kennel swung open and Blu turned the corner of the house, barking furiously. He plunged headlong into the fight with the men. He flew into the middle of Harrison's back and locked his teeth onto the fat man's side. With a twist and upward turn of his head he separated the flesh, causing a flow of blood to gush to the ground. Hardcore made a muffled cry and blindly swung his brawny fist in the dog's direction. The blow caught Blu on the side of his head, knocking him to the ground. Before Harrison could reach for him to deliver another blow, Bandit had his right forearm in his teeth, ripping as hard as he could.

From across the sheep pasture four hundred pounds of angry guard dogs flew over the ground in an attempt to rescue their mates. The criminals were getting an upper hand with the two Aussies due to the size and strength of the men. Hardcore grabbed Blu in both hands and was about to throw him against the side of the house. Spencer had Bandit down on the ground with his hands tightening around the black Aussie's neck to squeeze the life out of him.

In a blur of white the Great Pyrenees joined the fray. Mike attacked Spencer, nearly biting his leg in two. Gabe's powerful frame careened into Harrison, driving him off his feet and to the ground. Blu got up and grabbed the other leg of the man, clamping his powerful jaws around the ankle and biting the Achilles tendon almost in two.

Bandit rolled away from the fury and regained his feet. He ran headlong into the raging fight. He snapped his jaws shut on Harrison's upper thigh, pulling downward and ripping some of the tendons near the man's hip. As Spencer rose with the stick in his hand, the full weight of a guard dog knocked his legs out from under him and gave Blu a chance to again slash and rip at the outlaw's chest. It was as though every dog Harrison and Spencer had ever mistreated and killed was witness to the struggle and urged the dogs on in a punishing fight to the death.

Old Mate was howling in his kennel. Bayo stomped and neighed in his stall. The sheep assembled in the center of the pasture, afraid that the violence could some how spill over to them.

The sounds of the brawl were loud and awesome to behold. The fury of the death dance grew wit the men screaming in pain and the dogs growling and snapping in rage. Spencer, now afraid for his life, fought with a renewed intent. Harrison's bulk was a formidable foe in

itself. No matter how hard Bandit fought he could not
overwhelm the large man, whose brain was so alcohol-
addled he never realized the danger he was in. He blindly
swung at the attacking dog and screamed all the while, as if
the force of his voice could drive the animals away.
Bleeding and in severe pain, Spencer fell to his knees once
again, trying to quickly draw some life-giving air into his
lungs.

      Harrison's hand fell by his side and to his
amazement he felt the scabbard strapped to his belt, holding
the lethal hunting knife. He had forgotten he had the
weapon, and with his mangled arm he tried to dislodge it
from the sheath. His hand, weak due to the torn muscle of
his forearm, fumbled with the buckle. His right hand
closed on the knife's handle. Bandit attempted another leap
on the shoulders of his foe; Gabe dove at Harrison's legs,
trying to bring him to the ground again. The mangled arm
plunged the knife up into the black night toward the
attacking dog. Bandit was committed to the attack and he
gave a surprised yelp as he landed upon the blade. The
knife entered Bandit's midsection behind his right front leg.
The steel sought its mark, ricocheting off a rib before the
icy metal penetrated the dog's lung. There was a
whooshing sound as the air escaped his body. A cloud
formed over his eyes, blocking out all sight. Slowly Bandit
lost his hearing and fell into deep darkness at the foot of his
enemy. Gabe grabbed Harrison's knife-wielding arm and
flung him backwards. The overweight man, incoherent and
weakened by loss of blood, lost his balance and fell,
banging his head on the corner of the steps with a deadly
impact. His world instantly evaporated, a gurgling in his
throat his only utterance. He slumped down with the
corner of the step still settled in his broken skull. As the
dogs turned to finish off Spencer, he was nowhere to be

seen. They ran around searching for Spencer, and when they couldn't find him they returned to Bandit's side. As Gabe looked at the still form, Blu whined and lay down as near to his nephew as he could. Mike started licking Bandit's face in an attempt to stir him from his frightening stillness. Suddenly headlights slashed the darkness. Javier's truck pulled around to the back of the house. Jenny, on the tips of her paws, panted and looked frantically out of the windshield. As the truck screeched to a stop, Ron Spencer had successfully crawled back a-ways up the trail and was hidden from sight. Bandit lay still, lifeless it seemed. His eyes were closed and frothy bloody bubbles poured from the wound in his side and out of his nose. Javier and the dogs' hearts all stopped as the flashlight's beam fell on the inert and rumpled form of the black Aussie, who had committed himself to defend his family to the death.

James MacKrell

Chapter 57
"The resurrection…"

To his ears the voices and noise sounded like strings that were pulled too tight and vibrating too fast, tinny and thin. As hard as he tried his eyes wouldn't open. Each breath was a monumental effort as his sides barely moved. The pain in his midsection seared his nerve endings and to try to move a toe caused more pain than he had ever experienced before. His dry mouth and cracked lips hur, yet the soft and moistened touch of his mother's tongue soothed like a balm from Heaven.

"Oh my son, I believe you are alive. You are living, my puppy. I am here, and everything's going to be fine. I love you so much."

Jenny had dashed from Javier's truck to the injured and near-death Bandit. Falen was right behind as Jenny pushed her way through the other dogs. With low whines and careful licks around his mouth, she perceived the tiny breaths coming from his parched and split mouth. Falen started making circles, chirping as only an Aussie can. The frothy bloody bubbles were still gurgling in and out of the gaping wound. Javier appeared at his side in an instant. Thinking his beloved dog had died, he ran to the truck to grab some rope to tie up the unconscious Hardcore Harrison. Then Javier dashed into the house to call the Sheriff's office.

Quickly he returned to the yard and knelt by the dying dog with tears running down both cheeks. Blu moved alongside the grieving rancher as if he wanted to apologize for not being able to save his friend, Bandit.

Javier patted the head of faithful Blu while staring at the motionless body of Bandit.

"Oh Bandit, what have they done to you? Oh Bandit, please live, please hang on."

With a clean handkerchief from his pocket, he pressed on the knife wound in Bandit's side to stop the bleeding. Gabe and Mike milled in the background, whining and in their own way praying to the Spirit of the Day and Night, begging for their friend's life.

Blu, in distress and hurt after the battle, limped aside to lick his wounds. A huge knot appeared on his head where he had been smashed by the stick wielded by Spencer. The ground in the yard appeared ripped. Scuffle marks filled the area, and blood, both canine and human, was splattered over the porch and soaking in the dirt. Even though the fight had lasted only a few minutes, the amount of damage done to both dog and man was incredible.

"I must open my eyes. I need to speak to my family. I can't just lie here with the clouds over my mind. Oh, Spirit of the Day and Night, please rush to my side and assist me, for I am your servant dog."

Suddenly he could feel Javier's strong hands stroking his neck and face. With all the effort he could muster he moved. Not much, almost imperceptibly, but he moved. Life's spark was evident in the stricken dog and Javier's joy voiced aloud to anyone, man or beast, who could hear.

"Oh, Dear God, how grateful I am for your answered prayers. You heard my pleas and came to our aid. Mucho Gracias, mi Dios." He couldn't continue speaking, so his hands did the talking, gently caressing the face of his wounded dog.

A siren's wail filled the air and the red and blue spinning emergency lights lit up the blackened sky. Deputy

James MacKrell

Tommy Hampton's patrol had been near Javier's place on Highway 298 when the call came in, so he raced to the scene. Within a minute an ambulance screeched to a halt in the front yard. Tommy's flashlight cut a pattern through the night air as he rushed to Javier's side.

"Oh, my goodness!" He knelt beside the grieving herdsman. "What has happened?" "Who is the guy tied up?" Hampton played his light onto the face of the unconscious man. "Hey, that's the creep we've been looking for." He rose and tested the ropes binding Harrison to satisfy himself that he was well tied. A rope moored the unconscious man to the foundation of the house. Deputy Hampton returned to the side of the stricken dog and unbuckled his two-way.

Javier continued to pet and love on Bandit, who responded ever so weakly. Bandit was dying and it seemed only a matter of time until death overtook him. Two more Sweet Grass patrol cars skidded to a stop, with deputies running to the back of the house. They immediately handcuffed Hardcore while the EMS's did as much emergency ministrations as they could with him tied. The wanted man stirred because of smelling salts placed under his nose. Hampton on the two-way again to the Sheriff's dispatcher cried, "Call Dr. Kainer and tell him I will be bringing the dog to his office. Please meet us there. This is an emergency! Tell him it's Javier Coronado's dog, Bandit. We can talk again when I get rollin'. Gotta go. We're on our way."

One of the medics retrieved a blanket from the ambulance and Javier tenderly wrapped Bandit in it. His black body had started to shake as shock set into his system.

Two deputies had roused Harrison to his feet and marched him to the patrol car. Harrison mumbled as his rights were read to him. Being arrested wasn't a new experience for him.

Captain Walters arrived and followed Javier and Hampton to the cruiser.

"It's going to be all right. I'll remain here as long as I can." He leaned on the open window on the passenger side of the police car and patted Javier's hand. Bandit had been placed on the back seat and Tommy already had the motor running and the red and blue lights flashing. "A deputy will stay here with your animals and guard the place until you get back."

Captain Walters said, "Hamp, are you sure it was only this guy that we have in custody? Could his partner have been here as well and somehow escaped?"

Hampton started pulling out of the drive slowly as he shouted to the Captain. "I don't know, but I would bet he's around here somewhere. I don't think this one bad guy could have caused all this damage by himself."

By that time the car was rolling toward the highway and headed full-steam toward Big Timber.

Captain Walters began to walk the area with his deputies, carefully combing the yard for clues to causes of the turmoil. He carried a multi-directional flood light from his car around to the back, and the artificial light brightly illuminated the area. The blood splatter appeared worse than they all had thought.

"Hey, Captain, look over here!" Walters rushed over to where Deputy Stillwell was pointing. A large drag mark appeared on the ground leading up toward the hill. The trail wasn't marked clearly and was somewhat obscured by underbrush. Flashlights played their beams up the trail but because of the heavy growth and darkness they didn't see the blood track left on the trail. Ron Spencer wasn't even aware of the lawmen below. His pain was

344   James MacKrell

such that he was having a tough time just staying awake. He couldn't stand and while the lawmen were below looking up the trail he had half-passed out so he didn't move, let alone hear any noises. He was out and due to the loss of blood his breathing was slowed and he lay perfectly still.

"Captain, come over here!" One of the patrolmen had returned to the area of the porch and was pulling the gasoline rags from under the porch. In his hand he held the bloodstained book of matches from the Last Cowboy' Bar. "I hope you're wearing gloves?" The crime scene department arrived on location. "Drop that into this sack." The deputy pointed to where the gasoline soaked rags were and pointed to a cigarette butt crushed out in the dirt.

"Mr. Coronado was really lucky. From what I can see, it was those dogs that stopped this guy in his tracks."

"That seems to be the way of it. If they hadn't attacked when they did, this all could have been burned to the ground." The men looked at the Aussies in the yard. Jenny was taking it all in with her eyes filled with worry. Blu limped over toward the house and found a place to lie down and rest. One of the medics experienced in veterinary medicine gave the old warrior a good going over. He declared the Blu dog just needed some rest and good care. Gabe and Mike had returned, on their own, to the middle of the sheep, and old Mate still barked in his kennel wondering why he hadn't been included. Jenny whined and dropped her head. Falen eased up to her side and tenderly licked her face.

* * *

The sheriff's car squealed into a parking place in front of Kainer Veterinary Clinic. Dr. Kainer was waiting at the door with a gurney to lay the wounded Aussie on. His grim face told the story. "I am going to do everything I can to save him, Javier. I trust in my skills but let's keep a prayerful attitude. We are going to need all the help we can get."

Chapter 58
"The long road home...."

The morning's light started to break as Javier drove back to the ranch, leaving the mortally wounded Bandit at Doc Kainer's hospital. The loneliness of the preceding night covered Javier like a ragged blanket, offering no warmth and a smattering of cover. Deep sobs welled up in the herdsman's chest as he remembered pacing the waiting room while Dr. Kainer worked feverishly in the operating suite to save the injured Aussie's life. The possibility of losing Bandit was more than he could stand. A shudder pulsed through his body as his mind played over the tragedy of Jenny and the joy of finding her again, and then the excitement of Bandit's return to his home.

"What this poor puppy has been through. It's just not fair. He deserves to live." He placed his empty hand on his heart, "I plead with all the Saints and the Blessed Mother, to grant life to my brave dog."

Javier tried to continue his monologue but his grief overcame him. Tears prevented him from speaking anymore. He reached for the rosary hanging around his rear-view mirror, hoping its touch would ensure his prayers would be answered.

The night had been long. Doc Kainer called in two assistants, as the surgery proved complicated and stressful. The knife that had plunged into Bandit's side had ricocheted off a rib, and then slightly punctured one lunch. A lot of precious blood had been lost and the dog's system had started the dying process. Once the body starts to shut down, to reverse the course is difficult. Javier never left the waiting room. One of Kainer's assistants would come out from time to time to keep him abreast of how things were going. After Bandit was sewn up and placed in a recuperating kennel, Doc connected monitors to his heart and head.

Satisfied that all had been done that could have, Javier headed back to the ranch. He was still worried about the damage to Blu and he also wanted to check the brave guard dogs as well. As he drove home his hand absently reached over toward the passenger seat where Jenny usually rode to pat her and give her loving touches. She was so much a part of him that the fact she wasn't there didn't deter his rote action.

Yellow tape wound around the trees and buildings at Townsend Sheep Company ranch. As Javier pulled up in his drive Deputy Stillwell met him. "How's the dog doing? Boy, he sure looked in bad shape last night."

"I believe he's going to make it," Javier said as he extended his hand to the officer. "Say, I surely appreciate you staying with the animals and keeping an eye on things. I hope these dogs," he stooped to pat Jenny and Falen who had rushed out the open front door to greet him "weren't too much trouble."

"No sir. And I have to add, I felt a lot safer with them looking out for things." Jenny looked up. "They can hear and see things long before I notice noises."

Javier's look hardened, "Anything in particular?"

"Nope, just some rustling sounds up the hill, but I assumed the clamor was caused by animals and I got these two back in the house after giving the hillside a once over with my light."

Javier, Jenny, and Falen started walking around back. Blu was still asleep after his ordeal. It broke Javier's heart to look at the blood-splattered ground, knowing some

James MacKrell

of the blood belonged to his faithful Bandit. He almost wanted to collect the stained dirt in a jar to keep it in case Bandit didn't make it.

"Up there is where the racket came from." Stillwell pointed toward the crest of the hill near the road, over a hundred yards away. "From what I could see, and granted, it was dark, there was a little commotion and then it fell silent."

Javier looked up the hill, "Jenny, come back down here." She had started up the hill to where the deputy was pointing.

"About what time did this happen?" Javier turned toward the lawman, "cause if it was almost dawn, there is a family of deer who come down out of the woods trying to find some kibble or sheep grain left over. They've been doing it so long that Jeremy and I leave a little out each night for them."

Stillwell glanced at his watch as if it would have marked the incident. "Yeah, it was about five or five thirty. In fact only about an hour before you came home. Then as I said before, things quieted down and we went back into the house."

Falen's head bobbed up and down as if she was confirming everything the Deputy had said. With a rub of her head, Javier and the lawman turned back toward the house.

Javier was exhausted and bid goodbye to the officer. "Mr. Coronado, two detectives will be out this morning to collect clues and investigate the property. They will make it about noon so you can get a little rest."

"Don't worry about me. A couple of quick winks and I will be fine."

As the patrol car drove away, Javier gave one more glance up the hill. "I wonder?" he said to the dogs.

"Maybe we'll take a climb later, but now, let's try to get a quick nap."

The commotion Deputy Stillwell described was real enough. It had more serious consequences than both men figured.

* * *

As dawn started to break Ron Spencer was roused from a near coma by a small squirrel scurrying across his face. Weak from loss of blood he could hardly open his eyes, let alone take a swipe at the offending rodent. The tiny claws dug into Spencer's face as it dodged his hand and leapt away, causing him to yelp in pain again. He barely raised his head, but could see that he had fallen in the night over a huge tree branch across the trail. His whole body ached and the muscle tear in his leg started bleeding again as he tried to right himself. His right arm seemed useless. There was no feeling in his hands due to the torn nerves. The pounding in his head became unbearable. "I've got to get up. I can't just lay here. If I'm going to live I have to make it back to the truck." His voice was so weak no creature heard him except one.

Spencer struggled to rise to his hands and knees. The morning sun burst through the dark billows and a beam of extremely bright light hit Spencer in the face. His good hand covered his eyes, and he fell back down on the rocky trail.

As the clouds moved the sunlight dimmed and Spencer got his bearings again. He was determined to reach his truck. He didn't care what had happened to Hardcore. He thought only of his welfare and knew he desperately needed to escape. His left leg was the most damaged, and he figured he could drive using his right leg and foot, and his good arm.

He wiggled around to face the upward climb of the hill and pulled himself to a crawling position. The steep path with its twists and turns circled back just a few feet in front of Spencer. A large bush had grown across the track so he had to dip down almost to his belly to crawl through what he could have easily pushed aside if he hadn't been so injured.

With his good left hand he managed to shove the dense branches aside, so he could crawl through to the portion of the trail that flattened out a bit. The branch, stronger than he thought, repelled back into his face, almost knocking him over. Head down, he struggled a few feet and came out on the other side of the brushwood. Proud of himself for escaping, he believed if he could just make it a few dozen yards or so, the truck would be there, and he could flee.

A gasp lodged in his throat and he vainly mouthed a silent scream. He eased back down on his knees and wiped at his eyes to clear his vision.

About ten feet up the hill and right in front of the crippled man stood Sheena. Tall and proud with her timber wolf mate at her side, she lowered her head and stared straight into the eyes of the man she hated more than anyone else in the world.

Her white face housed her yellow eyes as they turned nearly crimson. Her fangs dripped with revulsion. Her head was lowered in the attack position. Steel inched slightly off the path to the right side of the wolf-dog. Spencer opened his mouth to scream, and again nothing would come out. The face of Sheena, fierce and terrible, was the last thing Spencer ever saw.

James MacKrell

Chapter 59
"The cleanup begins…"

After a full breakfast of sausage, eggs, and toast, the young deputy wasn't prepared for what he discovered. He pushed back the brush at the top of the trail and recoiled in revulsion. The stink of coppery blood permeated the area. He could barely get the words out.

"Captain Walters!" He waved an unsteady hand. Bending over he clutched at his stomach, afraid he would throw up.

Walters and another deputy raced up the hill. The crime scene investigator was a step or two behind.

Flies buzzed around the area, stirred up by the intrusion of the lawman. They had been nestled on the body that was twisted and tangled in the underbrush. All around the area were scuffmarks and blood.

Panting from the climb, Walters yelled, "What's up, Jason, what have you found?" Captain Walters looked around for his deputy, who by now was nearly lying on the ground about ten feet from the dead Spencer. He pushed through the brush and saw the mangled body for himself. "Oh, my God!" Even the seasoned Sheriff's Department official turned a shade of pale when he got a nose full of the stench around the site. The Crime Scene officer pushed his way through the brush and moved a little ahead of the sickened deputy and the captain. Reaching into his pocket he withdrew a surgical mask and whipped on sterile gloves. The corpse had a heavy deposit of insects crawling over it. The CSI judged the man had been dead only a matter of hours. His clothes were torn and ripped from the savage attack. Captain Walters stared at something on the ground. "Hey you guys, be careful where you walk or stand, there seems to be a lot of tracks here and I would like to preserve them." To the CSI he said, "Don't you have a camera in your bag?"

"Yes sir. What do you want shot, besides the condition of the victim?"

"Shoot me several pictures of those tracks and get a couple of close-ups if you can."

"Ten-four." The investigator carefully documented each and every track. The obvious animal prints and the drag marks where the man was apparently crawling."

"Look's like he tried to get away, poor devil.

"Cap, who is this guy?"

"Andrews," the CSI looked up, "rifle through those pants and see if there is any type of identification."

Before he could answer the second deputy called down from the road.

"Captain, there is an old piece-of-crap pickup truck up here. It looks like the F-150 Hampton had us on the look-out for."

"Be there in a minute. Don't go through anything until I get up there."

He turned back to the CSI and before he could speak, the investigator interrupted him.

"I swear to God I've never seen a body in this bad of shape before. Can I cut this brush out of the way?" Captain Walters nodded in the affirmative and took a step closer to the scene of the death. Even he was repulsed by the condition of the corpse.

"His wallet has a Mississippi driver's license issued to Ronald Wilson Spencer. The picture is a little old, but I guess it's the same guy. If only his face wasn't so torn up I could say for sure."

As the Captain moved in next to the examiner he uttered a slight gasp. The stomach and all of the intestines had been torn out and apparently eaten.

"Captain?" The officer didn't look up. He just stared at the body.

"I'm not sure, but this sure looks like a deer I saw once that had been killed by wolves."

They don't leave much. You think they ate him?"

"Sure looks like it. Let's get back down and get the coroner out here. You guys," he indicated to the other deputy and the CSI, "move on up to the truck and give that a thorough going over."

It took all day to clean up the crime scene. Javier tried to continue his daily chores with the help of Jeremy, but he couldn't stop thinking and wondering about what was happening up on the hill.

* * *

"Falen, I am so worried about our Bandit."

"I know, Mother. I pray to the Spirit of the Day and Night for my brother. If only I could play with him right now," she let out a little Aussie chirp as she thought of better times.

Blu limped over to his sister and licked her face. *"I believe Bandit will be all right. The Master has taken good care of us dogs all our lives. Did you see his face when he left? I have never seen him so saddened."*

Blu turned and started looking to the sheep pasture. He watched as the shaggy white giants slowly moved among their charges.

A shudder raced over the merle dog's body as he remembered how Mike and Gabe had risked their lives to save him and Bandit.

"I will never take you two for granted again." The guard dogs kept their concentration on the sheep. Blu moved over to the pasture gate, slunk down, and crawled under. He picked his way through the flock and walked up to the Great Pyrenees. He issued a low whine, *"My nephew and I owe our lives to you. We are grateful and will be forever in your debt."*

Mike scratched his left ear with his hind leg and if the Goliath of a dog could blush he would have. He nuzzled Blu on the shoulder and said, *"Good Blu, we each have our jobs and we each serve the Master. Gabe and I take pride in our ability to lay our lives on the line to protect those to which we've been given charge. We are family, my dog friend; we are a pack, working together for the Master, and the Spirit of the Day and Night."*

Then he turned away from the Aussie and slowly trotted over toward a fence in case a threat appeared. Blu watched as Mike and Gabe went about their business.

"How great it is to be a working dog! How great are our lives, how great to be of service to humans."

Careful not to frighten the sheep, Blu raced back to the ranch yard to rejoin his family.

As the afternoon faded into evening the police activity was completed and the equipment moved away. The Townsend Sheep Company seemed to slowly return to normal. The night's chill called for a fire in the house. Falen had twisted herself into a ball on the hearth to let the warm rays soothe her tired muscles. Jenny paced the floor. She went into the bedroom for a minute then came out. She took a turn through the kitchen, peered out of the glass on the back kitchen door, then moved back into the living room and plopped down not too far from Falen. She stretched out for a second but when Javier, with a cup of coffee in his hand, walked out onto the front porch, she quickly joined him.

"My Jenny girl," he said, his rough hand gently stroking her black head. "We've been through a lot me and you, my girl."

She looked up into his eyes. His old eyes brimmed with tears. She could read him like a book, and she whined under his steady caresses. *"Master, I understand. I love you and will always be at your side."*

Little Falen couldn't be left in the living room alone so she joined in and licked the other hand Javier rested on the arm of the rocking chair.

"We are a family, my dogs, and one of our own is missing."

He rose from the rocker and continued talking. "Let's head for bed. We know it's not going to come to us." He chuckled at his own joke. "Let's pray tonight for the speedy return of our Bandit. When he is home we will all be whole again."

With that they went to bed.

Chapter 60
"The end is just the beginning...."

His fingers tapped out a Mexican tune playing on his CD player as he rolled down Highway 298 on his way back to the ranch. Javier had never, to the best of his knowledge, felt so good. Well, maybe once when he discovered Jim Townsend had left him the ranch and all the livestock, his heart was pretty full, but he would be hard-pressed to believe any other day could possibly be as happy. "Blessed" was the word he repeated over and over as he drove along heading south toward McLeod.

His hand reached over to the passenger side of the truck cab and ruffled the black fur on Bandit's neck. The gentle dog made a murfing sound to signify his pleasure. Bandit never took his eyes off the road ahead, the road leading home.

"My Bandit, we are going home. Yes, my dog, we are going home to our family, our dogs, our friends, our home. Good Bandit. I love you so."

The big almond eyes glanced at Javier. The past month had been hard. There were times the black Aussie felt like giving up. But his great heart just wouldn't quit. He had to live; he had too many depending on him. A soft whine eased out, *My Master, it is good to be going home with you. It is good to be a dog who is loved by so many.*

Javier's hand dropped from Bandit's neck and the great Aussie gave it a lick, reassuring the herdsman of his devotion.

Javier would love to forget the restless times, the hard conversations with Dr. Kainer, and the volley of dread and hope that lobbed back and forth with each phone call or visit. As is usually the case with bad memories, they faded with the joy of Bandit's improving condition. As each day passed, Jenny and the other dogs, sensing a lightening heart in their beloved Master, seemed to grow more confident in Bandit's return. Over the years the herdsman and the other ranchers, who depended so much on their dogs for their livelihood, had learned to read and trust the varying moods and signs from the herding dogs. One rancher told a story about a great Aussie he owned who lived for a good long time. The day the great sire died, his daughter kissed on him all day soothing his pain just as if she knew death was approaching. The rancher laughed about a Border Collie he had also owned who hated the Aussie except when they worked cattle and sheep together. On the day the Aussie died the Border Collie lay by the dying dog's kennel moaning his passing. People who work with livestock know. The animals are aware and sensitive and would tell us in words if they could. As Jenny said a long time ago, *"You can say what you like; humans don't understand dog talk, anyway."*

Javier felt that it was too bad for the humans that they didn't understand. They could learn a lot from the honesty of dogs.

With each mile that rolled by a panorama of memories played across Coronado's mind. He thought of the bond that had sprung up almost overnight between the returning war veteran, Rick Gonzales, and Falen. Whenever Ricky visited, Falen never left his wheelchair. She was even allowed to enjoy sleepovers at the Gonzales home. She doted on Rick and could almost anticipate his needs and wants. Australian Shepherds need jobs and Falen seemed to have found hers.

Jeremy spent more time at the ranch. He not only did his chores but also loved to hang around to pet and love on Blu. There was something of a champion's nature in the Blu Merle dog and Jeremy believed the closer he was to the heroic Aussie the more the champion's nature would rub off on him. It was apparent that Jeremy was blessed with a deep love for animals and a respect for all of God's living things.

One day when Javier finally found out Bandit was going to pull through Jenny plopped down at his feet as he concluded the telephone conversation with the veterinary hospital.

"Oh my Master, it's true, our boy is coming home. My son, my prodigal son, is coming back from the dead again."

She reached up as far as she could and licked Javier's hand all over, even giving him tiny nips of love.

Each day the sun seemed to shine a little brighter as the folks and dogs at Townsend Sheep Company readied for Bandit's homecoming.

Now on the appointed day Javier sped along the highway and couldn't wait until they could rest again at home.

The sound of a siren jolted Javier from his daydreams. A sheriff's patrol car was on his tail with lights flashing and siren blaring.

Nervous he might have inadvertently done something wrong or somehow broken a traffic law, Javier pulled over, rolled the window down, and waited for the officer. He didn't look around for fear he would look guilty.

"Hey there, speedster what's going on?" Tommy Hampton appeared at the window with a smile as big as all of the Big Sky country. "I stopped by Doc's to see how our hero was and he told me you two were headed home. Damn, it took me a while to catch up with you."

Bandit would have wagged his tail if he had one. Tommy reached over Javier and petted the boy. "How long is he going to have to wear those bandages?"

"Doc says a couple more weeks, if he doesn't pull them off by himself." They both laughed.

The relief of not getting a ticket beamed across the herdsman's face. "And you, catching any more bad guys?"

"Oh yeah! One kid who didn't show up for school and a cat who decided to try to climb to the top of a cottonwood tree in Mrs. Daigle's front yard." "You guys head on home. I'll follow. I got a book on law enforcement Jeremy asked to borrow."

When Javier pulled back out onto the highway Hampton pulled around him and turned on the emergency lights to give them a police escort all the way home.

The truck pulled into the ranch's drive and parked just behind the Sweet Grass County police unit. A crowd had assembled in the front yard. The Gonzales family was standing on the porch next to Rick's wheelchair with Falen inches away. Ivyn Keske and his family came to greet the wonderful dog who had saved their son's life. Blu jumped up into the bed of the truck and clawed at the back window. Jenny chirped as only an Aussie can.

"Blessings to you, Spirit of the Day and Night" she barked, *"You have brought my son home for the second time."*

Javier chuckled, "Bandit, I never thought of you as shy, but I believe you would be blushing if you could." He opened the door and got down from the truck. Bandit stayed in the cab and peeked out at the assembled crowd. One of the reasons he didn't just jump down is that the wound still hurt, and probably would for some time.

Finally, he disembarked. He placed his front paws on the running board and Javier gently held him to make sure he didn't fall.

Once on the ground he was instantly surrounded by pats from the humans and licks from the dogs. Even Gabe and Mike had left the flock long enough to join in the reception.

Bandit stood and let everyone pet him and accepted all the love the dogs and people could pour out. There wasn't an inch of him that didn't feel joy.

Deep within his brain came a still, small voice. *"My son, my dog, I promised to be with you through all of your trials. Today my spirit shines on you in the joy you deserve."* As quick as the voice came, it left. The corner of Bandit's mouth curled into a little dog smile, knowing that the Spirit of the Day and Night had looked over him.

Several people moved aside creating an opening between Bandit and the back of the ranch house. Out into the sunlight stepped a strange dog. It was a black tri Aussie about Bandit's age with a black coat that shown like ebony, copper markings on her front and back legs that suggested burning fire, and a white collar surrounding her neck like a wealthy woman's stole. A white blaze divided her face in half with the copper markings like fine make-up enhancing the natural beauty of a movie star. The face is what Bandit's eyes locked on. Slowly she moved out into the open sunlight. It was as if the sun's rays shown just for her. With tiny and dainty steps she moved slowly toward the black Aussie. Bandit quickly forgot about all the commotion and all the well-wishers. He was drawn to the dog as if by a string.

He pulled himself up to his full height and his legs stiffened in a proud march of majesty. The dogs moved together.

"Who are you, strange female?" He circled her, sniffing each inch of her magnificent body.

"I am called Trip by my humans." She returned the acknowledgment by smelling every hair on Bandit's body.

"Your Master came to our place which is called Amistad Kennels seeking from my owners, Judie and Walt Manuel, a proper lady to move here and join your family." She raised her head just a little higher than Bandit's. *"I come from a family different from yours, but just as regal and just as noble. When your Master visited the Manuals at Amistad Kennels I liked him and trusted his smell. He thought I would like it here and Walt and Judie, my humans, agreed with him."*

She turned a bit and moved so her head was even with Bandit's. She gazed deeply into his eyes, *"I believe I will like it here too."*

With this she gave the wounded dog a lick on his muzzle.

"We are strong; my mother, Jenny, my uncle Blu, old Mate, and my wonderful sister, Falen. We are proud of our work, and we hold our heads high as we serve our Master."

Then he looked her in the eyes and said, *"Welcome, most beautiful of Aussies. I will defend you, and I welcome you to our family. We may produce great things you and I."*

Trip smiled and whined, *"You are wonderful, most noted warrior, but time will tell what we produce. I'm no pushover, you know."*

***

Dear Readers:

I hope you've enjoyed this story as much as I have loved writing it. Dogs have a special place in our lives and we must reward their devotion by caring for their needs. That is why we are setting aside some of the proceeds of this book to benefit these important canine foundations. Thanks for allowing us this privilege through your purchase of this novel.

Sincerely,

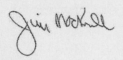

For more information please visit:
www.ashgi.org

For more information please visit:
www.wearethecure.org